KINGS OF THE RECS!

AN EVOLVING HISTORY OF FOOTBALL IN ARNOLD, NOTTINGHAM

VOL 1

ROVERS' AND MARYS' BATTLE FOR SUPREMACY

1946-1958

ROGER RANN

- - - - -

ISBN 0-9557305-0-4

PUBLISHED BY
JAMES HAWTHORN
EAGLE CLOSE
ARNOLD
NOTTINGHAM
NG5 7FJ

FIRST PUBLISHED SEPTEMBER 2007

Printed by Fineprint (Nottingham) Ltd.

Web: www.FineprintLtd.com
Tel: 0115 9111 700

CONTENTS

SUBSCRIBERS

A big, big thank you to everyone listed below who reserved a copy of the book having seen nothing more than a promotional flyer, and in some cases not even that.

MARK BUTLER
JOHN M PARR
MARTIN DERMODY
DAVID MATTHEWS
MARTIN WILLIAMS
GRAHAM TAYLOR
JOHN AND PAM LAMB
ANDY NOWAK
STEPHEN RANN
IVOR AND STEPH HOLLAND
DERRICK AND BERYL BARNES
ALF AND ANNE ASKEW
IAN JOHNSON
DAVID HOLLINGSWORTH
ARNOLD & DISTRICT CAMERA CLUB
PETER AND MARILYN TURNER
GEOFF BLACKWELL
RICHARD PANTER
MICK GRETTON
KEITH PARNILL
STUART J PYKETT
ANDREW AND PENNY MILLWARD
BILL COLLEY
JOAN JONES
RICHARD LANE
ANDY KEETLEY
MALC PENNYCOOK
THOMAS G HUDSON
TONY G HUDSON
ROY HILL
TOM AND AUDREY CHARLTON
ALAN SMITH
NICK STEVENSON
GERARD KELMAN
LESLEY BROCK (nee STONE)
TERRY BEARDSLEY
PHILIP HAYNES
JOHN R PARR
CHRISTOPHER PARR
REX BARKER
MICHAEL HOARE
JON CROSBY
DOUG DALE
DENIS KEETON
BRIAN JOHNSON
GLENVILLE CAMM
BRIAN HOWES
RODGER AND PATRICIA ARMITAGE
BOB TAIT
STEVE HASLAM

ACKNOWLEDGEMENTS

Thanks to all those members of the library staffs at Arnold, Belper, Ilkeston, Mansfield, Newark, Nottingham, Retford, and Sutton-in-Ashfield who provided unstinting support in trying to find old match reports or scores from their archives of local newspapers despite what seemed at times to be an epidemic of staff shortages and/or computer malfunctions.

Thank you to Philip Meakin of the Nottingham Post Group Ltd for organising a letter of access re their copyright publications.

A big thank you to Mark Butler for spreading the word via his excellent website **www.freewebs.com/theallnewarnoldwho**

A very large debt of gratitude to Martin Dermody for handing me the scrapbook that kicked off this whole project and whose assistance and support both before and since has been invaluable.

Thank you, too, to John Lamb for knowing a lot more about how to 'improve' a photograph than I do.

If I have forgotten anyone then please accept my sincere apologies for the oversight.

DEDICATION

Finally I must thank my darling wife Anna. Apart from having to listen to me rabbit on *ad nauseam* about obscure football teams and leagues from a bygone age for what must have seemed to her like an eternity she kindly offered to proof-read my final draft.

Armed with the dreaded blue pen she set about her task with a degree of zeal that I hadn't anticipated and I should have guessed, more or less immediately, that it was going to be a rocky ride when she struck out the very first word in the book. Well it wasn't a word as such, but I'd used 'WWII' as an abbreviation for 'The Second World War' and she was having none of it. "You can't start a book like that!" she said most indignantly, and I remembered too late that before we were married Anna had passed her Private Secretary's Certificate. Now she'd been given an opportunity to put what she'd learned to very good use and she grabbed it with both hands.

SHE WHO MUST BE OBEYED

Every night for a couple of weeks I was summoned to her presence so that she could take a little too much satisfaction for my liking in bringing the errors she'd found to my attention. Dutifully I sat there as she reeled off my indiscretions: a missed comma here, a spelling mistake there, and the worst offence of all, a paragraph that I'd dared to start with an 'and'! You'd have thought I'd committed a crime! Flushed with her success, this nightly interrogation became more and more intense until it reminded me uncannily of an occasion I'd almost forgotten way back in my schooldays.

It was a time of O-Levels, one of the precursors of the current GCSE exams. My lack of success in the subjects of Physics and Chemistry meant that I had to opt for the General Science paper, which whilst not expecting deep knowledge of its constituent subjects, also included Biology for good measure. My mock O-Level results in this particular exam were nothing short of disastrous; Biology, (relatively my better science subject), forty-five percent and FAIL; Chemistry, thirty-seven percent and FAIL; Physics, thirteen percent and, well, you know the answer.

Now it might not have been quite such a trauma if these abysmal scores could have been kept between me and the respective subject teachers, but there was no chance of that. My school of the time wasn't built on sparing my blushes. No, the papers were handed back to the pupils in ascending order of success, which put me close to the front of the class in Biology and Chemistry, and a country mile in front of, or maybe that should be behind, the rest in Physics. It certainly condemned me to have to listen to "Rann.....thirteen percent", delivered in a grimly sadistic tone by the Physics teacher, followed by barely suppressed sniggers of delight from my classmates. Sniggers that would normally only be silenced when the next mark was read out. Except that that day it seemed like I was the only one in class who'd bombed out so spectacularly.

I'd never, ever, scored as low a mark in any exam as thirteen percent. I knew that I was to all intents a hopeless duffer in the subject, but after all this was a time when neatness, good spelling, and the correct name at the top of the paper still counted for something. How could I have only scored thirteen percent? I pored over the paper; after all, there were still another thirty for the teacher to hand out, so I had plenty of time.

It suddenly became clear; my Physics teacher was almost as big a duffer as me. He couldn't add up. I became quite excited, and checked my paper over and over. Sure, he had made a mistake. He'd inserted the marks gained for each question in the margin on each page, and he must have missed a couple of pages when totalling them up.

When one of our class brain-boxes had received the last paper handed back, my hand shot up. "Yes, Rann" said our teacher in that very bored and condescending tone that all teachers adopt when they are thinking 'what are you bothering me for you hopeless duffer'. "Sir, I think you've made a mistake with my mark." The glare that shot back from him and nearly impaled me where I sat immediately told me that it was me that had made the mistake. "Come here!" he bellowed.

Undaunted, but still wishing to be anywhere but heading for the raised dais-type desk that he ruled from, I sheepishly handed him my paper and said in a faltering whisper, "Sir, I think I scored higher than thirteen percent" He proceeded to take what seemed like an eternity to agree with me, but had to concede that I was right.

Turning to the class at large, he engaged his rapt audience with the announcement of my corrected mark, delivered in a slightly less sadistic manner than his first declaration, but still with an undisguised element of *schadenfreude*. "Rann, twenty-four percent!" And if I thought that this was the last word on the matter I was wrong. Turning to me, he couldn't resist rubbing it in; "Twenty-four percent? Twenty-four percent? I think a little work might not go amiss, don't you agree?"

Now this was pretty much the same kind of impression that I was getting back from my lovely wife as she morphed into her role of pedantic proof-reader, but there was no getting away from it; a little more work was definitely necessary. So, with my tail firmly between my legs I diligently set about correcting my draft. If after my re-write there are still errors in the text then please remember they are mine; far fewer in number though than they would otherwise have been without Anna's efforts.

That she should have even given the task at hand the amount of attention and seriousness that she did is testament to her character. Everyone who knows her is in admiration of her stoicism and general good nature in the face of a condition that currently has no cure.

Multiple Sclerosis (MS), with which she was diagnosed back in 1987, is a degenerative and disabling condition. It not only attacks the central nervous system with many deleterious consequences but it can destroy lives too. It isn't a killer in the strictest sense of the word so it doesn't receive the publicity that other more pernicious maladies do but, make no mistake, it is still something you wouldn't wish on your own worst enemy. It is almost like death by a thousand cuts.

Given the fact that there are no drugs or relieving treatments available for the specific strain of MS that Anna suffers from, known as Primary Progressive MS, has meant that she realises that she can't 'beat it' no matter how hard she tries. However, her prodigious tenacity and sheer fighting spirit has resulted in a mindset that won't let it 'beat her' either. It is an understatement to say that I am proud of how she is handling a situation that would test the hardiest of us, but it really is true that she is an inspiration to not just me, but to all her extended family and friends. All the proceeds of this book will be donated to the MS Society, so do not lend your copy to anyone. GET THEM TO BUY THEIR OWN!

Finally, you don't often get a chance to say in public exactly how you feel about someone who has shared their life with you for over thirty five years and who you've known even longer than that, but this is a pleasing consequence of being able to write your own book.

Anna, you truly are the wind beneath my wings, and this book is dedicated most humbly to you.

xxx (noc!)

INTRODUCTION

(I) BACKGROUND

The background to this particular project was simply an idea of mine to research the history of football in Arnold. I started by initially concentrating on the years that Arnold FC played in the Midland League, 1963 to 1982, but gradually found myself picking up all kinds of information going back almost to the origins of organised football itself in the late nineteenth century.

I was already in danger of disappearing under a mountain of old cuttings, match programmes, photographs, booklets and other memorabilia when out of the blue Martin Dermody handed me an old scrapbook belonging to Peggy Whitt. Actually it was a photocopy of the original and the cover was a bit indistinct but it immediately grabbed my attention. There was a photograph of a football team right in the middle with the words 'FOOT' above and 'BALL' below and on closer inspection there were a few faces that I recognised; Jack Brace, Sam Archer, John Cunningham. Beneath the picture but almost obscured was the name of the team, 'ARNOLD ROVERS'.

I hurriedly flicked through the pages and was fascinated by what I saw and read. The cover photograph itself had been taken in 1953 and the scrapbook covered roughly the next five years. As a young football-mad boy growing up in the town in the 1950s I'd watched Rovers play when crowds were so big that I had to kneel, sit, or crouch right at the edge of the pitch at the feet of older and definitely taller spectators just to make sure I didn't miss any of the action.

Numbers of spectators were invariably much bigger than for comparable games today and when Rovers were playing their big crosstown rivals Arnold St Marys, games that were often scheduled to be played on key dates at Christmas or Easter or the August Bank Holiday, crowds flocked to see which team would prevail. The dates of the matches were chosen not just to maximise the number of spectators attending, but to ensure that when the collecting bucket went round at half-time it needed regular emptying before the players returned for the second half.

Although the scrapbook had jogged my memory in a most pleasant fashion, I would probably have put it to one side for later reference and carried on with my original research until, that is, a letter appeared in the Nottingham Evening Post early in 2006 stating quite emphatically that 'Arnold Rovers were far superior to Arnold St Marys'. When this piece of correspondence was quickly followed by one from Ken Renshaw, a Rovers' player whose name I'd seen in the scrapbook, confirming, naturally enough and as he readily admitted, that the original writer was correct in his judgment, I began to think that there might be a tale worth telling here. When, by complete chance, I bumped into Len Rockley, a Marys' goalkeeper of the same era only a few days later, I knew there was. Len, normally easy going and affable, had a trace of indignation on his face as he asked me if I'd seen the letters in the Post. When I confirmed that I had he gave a short, and not so sweet, assessment of the writers' opinions: "a load of cobblers" was how he put it. He was in no doubt that Marys had always been the better of the two sides. I didn't let on to Len but I made my mind up there and then to switch my attention to trying to find out just who was right.

(II) RESEARCH

THE AUTHOR HARD AT WORK

Having now decided that the story of the two teams' rivalry was worthy of investigation, I spent the better part of the rest of the year sifting through old newspapers for any item, no matter how small, to do with Rovers and Marys. Considering that, during the period that I was attempting to cover, Nottingham had no fewer than six publications (which for those of you of a certain vintage will recall were the Guardian, Journal, Evening Post, Evening News, Football Post and Football News) my self-imposed task rapidly became very much a labour of love. I wouldn't like to count the number of hours I'd spent in collecting information, but even though my workload was becoming very time consuming, it was also starting to be very addictive. I posted a few notices around the pubs and social clubs of the town, as well as the library, asking for information about football in Arnold in the fifties. The response was a big fat zero. I widened my horizons and the Nottingham Evening Post ran a very small piece mentioning what I was researching. This time I got lucky; one person phoned the contact number in the paper. It may not have seemed much of a breakthrough but it was. The call had come through from Brian Cunningham, a former player with both Rovers and Marys. Soon afterwards I spent a very pleasant evening with Brian and his wife and from then on never looked back. They gave me the name of Alec Casterton, another ex-Rover, as a contact who might be able to help me and they were right. Immediately Alec was a source of excellent information as well as a fascinating archivist in his own right. He was also extremely knowledgeable in letting me know just which of the players of the period I was interested in were still around. This led me to arranging interviews and telephone conversations with anyone and everyone who might be able to help my investigations and provide a little of the detail that wasn't available elsewhere.

What's more, especially after spending time with Alec, I found myself getting more and more immersed in the period that I was researching, and not just the football. If there was an element of nostalgia about my interest then I must stress that it formed just a very small part. I was drawn far more by a desire for a greater knowledge of those events that shaped or were shaped by the times.

(III) WRITING

Then someone asked me whether I was 'writing a book' and to be truthful I hadn't started my research with that in mind. However, by now I was gathering information at an alarming rate and the thought of sharing it with the world at large seemed like a good idea. Well maybe not quite the world, but at least the people of Arnold or even just a few of them. I realised though that if what I was doing was ever going to have a life of its own outside my own scholarship, then I would have to try and make it interesting not only to those who follow football but to a wider readership as a whole.

I decided to take the plunge. With my desk barely visible under all the paraphernalia that I'd accumulated I started the slow process of typing. Now my typing speed is pretty slow but it was still usually far faster than my thought process. I wouldn't say that I suffered from writer's block because that would be making the rather absurd assumption that I was a writer, but it did prove to be a bit of a struggle. I remember my uncle once working his way through a whole new pad of Basildon Bond and almost wearing out a brand new biro before he was finally happy with a letter he was sending his fiancée. My mother too, a more than capable writer once she gets up a head of steam, told me that sometimes she finds it difficult to start a postcard. Luckily, I came across the following quote that made me feel a whole lot better.

"I was working on a proof of one of my poems all morning, and took out the comma. In the afternoon I put it back again." [Oscar Wilde]

I was obviously in good company and this knowledge spurred me ever onwards; slowly admittedly, but still generally onwards. It was just a matter of trying to produce something coherent from the mass of notes and scraps in my possession.

Football doesn't exist in a vacuum and although the game hasn't changed fundamentally during the one hundred and fifty or so years of its official existence it is always very much the product of its time and place. Although the Rovers' scrapbook only began in 1953, I'd ascertained that the story of their rivalry with Marys went back to their formation in 1946 just a year after the Second World War ended and that there was a direct connection between the two events. The re-emergence of football after six grim years of global conflict gave an entertainment starved British public a focal point for their leisure and pleasure. Arnold as a town was very much like any other place in the UK and its inhabitants no different to their fellow countrymen and so it was into an atmosphere of optimism for the future and a desire for change that on the very last day of August 1946 Rovers, consisting in the main of young ex-servicemen recently demobilised, first made their appearance on the football field and in the town's sporting annals.

The football story itself ends in 1958 for reasons which will be made clear later, but the years between then and 1946 were times of significant change and each chapter contains references to key events of the period; do not be put off by the presence of Mussolini in the same paragraph as Stanley Matthews. There are lighter moments as well. Those new fangled items like the bikini and the ball point pen get a mention, together with crazes like jitterbugging and the hula hoop. I've also tried to cover the cultural changes that led to the word 'teenager' becoming the normal term for those who had previously and variously been referred to as just adolescents or young adults so don't be surprised to see Elvis or Marlon Brando make an appearance here and there either.

Sporting achievements other than football pop up as well. In fact it would be quite difficult to avoid saying a few words about the conquest of Everest, the first sub-four minute mile and Jim Laker's record breaking nineteen wickets in one test match when trying to provide an overview of the times.

Essentially though, the story is about football **in** Arnold, which is not quite the same as football **and** Arnold. Writing the history of the town is best left to someone more suitably qualified for the task. Even though I was born at James Street and have lived here all my life, I have to admit that I've only just found out that the old lane at the back of our house when we lived on Hawthorn Crescent was named after 'The Howbecks'. I only knew it as the 'obbucks and I'd never once made the connection until recently. I'm not totally lacking in credentials though; I know the difference between an entry and a twitchel and I can still remember when a pavement was called a corsey. No, the accent is firmly on the achievements of the players and the clubs themselves, with a little bit of old 'Arna' thrown in occasionally, and I hope that as the story unfolds the original conundrum as to which of the sides was the better becomes a little clearer. I also hope that it is one that will be sufficiently interesting to encourage you to carry on turning the pages.

Finally, the eagle eyed amongst you will have noted that the subtitle of the story contains the reference to 'Vol 1'. This was included with tongue firmly in cheek. There won't be a second volume if this one isn't well received so I'm keeping my fingers tightly crossed that it is. I leave you with one more literary quote about the trials and tribulations of getting the story into print.

"I never trust people who say how much fun writing is. The only thing that makes it fun is the anticipation of applause." [Tom Wolfe]

I do so hope that you'll like what you read sufficiently enough to be generous with yours. Anything other than the dreaded slow handclap would be greatly appreciated. Then I would truly be able to say that it really has been fun.

Roger Rann
Arnold, Nottingham, September 2007

THE INTERVIEWEES

A delightful and quite unexpected side effect of carrying out the research behind this project has been the pleasure generated for both parties in the listener / storyteller process. Certainly I have been enthralled by the reminiscences of all those who I managed to get to meet in person or speak to on the phone and I am reliably informed that the experience was just as pleasant for many of them too. The chance to wander down memory lane, to chuckle about past events and to be reminded about the exploits of their youth seems not to have been too much of a chore.

Of course not every bit of information that I've been told could possibly be included as it would need to be as thick as a telephone directory as a consequence. Nor have there been any 'off the record' or 'don't quote me on this' caveats. What has shone through is the very good naturedness of all those I have spoken to, and that includes wives as well, and the great sense of camaraderie of the time. 'Happy days' was a phrase used more than once.

As to the content of what was discussed, not everyone of course had the same power of recall as others. Given that the span of years under review began in 1946 and ended in 1958, and that the players of the era would generally be only in their twenties at the time, it would have been difficult to cast the net over all those available and haul in anyone under seventy years of age. As a result memories have had to withstand the unavoidable march of time and some were patchy, some conflicting, and on the odd occasion completely gone for good. Happily many were not only intact but surprisingly sharp and on many occasions a researcher's dream, either leading to information that could be corroborated via other sources or fleshing out the detail of the skeleton of what was already in the public domain.

Even when discussing the inevitable loss of memory there was a great deal of humour shown. Albert Trash, eighty-something supporter, told me with a big grin on his face during one of my gentle interrogations: "I can remember those days quite clearly, but then I'll forget where I've gone and put my shoes." I nodded sagely, but didn't tell him that even in my fifties I've already experienced more than one or two 'senior moments' of my own. His dry appreciation of his predicament was echoed by ex-Regent player Eric Woollacott who, at ninety-one, was the oldest of my interviewees. When I remarked on the precision of the information that he was giving me over the telephone, he thanked me for my kind words but said: "You do remember these things, it's true, but then you'll still find you've left your glasses in the fridge; I think it's best just to laugh about it."

In fact I am extremely grateful to everyone who found the time to talk with me, both in person and on the phone, especially those who I rang so often that they would have been forgiven for thinking "Oh not him again". So many of the calls would start with me saying "Have you got a minute, I've just got one quick question..." and would end up lasting half an hour. Then there were the 'twenty minute' visits that took up what seemed like the entire afternoon. In many respects I wish I'd started the project much earlier so that many more of the 'Kings of the Recs' were still around, but I'll content myself with the knowledge that my search for information has still managed to raise a few smiles and laughs along the way from those that are.

For my part, the chance to have made their acquaintance, to have spent time in their company, and to have been able to listen to their stories about a time when I was 'nobbut a lad missen', has been nothing short of an absolute pleasure and a privilege; for which I thank them all.

INTERVIEWEES

SA	*SAM ARCHER*	*Player*
KA	*KEN ATHERLEY*	*Player*
AC	*ALEC CASTERTON*	*Player*
BC	*BRIAN CUNNINGHAM*	*Player*
FG	*FRANNY GREENSMITH*	*Player*
AM	*ALBERT MOORE*	*Player*
GP	*GEOFF PARR*	*Player*
JP	*JOHN PIKE*	*Player*
GR	*GWEN RANN*	*Author's Mother*
LR	*LEN ROCKLEY*	*Player*
ET	*ERIC THOMPSON*	*Supporter, Committeeman*
RT	*ROY THOMPSON*	*Supporter*
PW	*PEGGY WHITT*	*Supporter*
RW	*RON WHITT*	*Player*
BW	*W 'BILL' WHITT*	*Player*
EW	*ERIC WOOLLACOTT*	*Player*

CHAPTER ONE 1945-46

The Second World War finally came to an end in Europe with the German surrender on May 7 1945 and three months later in the Pacific when Japan did likewise on August 14. Organised football had been put on hold for the six years' duration of the conflict, even though at the full-time professional level attempts had been made to provide some element of continuity, albeit in a very makeshift manner compared with the long established league and cup competitions of the pre-war years. Many young footballers, both professional and amateur, had served their country during the war, and were still on active service well after its conclusion. Not enough of them could be demobilised fast enough for the Football League to be able to resume its normal structure by the start of the 1945 season in August.

This didn't stop the two main knock-out competitions from being reintroduced. The Football Association's Challenge Cup, better known as the FA Cup, and its non-professional equivalent the FA Amateur Cup were both played for in the 1945-46 season. Derby County beat Charlton Athletic 4-1 at Wembley in the senior final, whilst the amateurs of Barnet overcame their Durham rivals Bishop Auckland by the odd goal in five at Stamford Bridge, home of Chelsea Football Club. The crowds of 98,215 and 53,832 showed that the desire for viewing the game hadn't diminished. In fact, the absence of competitive action through the long hard years of the war had whetted the appetites of the paying public. Attendances in the post war years were the highest in the history of the organised game in this country, peaking with an audience for Football League games in 1948-49 of over forty one million, a figure not even bettered in the days of the Premiership, Champions League, and wall-to-wall television coverage. The man in the street back in 1945 was eager to be entertained, and football was one of the main beneficiaries.

It wasn't just watching the game that was an attraction, but playing it too. One of the immediate problems for the professional game was that many grounds had been directly damaged as a result of enemy action. Manchester United's Old Trafford was severely hit by a German air-raid in March 1941 and it wasn't until eight years later that it was rebuilt. In the meantime, they had to share the Maine Road ground of neighbours Manchester City. The problem for the amateur game, especially in and around Nottingham, was a lack of grounds, rather than damage to them. Many had been used for alternative purposes during the past six years and others had been rendered unavailable due to neglect.

Of course, this small inconvenience was just one of many felt by the population as a whole. The war may have ended but its impact on the country certainly hadn't. In fact the cessation of hostilities ushered in an era of austerity that would last longer than anyone could have envisaged at the time. Enemy planes and doodlebugs might not be threatening the skies above Britain, but the hardships of wartime rationing of foodstuffs, clothing and furniture remained. Petrol, too, required coupons, but as private motor vehicles were a bit thin on the ground in Arnold, this wasn't a matter of great concern for the majority of the town's inhabitants. For them 1945 was a time of coal fires and outside privies, of a bath in a tin tub in front of the open fire or else a trip down to the Public Baths that used to be housed in the same building as the Arnold Swimming Pool when it was situated on Arnot Hill Road. Television sets were not yet available to the masses and refrigerators, vacuum cleaners and other labour saving devices were still some way away too. At least before the year was out ball point pens would be on sale for the very first time in England, just a couple of months after they'd appeared in the USA. Unfortunately they were more expensive than a decent fountain pen.

It wasn't all doom and gloom though, especially at street level where the summer saw thousands of parties thrown to celebrate the victory in Europe. It is popularly believed that impromptu street parties were the norm on VE Day itself, 8 May, but the reality was somewhat different. Although there had been an anticipation of the end of the war for some while, the rumours and delays led to a sense of anticlimax, especially when the day of the German surrender came and went. It wasn't until three o'clock the following afternoon that Churchill formally addressed the nation to officially announce the end of the war in Europe. In amongst the more sombre matters his speech covered he mentioned that "we may allow ourselves a brief period of rejoicing".

He was taken at his word. The occupants of the place where I would be born three years later, James Street, like many others in Arnold, put in plans for a street party so that they could all have a bit of 'rejoicing' of their own. It required a lot of organisation, but just a few weeks later the families of the fifty or so terraced houses that faced each other down the length of the street could be proud of their efforts.

GR : Someone had managed to get hold of some trestle tables which were placed down the middle of the street. Bunting was strung across from the front upstairs rooms of the houses on either side. Mr Bernard Turner, who lived straight opposite, came from a musical family and was encouraged to bring his piano out onto the street. Our next door neighbour, Mrs Fanny Booth, had a barrel of ale just inside her front door and everyone was welcome to help themselves to a drink. The food was by no means extravagant because of the rationing and shortages that we were experiencing, but there was plenty to go round. It was a memorable day that showed just what a close community we were in the street. Later in the evening with the festivities still going strong, a bonfire had been started just around the corner at the bottom of the street and torches were lit and paraded up and down. I was eighteen at the time and it was a memorable day even at that age. I imagine that for the younger children it would have made even more of an impression.

JAMES STREET : VE STREET PARTY SUMMER 1945 (Joan Jones Collection)

So successful were the events of the day in James Street that when the Japanese surrendered later that August they did it all over again.

GR : The second party wasn't quite so grand, but it was another lovely occasion. This time my future mother-in-law came up to stay with us. She lived in Epping, Essex, just off the main

Harlow to London road, and she hadn't even been to a VE party. If I had any doubts about how she would take to our neighbours, I needn't have worried. Before long, she disappeared with Mrs Booth only to be found later down at the Lord Nelson pub. She remarked just how much more friendly people were up here than back down where she lived.

In between these two public displays of celebration, there had been the small matter of a General Election in July. As a direct consequence of the war, Parliament had been sitting for ten years without the politicians having to go to the polls, but when they finally did it resulted in the shock defeat of the Conservatives, with Churchill still their leader, by Clement Attlee's Labour Party. It wasn't a close run affair either, as the winners ended up with a 145 seat majority.

Of course wars change people and societies and there was a general feeling in the country, reflected by the election result, that social improvements were needed. Labour had gone to the nation with a policy of reform and the promise of a Welfare State that embraced full employment, a national health scheme, expansion of education, and what was considered to be the single most important issue facing the country, a new housing policy.

Churchill was reported to have been surprised and stunned by his party's crushing defeat. His wartime leadership meant that he had been held in high esteem by the country at large and his personal popularity had remained high right up to the election, but the voters' belief was that the Labour Party's raft of pledges would better meet the urgent requirement of rebuilding the country. Its manifesto was clear also in its intent to use public ownership as part of its economic strategy, and some six months later the Bank of England was the first, but not the last, enterprise to be nationalised.

Whilst the serious business of reconstruction was at the forefront of everyone's minds, all work and no play would have made Jack and Jill a very dull pair. Popular entertainment steadily expanded, especially the frequency of trips to the cinema and the dance hall. A modern dance craze, brought into the country by American GIs, was sweeping the nation's ballrooms. Variously called swing, street or jazz dancing, and with variations such as the Lindy Hop, it was far removed from old style ballroom dancing. So much so that it was deemed alarming enough to result in 'No Jitterbugging' signs being posted at the more sedate and traditional dance establishments. There was of course a greatly increased enthusiasm for another form of vigorous activity; football. However, a clear distinction could be drawn between those wishing to be on the field of play itself and the larger number content to take their places on the terraces and in the stands. The reorganisation of the game at the local amateur level was essentially of most importance to young men wishing to actually play. For those just wanting to watch, and not forgetting a sizeable female following of the game, Nottingham was well served in the professional ranks by the two city clubs, Forest and Notts, with Mansfield Town just up the road.

The Midland League, a competition for part-time professional teams and the second elevens of Forest and Notts among others, managed to reform in time for the start of the 1945/46 season. Two Nottinghamshire sides, Ollerton Colliery and Ransome & Marles of Newark were members of this league, but the majority of local teams below this level would generally have to wait another season before they could return to the competitive playing field.

Lack of grounds and delays in demobilisation have been referred to earlier, but there were other obstacles of an even more essential nature to be overcome. A shortage of leather and rubber lead to a lack of footballs themselves, and the rationing of clothes meant that it was extremely difficult to kit out a team in the first place. Two clothing coupons were required for a pair of socks, three for a pair of shorts, four for a shirt, five for a pair of boots, and the specialist position of goalkeeper needed eight for a knitted jersey; one hundred and fifty eight in all and not an easy task.

If these inconveniences were a contributing factor in delaying the debut of Rovers and the return of Marys until the 1946/47 season, there was another Arnold side that had been spared the widespread problems elsewhere and who made the most of their opportunity. They were the 1827 (Arnold) Squadron Air Training Cadets team who were unbeaten winners of the

Notts ATC Championship in 1945/46. They finished with the outstanding record of twenty one wins and a single draw from twenty two matches, scoring a hundred and fifty three goals in the process, around seven a game, whilst conceding only thirty. Many of the players involved would subsequently go on to play for either Rovers or Marys or even both, and one or two at a higher standard than that; they included the brothers Geoff and Denis Parr, one of the Cunningham brothers John, one of the Hazledine brothers Don, as well as Les Peel, Jack Brace, and Roy Carter.

ARNOLD ATC 1945-46 : Back Row (l to r); F/Lt H G Waltho (Commanding Officer), Cdt D Parr, P/O L A Cox (Sports Officer), F/Sgt J Armson, Cdt J Bailey, Cpl J Cunningham, F/Sgt A Berridge, Cpl F Crane. Front Row; Cdt L Peel, Cdt D Hazledine, Cdt J Brace, Cdt R Carter, Cdt G Parr.

(Geoff Parr Collection)

GP : Coming from Arnold and being of the same age group, we'd all known each other even before we joined the ATC. My brother Denis, who was a couple of years younger than me, was the only one of us who wasn't born in 1928 or 1929. Our HQ was located in what became known as the 'Oxo' building on Mansfield Road, just up from the Old Spot pub, where we were taught the basics like aircraft identification and so on, and we did our drilling in another building on the opposite side of the road.

Our home ground was the 'Top Rec' and we played against other ATC teams from the area such as Beeston, Hucknall, and Stapleford. Transport to away games was by bus or we might get a lift in one of the officers' cars. We had gone to Stapleford during the winter and when we arrived it was obvious that the pitch was in no fit condition to play a match on. There had been severe frosts and neither team wanted to play but for some reason the referee disagreed and the game got under way. I used to play on the left wing but on this particular day I was in goal. Football was impossible and I hardly saw any action. Eventually the game had to be abandoned, but not before I had frozen to the bone. I was so cold that after the match Mr Cox, the Sports Officer, drove me straight back and dropped me off right outside the front door of our house. I had hot aches for three weeks afterwards.

The training that Geoff and his mates' received as cadets in the Royal Air Force would prove to have been a good grounding when they were later called up for their National Service, but for most of them back in early 1946, those eighteen months in uniform could wait. They were more interested in the next season, when football's normal service would finally be resumed.

CHAPTER TWO 1946-47

If any one of the thousands of young men in the armed forces who were still making their way back home over a year after the war had finished had found himself in Paris in July 1946, he may have spotted a small item in the news. Despite claims to the contrary, bikinis went on sale in Paris for the first time. It was a small item in more ways than one, but it showed that in some aspects of the world at large, in this case French fashion, the shadow of war was showing signs of receding. A month later, followers of football in Nottinghamshire could finally begin to look forward with some confidence to brighter times too as the various local leagues in the county resumed their programmes almost seven years after they had been rudely interrupted back in early September 1939.

As it turned out, Marys' re-emergence would not take place until the following Saturday, but on August 31, 1946 Rovers made their first ever appearance and gave immediate notice of their arrival with a resounding 12-0 victory. Admittedly, the setting was only the second division of the Notts Realm League and their opponents the reserve eleven of a club called Carlton Stars, so a certain sense of perspective needs to be maintained, but when they repeated the feat with another double figure victory seven days later, there was no doubt that the seeds of a rivalry with their town neighbours had already been sown.

The movers and shakers behind the formation of Rovers were Harry Redgate, Charlie Kirk, and Joe Turton. Not only did they have to deal with the administration of the club in its earliest days but they also donned the playing kit every Saturday too. Lining up as goalkeeper, right back and left back respectively, they had probably been far busier off the pitch than they were on it in those first couple of one-sided matches.

Not to be outdone, Marys had started with a bang of their own, winning their opening game 8-4. Centre forward Albert Allcock, a leading player and prominent goal scorer for the club before the war, continued where he had left off by accounting for all but one of his side's goals. Marys had been in the Realm League themselves back in 1939, but had joined the Nottingham Spartan League on resumption of activities.

Both of the competitions that the Arnold clubs were now members of were long established. The Spartan League was the older of the two, having been founded in 1909, whilst the Realm League had originated in 1925 under the title of the 'Boys Realm' League, named after the popular publication of the time. Not only was the Spartan League the senior in age, but it assumed a higher status too.

Nottinghamshire teams outside the Football League were eligible to play for one of the Notts Football Association's three county cups; Senior, Intermediate, and Junior. Whilst Realm League sides would play in the Junior Cup, members of the Spartan League would take part at Intermediate level.

If this set the two teams apart somewhat, it was echoed by their respective locations at either end of the town. Marys, as was befitting of their name, had as their home ground the playing field adjacent to the parish church, known to all and sundry as the 'Top Rec', an abbreviation for the 'recreation ground at the top end of the town'. Rovers' home pitch was on the 'Bottom Rec', the meaning of which needs no elaboration. It was surrounded by housing on all four sides; accessible from Charles Street and George Street behind the goals and sandwiched between Arnot Hill Road and Nottingham Road down its flanks.

Both were in public ownership, and neither had any changing facilities. Marys' dressing rooms were at the Seven Stars pub, situated at the far end of the footpath that led from the pitch, down alongside the church's graveyard and onto Calverton Road. Rovers' players had use of a pub too, in their case The Greyhound, more or less opposite the junction of Charles Street and Nottingham Road, with washing facilities provided by an outside tap in the car park.

What both teams also had in common was the distinctive sound of the studs of the players' boots on the hard surfaces beneath them as they beat a path on their way to their respective pitches. The boots of that era, toe-capped and high-ankled, had leather studs that were secured to the sole of the boot by small nails, three to each stud, or 'nog' as they were usually referred to. The abrasive action of roads, pavements and paths between the pubs and pitches soon began to wear the leather of the studs down, exposing the three nail heads. The use of this type of stud has now effectively been outlawed, replaced by the modern screw-in plastic version and the even newer preference for a cleat style sole. As it happened, the use of the old leather stud was fairly dubious even during its lifetime. The last of the original thirteen Rules of Association Football, drafted in 1863, stated that 'No player shall wear projecting nails...on the soles or heels of his boots'. The exposure of the nails was made worse during the routine cleaning of boots between games. More often than not a small wire brush would be used to get rid of the previous match's mud on the upper and sole before the upper was lovingly lathered in Dubbin to help keep the leather soft and protect it from the elements. Whilst the wire brush was effective in the cleaning process, it also had the additional effect of wearing down the stud whilst shining the nail heads and giving them a rather menacing look.

Not that this practice was just the lot of the local footballer, with its inevitable and deleterious effect on shins and calves. During his own playing days the author found out that at the highest level of the professional game it was actively encouraged. He was putting in a shift in the boot room of a then First Division club and had just finished cleaning a number of first team players' boots in the manner outlined above. Dubbin had by then been replaced by good old fashioned polish, toe caps and ankle protection had disappeared, but leather studs were still in use. One of the coaching staff came in to the boot room to check the quality of the work. Pleasantries exchanged, he picked up a boot, turned it over, rubbed a finger over the exposed metal and said, with no small degree of relish, "my little beauties". The glint in his eye as he repeated the words was matched only by those flashing off the nail heads themselves.

If the choice of footwear might be a shared experience between professional and amateur, the job of putting up the nets and marking out the lines of the pitch before the game certainly wasn't. These tasks invariably fell not only on the shoulders of the players but also various committee men of both clubs. Back in 1946, before the introduction of wheelable line markers capable of applying a standard and consistent width of whitewash, both teams visited the local joinery firm of Henry Jew & Sons Ltd on the morning of a home match to cadge a plentiful supply of sawdust to do the job. Nobody hung around at the firm's Arnot Hill Road premises at the rear of the Bonington cinema for too long because they were also home to the company's other function as funeral directors, and there was always the worry of stumbling across a cadaver laid out in the front office.

Half time wouldn't of course be spent back in the warmth of the dressing room but instead amounted to no more than a quick huddle in a group on the side lines, sucking the proverbial oranges whilst well meaning advice went in one ear and out the other. The trainer would hover over any player that looked in need of a bit of attention but just the thought of the standard remedy of the time, a cold sponge more often than not applied down the shorts despite the damage being elsewhere, was enough for most guys to decline the offer. It wouldn't always be this way as improvements in facilities would be made down the years but for now at least it was against this backdrop that the two Arnold teams tried to establish their credentials where it really mattered, out on the pitch.

Neither of the two sides' cracking start to the season was a flash in the pan. By the end of October, both remained unbeaten in league games with Rovers heading their division with a one hundred percent record. Marys had dropped just a single point but were still only fourth, mainly as a result of being games in hand of the top three, but also because the two leaders, Linby Colliery and Worthington Simpson had made terrific starts of their own. Both appeared capable of providing a formidable barrier to success for the maroon and golds and when the works side from Newark visited Marys early in November, the game promised to be a cracker.

It didn't disappoint. The Nottingham Football Post reported that 'no one could wish to see a finer game' and that it was 'truly great'. The fact that the two sides shared nine goals probably helped the paper's reporter come to that conclusion, but it was the old cliché of the ninety minutes being a distinct 'game of two halves' that added to the enjoyment of all those present. Marys were under the cosh so much during the first half that they turned around four goals down and with the game seemingly beyond them. The half time oranges and threat of the cold sponge obviously worked a treat because with Albert Allcock notching a hat-trick, the second half was spent camped in the visitors half. It was 'all but the kitchen sink' stuff and two of Marys' players failed to finish the game through injury. These being the days long before substitutes were allowed Marys' remaining nine men just couldn't find a way through as the minutes ticked down to full time and eventually had to concede defeat. It finished 5-4 in the visitors favour; a valiant comeback by the home side but a setback for their title hopes for the season.

It's an old adage that good attacks win games but good defences win championships and even this early in the season it was obvious that Marys would need to score quite a few goals each game to be sure of victory, so difficult had they found it to keep the opposition out. Averaging five goals per match at the right end, courtesy mainly of the exploits of their prolific centre forward, they had unfortunately conceded twenty one in just seven matches, three a game. By comparison, Linby's goalkeeper, with his team topping the table with ten wins out of ten, had only had to pick the ball out of his net a mere eight times, a tremendous achievement at any level. By the end of the month, Marys' weakness had become their undoing. Two games against mid-table sides saw them pick up just a single point. Despite scoring five times, three goals were again conceded in both contests and they slipped down to fifth with the leaders pulling away ominously.

On the other side of town, matters were distinctly more promising. Their double figure victories in the first two games hadn't been repeated, but Rovers were continuing to win comfortably. More importantly, whilst scoring as prolifically as their 'top o' town' neighbours, they were also managing to deny the opposition far more easily and were conceding just a goal a game. Not only that, but in seventeen year old Don Hazledine they had unearthed a player destined for a much higher level of football. Playing both as a wing half and as a forward, Don had been receiving glowing reports, with the Football Post already referring to him as 'one of the cleverest players in the league'. His emergence wasn't a total surprise because he had been a member of the successful Arnold ATC side of the previous season. Indeed, most of those young cadets had made the transition into adult teams; Don with Rovers, John Cunningham with Marys, and a number of others, including Geoff Parr, with Notts Regent in Division One of the Realm League.

The latter will feature in future chapters, but for the time being it will suffice to mention that they were a long established club that were then using one of the many pitches at the Highfields recreation ground as their home venue. Before long they would relocate to the Top Rec and share the two-pitch facilities at Church Lane with Marys. As quite a few of their players had connections with Arnold, this created a genuine triumvirate of town sides competing alongside each other for honours. Not only that, but the clubs vied with each other for local players too, with at least a couple of guys having spells with all three outfits and a large number turning out for the various permutations of any two of the rival sides. This 'fluidity' between teams was of course linked with the times in a way not seen today. Back in those immediate post-war years, and indeed for quite a while to come, players, just as the majority of the population they came from, had no cars of their own, and the prospect of playing for a side outside your own locality was hardly an option. Buses, trolleybuses and trains were all well and good, but eventually private vehicles would prove to be the most preferable means of personal transport and would herald the demise of the local team being the preserve of home town players. For now though Rovers and Marys didn't need to cast their nets too far afield.

By the time the hectic Christmas programme of matches began, Rovers remained top of their division with nineteen points out of a possible twenty, their only hiccup being a 2-2 draw with one of their nearest rivals, the still unbeaten Cotgrave. Three games later, amazingly played in just four days, they had consolidated their position as leaders with a maximum haul of six points. In the days when men were men, they won 9-0 on Christmas Day, a Wednesday, 2-0 on Boxing Day and 10-0 for good measure on the Saturday. This latest victory was their fifth in a row without conceding a goal. Marys weren't quite as successful, winning just two of their three fixtures during the season of goodwill. Albert Allcock's run of personal success continued with five goals on Boxing Day, but his efforts weren't enough to prevent his team from slipping down to sixth place as the year drew to its close.

ALBERT ALLCOCK RECEIVING AN AWARD FROM REFEREE JOE WILLIAMS

(Geoff Parr Collection)

Even at this approximate half way mark in the season, it was obvious that any hopes that Marys might have in picking up any silverware would have to come from success in a cup competition. Having already been knocked out of the Notts Intermediate Cup by Hucknall Collieries of the Notts Amateur League, their last chance of honours depended upon winning the Spartan League Cup. A first round home tie against next to bottom Burton Joyce presented the club with a real likelihood of progressing to the next stage. Unfortunately, the game, played on the last Saturday in January, provided more evidence of the old saying that 'the cup is full of surprises'. Despite yet another hat trick from Albert Allcock, taking his tally to thirty five for the season, Marys had another bad day in defence and again succumbed to a high scoring defeat by five goals to four. If only the side had been as stingy in conceding as Albert had been prodigious in scoring the table would have painted a different picture. This was the sixth game where he had registered three goals or more and he had the remarkable record of accounting for more than half of his side's total so far this season.

Rovers on the other hand went from strength to strength. Three straight league wins in the first month of 1947 saw them comfortable leaders of the division with just that single point loss to Cotgrave their only blemish in fifteen outings. By contrast with their neighbours, their last match in January saw them hit double figures once again and take their average goals per game up to six. Rovers had a sharpshooter of their own in Ernie Barber. He'd played in fourteen matches and achieved the remarkable feat of scoring in every one whilst racking up forty goals for the season so far. The boys in the Arsenal colours of red and white could hardly wait for the next game to come to maintain their hot streak whilst the maroon and golds might be wishing the same thing but for an entirely different reason; in their case a quick chance of a return to winning ways and some redemption for the cup defeat. As it happened, both would be kept waiting, and for some while too, but not for any reasons to do with football.

On that last Saturday in January, no one at either club could have imagined that it would be almost two months before they were to play their next game. Bad weather had tried to bite on a couple of occasions prior to this, once before Christmas and again during the first week of the New Year, but had failed to make a lasting impression. As January turned to February, it returned with a vengeance, and the football boots stayed in the kit bag.

Snow came to the northern and southern extremities of the country first on the 22 January and eventually left no area unscathed, falling every day somewhere in the United Kingdom for the next fifty five days, with the weather so cold that the snow accumulated. The temperature seldom rose more than a degree or two below freezing and across Britain drifts more than fifteen feet deep blocked roads and railways, often needing the armed services to help clear them. People, and not just those in isolated villages and farmsteads but in towns such as Buxton and Bridlington, were cut off for days at a time and relied upon supplies being air lifted in by helicopter. And if snow was the major problem, the lack of sunshine that went with it only added to the gloom, with the citizens of Nottingham particular sufferers. The city didn't see a single ray of sunshine on twenty two of February's twenty eight days.

GR : I remember the snow being piled so high at the sides of Mansfield Road from the Thackeray's Lane junction down to Valley Road that it was impossible to see over the top. Even though the sky was still visible, the effect was almost the same as passing through a tunnel.

Demands on coal and electricity supplies were intense. Both these industries were nationalised in 1947 as part of the Labour government's drive towards state ownership but it wouldn't have mattered who owned them as Mother Nature wreaked havoc. Four million workers were made idle by power cuts caused by coal trains being unable to reach power stations as a result of deep snow drifts, the disruption to road transport was huge with even major highways such as the A1 blocked, and the fishing industry was crippled. As a result fish, one of the few food items not rationed, became scarce.

The severe weather and the misery that went with it continued into March with even greater ferocity and temperatures fell to as low as minus twenty degrees centigrade. Not until the middle of the month did it finally relent when milder weather broke through to all areas, but the subsequent rapid thaw created devastating problems of its own. The ground had been frozen hard after weeks of frost and the rain and meltwater couldn't soak away. As a result the surface water ran off and river levels rose relentlessly. Vast areas of southern England were quickly under water but if the snow and resultant flooding weren't bad enough then the weather gods decided a final flourish might just be in order. Severe gales swept the country, breaching dykes in East Anglia and Lincolnshire and causing rivers to burst their banks. Most of South Yorkshire was awash, and in the middle of the month the Trent's defences were overcome at Nottingham and hundreds of homes were flooded. The city's Meadows area was particular badly hit. The streets between the rows of old terraced houses resembled the canals of Venice, though not of course that famous city's beauty. For several days, transport in the worst affected areas had to be by boat and even amphibious army vehicles and a number of families remained marooned on the upper floors of their houses until the water subsided.

GR : As we didn't have television, we relied upon the newspapers and radio for information. There were no twenty four hour news services bringing us 'breaking news' and up to date pictures to go with it. When we'd heard that the Trent had burst its banks quite a few of us decided to go into Nottingham to see the flooding up close. I'd never seen the river in such condition before. Trent Bridge was still crossable, but there wasn't much of a gap between the water level and the top of the bridge's arches. Although we didn't use the term back then, a youngster of today viewing the scene would probably have called it 'awesome'.

The country, struggling anyway with the aftermath of war, had suffered a setback that no-one could have foreseen. Industry and commerce had effectively ground to a halt during the severe weather and the impact on the man and woman in the street was pronounced. The government had announced 'profoundly gloomy forecasts of Britain's food position', cutting the fresh meat ration. Vegetable supplies were blighted by frosts and even beer production had to be halved. By the time Rovers and Marys took to the field again on 22 March, the economy was on its knees.

Help would eventually arrive would be some months in arriving. In the meanwhile, for our local footballing protagonists, normal service was resumed once more. Except of course for the fact that there were only seven Saturdays left in the regular season and both teams were faced with an extremely demanding task of fitting fixtures in. Rovers had only played fifteen league games in seven months and now had to cram in thirteen in less than two to finish the season. Marys were in an even worse position, having completed just twelve of their scheduled twenty six matches by the resumption. Even the big boys of the first division of the Football League were similarly affected. By the time a full fixture list was possible, Sheffield United found themselves eight games in hand of Blackpool. As a consequence, The Football Association extended the season and it eventually finished on 14 June when the Sheffield team finally caught up with the rest. Of course matters were less straightforward in local football because many public pitches were traditionally turned over to cricket at the beginning of each May. The two Arnold sides didn't have that particular obstacle to overcome for their home fixtures but it still impacted on their schedule during the extended run-in.

For the time being though it was business as usual in the first game following the enforced break. Rovers had a comfortable four-one win whilst Marys unsurprisingly conceded their customary three goals. Happily, their forward line was continuing to fulfil its part of the bargain and rattled in six at the other end to guarantee both points. Amazingly, and despite the pressure to complete fixtures, Marys' next game was to prove to be another three weeks away. In truth the championship had long been conceded and it was just a matter of which of the two runaway leaders, Linby or Worthington Simpson, finished top. When their next game finally came around, Marys certainly did the Newark club no favours by losing six-nil to the colliery side. It was no more than a true reflection of the gulf between the two teams.

The rivalry between the two best sides in the Spartan League continued right to the end of the season. Games between them attracted large crowds with thirteen hundred turning out for the league match at the Gatehouse Ground, Hucknall. When the two teams met in the Spartan League Cup and Notts Intermediate Cup semi-finals, sixteen hundred saw the first game at Linby and two thousand attended the county cup tie at Newark. Linby were winners in both the cup clashes and went on to claim the Intermediate Cup whilst their Newark rivals had to be content with the Spartan League championship in which they remained unbeaten. Worthingtons would remain to lock horns with the maroon and golds in the Spartan League again the next season, but Linby, under the guidance of former Arsenal professional Tim Coleman, were on a fast track for success that would see them move up the leagues, win the Notts Senior Cup three times in five years, and make it through to the first round of the FA Cup proper and meet Football League opposition in the form of Gillingham. Although the full-time side proved too strong in the end, a crowd of six thousand three hundred packed the Gatehouse Ground to witness the event. In this first season of post-war football it had been Marys' misfortune to have had to battle it out with two teams destined for success at a higher level.

The only really memorable event of the Saints' year came when they hosted a match against a German Prisoner of War (POW) eleven towards the end of the season. Because of the impact of the atrocious winter it was well into the middle of May when this most unusual of games took place. Unusual but not unique as it was actually one of a number of matches in the summer of 1947 that were arranged between teams from the Nottingham and Mansfield areas and sides made up of POWs still awaiting repatriation. There were at least seven camps in Nottinghamshire as a whole, maybe more; even now a fully documented record doesn't exist. What is known is that most of the POWs were put to work mostly on the land or in support of the British Army when it was called upon to provide extra labour in times of crisis. In fact it had only been a couple of months earlier that POWs had helped the Army clear railway lines made impassable by drifting snow. Not only that, but they accounted for one-fifth of all farm work carried out in the previous year and were also used extensively on road work and building projects.

Once the war had ended, the lengthy task of reuniting them with their homeland began. It was a slow process, one that wasn't finally completed until November 1948, over three years later. It was little wonder considering that estimates as to how many POWs were actually in Britain varied between three hundred thousand and half a million, and not all of them were in a particular hurry to head east anyway. If Britain was hardly an earthly paradise in the post-war years, it was heaven in comparison with large parts of Europe.

At least once hostilities ended, the POWs had a certain degree of freedom to come and go as they pleased. They were often seen in Arnold itself, Italians and Germans, and were normally distinguishable by a distinctive patch or patches sewed onto their clothing. There was no great hostility towards them in the locality, especially the Italians, but there had been a degree of resentment rippling through the country when it was learned that POW rations, especially meat, were greater than those of the civilian population. This was a consequence of the Geneva Convention that stated that POWs should be allocated the same rations as those enjoyed by the British Army though whether the clause was strictly adhered to remains a moot point. Other than that, animosity never appeared to be an issue in the Arnold district. In fact a number of local POWs even turned their hands to crafting a variety of goods and objects from scrap metal and odd bits of material and successfully offered them for sale on a door to door basis around the town.

The series of POW matches played over the summer of 1947, however, were the most prominent examples of genuine attempts at reconciliation between sets of people who had been bitter enemies not long before. The concept certainly caught the public's imagination. Just the week before Marys' own game, The Forest recreation ground had seen a match between Notts Corinthians and a representative side made up of POWs from 51 Camp, based at Allington, near Grantham. A tremendous crowd of six thousand saw the visiting team win comfortably by three goals to nil. Maybe the difference in rations had been a decisive factor; it could even have been the rumoured presence in the POW eleven of a German international player. It has recently been reported that August Lenz, who'd starred for Borussia Dortmund before the war and had scored nine times in fourteen appearances for his country, had definitely been based at 51 Camp but he appears to have been repatriated some time during 1947 so his actual participation in the Corinthians game is questionable.

Such was the amount of disinformation at the time that many recollections of the POW XI that faced Marys, always mention the inclusion of at least one international amongst the opposition, sometimes even more. Chairman Walter 'Kegga' Parr, father of Geoff, gave an interview in 1981 in which he averred that the POW team had 'included three internationals' in their side. 'Kegga' was never one to miss a chance to talk up his beloved Marys, and the story doing the rounds at the time regarding guys from the German national side playing for the various POW outfits was too good an opportunity to miss. Peddling it in the run-up to the game would quite obviously increase the public interest in the match, whilst repeating it after the contest had finished only served to reinforce just how well 'our boys' had done. Win, lose, or draw, the result would only have been accomplished despite or because of the presence of these 'internationals'.

For the record the POWs were actually from 166 Camp at Wollaton Park and a contemporary newspaper report of the time gave the result as three-two to the Germans, watched by a crowd of four thousand. Walter had the visitors scoring another two goals, saying 'not surprisingly they hammered us' and the attendance higher by a couple of thousand. Given that the Church Lane ground had, unlike The Forest, no natural terracing or embankments, the prospect of the crowd at Arnold being of similar size to the earlier Corinthians game was highly unlikely. However, irrespective of the actual number, it was without doubt the largest crowd which had yet assembled to watch a game on the Top Rec and when the half-time collection was made, it was necessary to use a bucket rather than the normal wooden box; 'easier to catch the cash as they threw it' according to 'Kegga'.

The doubtful possibility of catching a glimpse of an 'international' or two wasn't the only reason why such large crowds flocked to see these POW games. In those days England didn't participate in the World Cup and competitions amongst European clubs and nations hadn't yet begun. With blanket coverage from television still a long way away the only chance for many of seeing an actual game against teams from abroad came with a trip to the local cinema to see the odd friendly international. Even then the event would be distilled into a couple of minutes of newsreel footage that in itself followed a rather predictable pattern and left the viewer hardly any better informed about the opposition than he had been before. Invariably, the clip would start with the kick-off and a couple of passes, fast forward to the ball in the net following a goal, the cameraman seemingly having missed the crucial act of the actual scoring shot or header, cut across to a sea of happy faces in the crowd with hats and rattles in plentiful supply, and back to the action just in time for the final whistle, irrespective of the final score. All shown with a commentary delivered in the kind of accent never heard 'round our way'.

That the rare chance of seeing 'Johnny Foreigner' in the flesh held a great fascination amongst the British footballing public had never been more obvious than during the previous season. In November 1945 a party from Moscow Dynamo had travelled to the UK for a series of four games against its top professional sides. A month later they'd left unbeaten, having been watched by a total of two hundred and seventy thousand spectators with tens of thousands more locked outside the stadia. Even back then the media coverage, mostly confined to radio and the printed word, rivalled anything that a much later obsession with the damaged metatarsals of England's David Beckham and Wayne Rooney could offer. Such was the clamour to view these 'aliens' that fans amongst the eighty five thousand jammed into Chelsea's Stamford Bridge ground for the opening game even resorted to taking their lives in their hands by watching the match from a standing or sitting position on the actual roofs of the various grandstands.

Amongst the spectators similarly straining for a view of the action in the POW games would have been one or two local scouts on the look out for talent; from either side. Internationals in their ranks or not, it was generally acknowledged that all the various POW teams played skilful football, much like Dynamo had done, and there is a fair chance that for some of them a decent career in the game awaited them on their return home. Roy Thompson, who with his brother Eric followed Marys home and away for over thirty years, saw the game on the Top Rec.

RT : I was just a lad then but I remember the POW team looked like a semi-pro side, like they'd dragged in players from other camps. It was like an Intermediate side playing a Midland League team. They made such an impression on me that when there was another match down at The Forest against Christ Church, I went there as well. There must have been five thousand there, the embankment was full. I think half the crowd were POWs on a day out.

Two of the POW players who didn't make the journey back but preferred to stay and play their trade in this country were the Manchester City goalie Bert Trautmann, famous for his heroics in the closing minutes of the 1956 FA Cup Final after he'd broken a bone in his neck following a collision with an opposition forward, and winger Alec Eisentrager who went on to play over two hundred games for Bristol City. Both of these players though would start by playing for non-league sides, the keeper at St Helens Town and the forward at Trowbridge Town, before making their Football League debuts. Back in 1947, it was prohibited for POW teams to play in competitive football and forbidden also for an individual POW to sign for and play with a civilian club.

As well as the two POW sides already mentioned, there were at least two other local camps that managed to raise decent teams; 174 at Norton, Cuckney and 262 at Langar. In terms of results, the German sides appear to have won more than they lost, but the outcome of matches truly didn't matter in the circumstances. If proof was needed of this and that the games between the old enemies were of a greater significance than just the result, then a letter from one of the members of the Norton POW side went a long way to providing confirmation. From his home in Rosenheim, Bavaria, Robert Freissinger wrote: 'Now back in my home country I should like to send all our English friends heartiest thanks and regards for their kindness and hospitality shown during the hard time of the past years behind barbed-wire.'

Whilst third place behind Worthingtons and Linby was the highest Marys could finish, over at Nottingham Road the situation was much different; Rovers were still in with a realistic chance of a league and cup double. Unfortunately, in just the second game after the restart their interest in the Realm League Divisional Cup came to an end at the semi-final stage in a close game lost by the odd goal in three, but in the old footballing parlance that setback left them able to 'concentrate on the league', which they duly did the following Saturday by winning their sixteenth game for points to take their tally to thirty three out of a possible thirty four. The championship looked theirs for the taking, except fate was to lend a hand in making the run-in far more interesting than they would have liked.

Before the mini ice age only Cotgrave, the sole team to take a point off Rovers all season, looked to be in with any reasonable chance of challenging them for the title. Even then, with Rovers two points ahead and two games in hand it would have taken a major reversal of fortune to deny Arnold's newest club a trophy in their very first season. When Cotgrave managed to sneak in two games and two victories whilst Rovers were inactive due to the weather their positions at the top of the table were reversed. Cotgrave were now two points ahead, admittedly having played four more games. When the news came through that a team had had to resign from the league and its record would be expunged as a result, Rovers had the worst of the deal. The Arnold side had taken four points from the outfit in question, whilst their closest rivals had only met them once. Even though Cotgrave would lose the two points from that clash, Rovers would be deducted four. The restated table showed that Cotgrave were now four points ahead, and although Rovers' five games in hand were in theory an advantage, many people in the game at all levels will always say that 'points in the bag' are what matters when the home stretch of the season is reached and tension and tiredness begin to tell.

Just four matches later, the advocates of points over games in hand looked decidedly the wiser. For some reason, Rovers hit the skids at the very point of the season when they could least afford to. The first shock came on Easter Monday when they visited Shelford United. The Trentsiders were a decent enough side but even so it was a big surprise when they edged Rovers by the only goal of the game and became the first side to prevent them scoring in the league this season. That unexpected defeat appeared to have cost Rovers more than just the loss of points; it seemed to induce a crisis of confidence. The next three fixtures of this indifferent spell produced just two goals, two draws, and two points, though thankfully one of the tied matches was the crucial return game against Cotgrave. With their south Notts rivals winning their other four games during the same period, the table published in the penultimate edition of that season's Football Post painted an alarming picture. Rovers had slipped to eleven points off the top spot and their six games in hand certainly didn't look that attractive at that moment; they would need to win all of them to have any certainty of reclaiming pole position. In addition, the odds were also stacked against them as Cotgrave had just one more game to play compared with Rovers' seven. With their rivals scheduled to complete their fixtures on the last Monday in April, extremely early in comparison with other sides in the division, it was beginning to look like Rovers' season was destined to end in anti-climax.

Cotgrave had lost just once in the league all season and not at all since the turn of the year, so it was a great surprise and relief when the news came through that they had gone down by three goals to two in their last match. At least now Rovers' fate was entirely in their own hands. They had seven games left in which to muster the twelve points necessary to snatch the championship, but considering their abysmal form of late, it looked liked a challenge beyond them. Still, they had every incentive if only they could find a bit of form. When they won their next game four-one hopes were raised slightly and having struck something like their form of old with a nine-nil thrashing next time out it seemed that the corner had been turned. So it proved, and even though they drew a couple of games along the way, in the best traditions of fictional boys' magazine stories, quite apt considering that the Realm League was started as a result of one such publication, Rovers finally arrived on the very last day of the season, physically drained, but with a great chance of the clinching the championship at the death.

Although lying second in the table and a point behind the leaders Cotgrave, Rovers only needed one more point to take the title on goal average. Goal difference wasn't used to split teams back then, but by either measure the advantage lay with the Arnold side. May was almost out by the time the red and whites travelled to Radcliffe to face the reserve outfit of the very strong Radcliffe Olympic club, or at least that was what was expected. Olympic's first team had already run away with the championship of the top division of the Realm League, remaining unbeaten in the process, and had added the divisional cup for good measure, so there must have been a temptation for them to strengthen their second string for this final fixture; it wouldn't have been the first, or the last, time that this happened in local football. A counter argument to this was that, given the fierce and sometimes irrational rivalries that exist between close neighbours, hardly anyone at Radcliffe would lose any sleep should Rovers prevail at the expense of Cotgrave, which after all was just three or four miles down the road.

Whichever eleven the hosts would eventually put out, a very large and interested crowd would be there to see for themselves. It was reported in the pre-match build-up, possibly with a hint of journalistic exaggeration, that Cotgrave itself would be deserted during the game, all its inhabitants having decamped for the short journey across country to see whether their hopes for their own side's success would be dashed at the eleventh hour. On reflection, they probably travelled more in hope than expectation.

Rovers had thrashed Radcliffe nine-one earlier in the season and even if their hosts were to tinker with the team it was still thought that they were capable of picking up the point they needed. In true boys of the Rovers style, they did better than that and ran out four-nil winners. All the earlier ifs and buts were now academic; at the very end of a long drawn-out and extremely arduous season, the first piece of post-war silverware would be heading its way to Arnold.

When Harry Redgate, Charlie Kirk, and Joe Turton had decided to start their own club just a year earlier, the rapid success that their team had achieved at the very first attempt was probably at the top end of their expectations. Although in the annals of football, even at local level, the winners of the second division of a league at Notts Junior Cup level would hardly merit a mention, in the context of this particular story, it was a significant start to the proceedings. Arnold's new kids on the block had laid down a marker for the bragging rights around the many pubs and workingmen's clubs that occupied the mile or so separating their spiritual homes on the Top and Bottom Recs.

Walter Parr and the rest of Marys' committee would definitely have taken notice of Rovers' arrival even without their initial success. It was inconceivable that they would let another club usurp Marys' position as number one in the town. That the two teams hadn't yet met was probably a good thing, and anyway, there'd be plenty of time for that later, but the rivalry had certainly started. As the elongated first season of local football in the post-war era finally drew to a close, the honours board looked like this:

ROVERS : ONE CHAMPIONSHIP

CHAPTER THREE 1947-48

There is little doubt that the combination of the ultra severe winter of 1947 and the attendant shortages of food and fuel had left the country mentally and physically weary and exhausted. If that wasn't bad enough, the economic and financial implications were beginning to bite hard too.

The Realm League had reported that a record number of players registered with their clubs had made claims on the league's benevolent fund as a result of 'many accidents' in the closing weeks of the previous season. Given the state of the country as a whole and the hectic schedule of playing so many matches in such a short time, and on pitches that had hardly been improved by their exposure to the elements, it was little wonder that guys who also had to hold down full time jobs were dropping like flies. An injury in a game that they all played for the love of it more often than not meant time off work. And that in turn meant no pay; in 1947 there was hardly an employer in the land that had a sick pay scheme in place.

It wasn't just these unfortunate footballers who had to go cap in hand to survive. The country, along with the rest of Europe, was on its uppers. Agricultural and industrial production hadn't yet recovered to their pre-war levels and exports had been decimated. Help was needed urgently and by the middle of the year the cavalry arrived led by the USA Secretary of State George C Marshall. In his original June 5 speech at Harvard University he outlined the problem: "Europe's requirements are so much greater than her present ability to pay that she must have substantial additional help or face economic, social, and political deterioration of a very grave character." Giving his name to a massive programme of lending, 'The Marshall Plan', he oversaw the provision of a $4.34bn loan to the UK at two percent interest repayable over fifty years by annual instalments.

In essence the aid was massively crucial in helping rebuild the country and the Chancellor of the time, Stafford Cripps, no doubt viewed the plan with a mixture of relief and delight. Which is probably just what his counterpart in the government of the day, Gordon Brown, felt as he raided the Treasury's piggy bank to the tune of £54m in order to finally sign off the very last repayment of the loan on 29 December 2006, almost sixty years after its inception and nearly a decade behind schedule.

And just as the country's finances were about to take a turn for the better, the early summer of 1947 saw a massive improvement in the weather too. On May 31, the event that would one day enable me to be sitting here writing this took place rather appropriately at St Marys' church in Arnold. My parents' wedding vows were exchanged, I am reliably informed, under clear blue skies and a scorchingly hot sun.

Of course every silver lining has a cloud for company and the assistance from Uncle Sam couldn't come quickly enough to avoid a worsening fuel crisis and the announcement in late August, just as the new season was starting, of the abolition of basic petrol rationing, already meagre to begin with, from the beginning of October. To make matters worse, the weather on my parents' special day wasn't a one-off either. It heralded the start of the lengthiest drought then recorded for that time of year, continuing mercilessly for over three months until well into September. Supplies became so scarce in parts of the country that a village in Cornwall even had to buy its water at a penny a bucket from a horse-drawn tank.

If the effect of the government's reaction to the fuel crisis wouldn't be seen for another month or so, the impact of the sweltering heat, particularly on football, was immediately noticeable. When the season kicked off on 23 August, after the shortest close season in history, games were not only played in a heatwave but on pitches that had been baked rock hard. Even before the season started, Rovers had already lost a player to a broken arm picked up in a practice match, and the prospect of rain refreshing the burnished turf was some way off.

The condition of pitches wasn't the only concern either. Just as problematic was the distinct lack of them. This had been a difficulty the previous season, but now, a year later, as the pace of demobilisation quickened, the situation had been exacerbated by the significant increase in the number of clubs registering to play. Both the Spartan League and its Realm counterpart had added an extra division, and theirs wasn't the only example of expansion; Rovers' success had already enabled them to sign on enough extra players to run a second team.

When Radcliffe Olympic hammered Rovers on the opening day of the season by six goals to one it looked as though competition for places in the first eleven might just be what was needed. Of course it was to be expected that Rovers, having automatically gained promotion to the top division of the Realm league, would find it that much harder this time around. Even so, it was disappointing that when, a week later, they met last season's main rivals Cotgrave, promoted too as runners-up, they stumbled to their second defeat in two games, losing three nil. As their third match saw them scrape a victory over Carlton by the only goal of the game, it appeared that Rovers may have found their level.

Unfortunately, over on the other side of town, things weren't looking any brighter. Marys' only two points in their first three games came in a two-one win on the opening day of the season but they then proceeded to go down heavily in their next two outings, conceding six goals in each of them. The defensive problems of the previous season didn't appear to have been remedied, and although Albert Allcock was missing from the first defeat, his presence in the last of the three games couldn't prevent his side from drawing a blank. Not only that, but the ploy of having John Cunningham, a half-back good enough to have had a trial at Forest at the end of the previous season, line up at outside left, was an indication that Marys were already struggling to find the right balance even this early in the calendar.

Seven days later, the gloom lifted slightly. Rovers prevailed six-three in their game and Marys went two better in their eight-three victory over Barlock Typewriters. Albert Allcock continued his personal vendetta against the works team with yet another hat trick, taking his total against them to thirteen in three games. His achievement on the day though was surpassed by newcomer 'Jock' Neville, who notched four times from the inside right spot.

Marys' game the following Saturday was another eleven goal affair, a nine two win in the local derby against Edwards Lane Estate on the Bulwell Forest ground. Their opponents had provided few problems for Marys in the previous campaign and none this season so far for anyone else either. Bottom of the division they had conceded twenty goals without reply in their two games to date, so the maroon and golds' win was really nothing to get excited about. In fact, there was still much to cause concern, especially at the back. The Estate team's secretary was reported as being 'delighted that the opposing defence had been pierced for the first time this season' but truth be told it would have been a surprise if they hadn't managed to break their duck against Marys' porous rearguard. To make matters worse, Marys' last two victories would ultimately prove to have been in vain and end up counting for nothing at the season's end. Both their opponents were destined to resign from the league at some point and have their records expunged as a consequence.

At the time however, the two high scoring victories had brought a bit of optimism to the proceedings; which is just what was needed, considering that their next opponents were last year's outstanding champions, Worthington Simpson. The Newark side had got off to an indifferent start of their own, victims of their own success in so far as the attention their achievements received had led to the loss of a number of their players to a higher standard of football. As the game kicked off at Church Lane, hopes were high in the home team's camp that this was as good a time as any to meet Worthingtons. In fact it was reported that there was 'some trepidation' amongst the visitors about the task ahead. They needn't have worried. Ninety minutes later Marys left the field with their tails between their legs, smarting on the wrong end of an eight one scoreline. These were gentler and more civil times though. The Football Post put it thus: 'The match had an exceptionally happy ending, the teams partaking of tea and spending a convivial evening together.' Presumably, I suppose, an early example of tea and sympathy.

Infuriatingly, a couple of weeks later Marys turned in their best performance of the season yet when they beat Linby by four goals to two. Well actually it was the colliery's 'B' team because their first eleven had decamped to the Notts Alliance, but even the second string had proven too good for their opponents so far, winning all seven of their matches. 'Jock' Neville scored and again received glowing praise, as did fellow forward Ron Dawes who weighed in with a couple of goals of his own. Unbelievably, this excellent result wouldn't appear in the record books either, as Linby would make it an astonishing five teams who would withdraw prematurely from the league before the season ended; this from a starting line up of only fourteen teams too. Actually, this first couple of months of the season was a perfect microcosm of Marys' year as a whole; a leaky defence, inconsistent performances, and the costly ramifications of matters away from the playing field.

MARYS 1947-48 : Back Row (l to r); A Evans (Committee), J Mason, K Hoskins, W North, J Scattergood, J Atkinson, R Dawes, H E Walker (Treasurer), S Gray (Committee). Front Row; J Pearson, T Dickinson, J Neville, A Allcock, R Carter.

(Courtesy Football Post)

The only other highlight of the season was a good run in the Notts Intermediate Cup. One game in particular stands out, the second round tie away to the strong North Notts League side Retford Grove Lane, who were the current holders of the Notts Junior Cup. Despite the reputation of the home side, Marys went up the A614 with high hopes of causing an upset. So confident of victory were the Committee that two of its members, Chairman Walter 'Kegga' Parr and Syd Gray, even had a five pounds wager, a very decent sum back then, with a Grove Lane supporter that Marys would win the tie.

GP : I'd been drafted into the team as a replacement for John Cunningham. I'd just turned eighteen and was due to go into the RAF for my National Service just a couple of weeks later. Apart from my dad's and Syd's bet the thing I remember most was the poor old referee. The

Retford supporters blamed him for the defeat and things turned really nasty. He had to be escorted out of the ground and was last seen driving away into the distance on his motorbike and sidecar flanked by police. And that Retford supporter who'd taken the bet had left early too, so Syd and my dad never did get their money.

Supporters Eric and Roy Thompson were amongst the Marys contingent as usual.

E&RT : Geoff Parr was given the job of following their best player all over the pitch. Geoff never took part in the game, just followed this player who'd been with Manchester City before the war. Geoff did a good job. Teams that aren't used to losing don't like it when they get beaten. They can't stand it.

Safely negotiating the next round, they reached the quarter final stage where they were drawn at home against the reserve side of Raleigh Athletic. They put in an excellent performance in winning six-two and a place in the semi-finals was theirs, or so everyone thought; everyone other than the Notts Football Association, that is, who ordered the tie to be replayed following a breach of the competition's rules. In keeping with the rest of their season, the maroon and golds' proceeded to lose the rematch six-four.

Their season, what little was left of it after the decimation of the fixture list by the mass withdrawals, was a complete anti-climax, one let down after another. In the two weeks following their cup exit, Marys were humiliated in back to back defeats by Stapleford Villa, themselves hardly contenders for the championship, eight-one and nine-one. These pastings meant that Marys had conceded an awful twenty-eight goals in their last four matches. When they travelled to Newark late in the season for the return game with Worthingtons, it looked as though the end of the campaign couldn't come quickly enough. The post-match hospitality of the first encounter was reciprocated by the Newark club, but the chances are that after another trouncing, this time by a mere seven goals to one, Marys' players and committee couldn't wait to hot foot it back across the Trent.

The town's senior outfit eventually finished a lowly seventh out of nine. It was no consolation at the time but thankfully it would be over thirty years before the club would again suffer the ignominy of ending a season propped up by only two other sides at the foot of the table. At least for the Notts County supporters in Marys' ranks, the signing of the great Tommy Lawton, then England's centre-forward and one of the finest to ever wear the 'Three Lions' badge helped lift the gloom a little. His transfer for a record fee of seventeen thousand pounds from Chelsea only went through in November but by the end of the season he had finished as the club's top scorer, averaging a goal a game in his twenty four appearances. The real impact that he would make was a little while away yet but there was no doubt that his signing by Notts, a third division club at the time of course, had brought an immediate and tremendous excitement to the city and given a big lift to its sporting fraternity.

GP : Whenever I was back on leave from the RAF and I wasn't playing, I'd go and see either Notts or Forest play. Tommy Lawton signing for County was brilliant and after I'd finished my National Service in 1949, I'd always try and get off work early to see the Magpies play their mid-week matches.

GR : All my family were Notts fans even before Tommy Lawton arrived. In fact I think that everyone on James Street who was interested in football were Magpies supporters too. My good friend from a couple of doors down the street, Joan Berrington, knitted what must have been the longest County scarf in existence; it must have gone round her neck about twelve times.

Tommy Lawton's signing for County was big news in Nottingham, maybe even the country, considering he was playing for England at the time. With his fame and his Brylcreemed hair, it was a bit like royalty coming. I remember queuing for hours once down at Meadow Lane for cup tickets.

I'll never forget him joining Notts because it was the month that my husband was demobbed. We'd gone down to Epping to visit my in-laws and while we were down there we went up to

London to see the Queen. Well, not quite, because she was still Princess Elizabeth then, but she was getting married to the Duke of Edinburgh and it was a good time to make the trip. From a personal point of view I look back now and think that things started to pick up from then.

Back in Arnold a few weeks before the David Beckham of his day would arrive in the city, Rovers, unlike their town rivals, had managed to recover from their own less than auspicious start and make something of their season. After six games their record mirrored that of Marys almost exactly. Both had averaged just a point a game, had a goal difference of minus four, and were labouring in mid-table. I don't suppose there was any connection, but as soon as the basic petrol ration was withdrawn at the beginning of October, Rovers form improved beyond all recognition from that which they'd shown so far.

Their first six points had been rather hard to come by. After being well beaten in their opening two fixtures and edging the next couple, one unimpressively, they only managed to scrape a couple of draws as September drew to a close. Still, it did mean that they were undefeated in four games. That was nothing compared with what followed. Four months later, their unbeaten spell had been stretched to an extremely impressive seventeen games; a remarkable spell that had yielded thirteen wins and just four draws, a tremendous achievement especially after the early hiccups. It was the Chinese that are accredited with the proverb that says 'even the greatest journey starts with one small step' and it certainly rang true in Rovers' case. The first game of the run had been that indifferent one-nil win over Carlton, a result put into perspective by the fact that in the return fixture the double over them was completed with a more realistic five-one scoreline.

The margins of victory were impressive too, especially in the early winter months, when wins of nine-two, six-one, and nine-three were recorded in consecutive weeks. The first featured the unusual feat of three separate players each scoring a hat-trick; Jack Surgey, 'Nobby' Clarke, and Ken Atherley.

One of the three, Jack Surgey, was a 'Bevin Boy'. These were young men conscripted by the wartime coalition government to work in the coal mines. In 1943 a shortage of both coal and the labour to mine it had reached a crisis point. The Minister of Labour and National Service, Ernest Bevin, introduced a programme whereby a certain percentage of draftees would have to work in the pits. The selection process was random; a member of Bevin's staff would draw one or more digits from a hat and those guys whose draft number ended in those digits would end up digging for their country rather than fighting for it.

It was a hybrid kind of existence for those chosen by chance, and for whom refusal to accept their lot would have resulted in prison. Whilst effectively being fully conscripted, they were never regarded as servicemen, yet they had to work at the coalface just like the industry's existing workforce. It was the worst of both possible worlds especially when, as non-uniformed men of military age, they were inevitably stopped by police and questioned about avoiding the call-up.

The programme outlived the war that caused it, finally ending in 1948, and in the process led to a great deal of resentment amongst those for whom it had been a way of life for the duration. No 'Bevin Boy' ever received a medal until a belated campaign saw that wrong righted in 2007, nor did they have the right to return to their original job, a privilege granted to other servicemen. They missed out on a war pension and to add insult to injury their service to the nation wasn't fully recognised until 1995, fifty years after the end of the war, in a speech by the Queen.

Acknowledgement by the country or not, Jack was highly thought of by his fellow players and played an integral part in the long unbeaten run and the purple patch right in the middle of it. Of those three free-scoring matches, it was probably the second game against Cotgrave, avenging the early season reverse, that was the most satisfying. When Radcliffe Olympic, the only other team to have lowered Rovers' colours, were also defeated later in January, the slate had well and truly been wiped clean. As they had also successfully negotiated the first two rounds of the Division 1 Cup, all that realistically stood between Rovers' and a league and cup double were their only genuine rivals, Keyworth United. And by a quirk of the fixture list, the two teams hadn't yet met in the league and had been drawn against each other in the semi-final of the cup. The season was set for a thrilling climax.

By the time the two teams met at Keyworth at the beginning of February, the hosts had dropped just two points, but their success in knock-out competitions, where they had also battled through to the semi-final of the Notts Junior Cup, had seen them fall six games behind Rovers in the league. Unlike the position at the end of the previous season where they were playing catch up to Cotgrave, now it was Rovers' turn to head the league table with the points in the bag. It just remained to be seen whether their closest rivals could do what Rovers had done the year before and pip them at the post.

Buoyed by an eight-one win the previous week, which had followed the excellent victory over Radcliffe, Rovers entertained very reasonable thoughts that they could get something from their top of the table clash. Disappointingly, their ambitions of adding the Division One Championship to their success of the past year were badly upset when Keyworth ran out four-one winners. Whilst it was by no means the end of their challenge, the result had certainly been a setback.

Rovers suffered a bit of a hangover the following week when they played Castle Imperials on the Bottom Rec. This was the team they'd beaten eight-one just a fortnight earlier, but the return game was a much closer affair. The visitors were less charitable in defence and the home side had to be satisfied with just a three-one victory in securing both points. Unfortunately, Rovers had two blank Saturdays coming up, a marked contrast to the previous year when they had to cram in game after game at the end of the season. Now they only had three more league games to go and a whole eleven weeks in which to play them.

Three weeks of inactivity was probably not the best way of preparing for their next game, especially as it was against Keyworth in the Divisional Cup. The luck of the draw hadn't favoured Rovers in terms of both opponent and venue, but at least it gave them a swift chance to avenge the recent league defeat. The result of the first meeting certainly didn't seem to overawe Rovers because, once it got underway, the game developed into a classic cup clash. It was end to end stuff with both defences under severe pressure. Once more, however, it was their opponents who ultimately held the upper hand and advanced to the final, winners of an eight goal thriller, five-three. When Keyworth won their Junior Cup semi-final too, there was a very good chance that they might achieve a rare treble.

Even so, all was not lost for Rovers. Having won their next match, some good news came their way in the form of a surprise reversal for Keyworth. Their rivals had gone down by the only goal of the game to a resurgent Radcliffe in the final of the Divisional Cup at the City Ground on April 16, a Friday evening fixture watched by a crowd of two thousand, and then had to play less than twenty four hours later in the league. The physical effort and disappointment of the previous evening were probably mitigating factors in them then losing three-one to Carlton, a team they would be expected to dispose of easily in normal circumstances.

So, a chink of hope had appeared for Rovers, and when their crucial home game with Keyworth took place in the very last week of April, the championship was still very much up for grabs. If Rovers could claim victory, Keyworth would remain three points behind with only three games to go. With their opponents' eye also on the Notts Junior Cup, there might just be a chance for Rovers to take both points and make Keyworth's run-in a little more tense than they'd like.

The game was by far the tightest of the three contests, but despite putting in their best performance in the series of matches, Rovers ultimately had to settle for just a point as Keyworth held out for a one-all draw. Arnold's new boys would now have to sit back and await the outcome of Keyworth's run-in, naturally more in hope than expectation. The south Notts outfit had really been the team of the season in the Realm League, and despite losing for a third time, they won their other games and clinched the title by three points. Radcliffe's late run of form almost saw them catch Rovers up, but in the final analysis they finished one point shy. When Keyworth annexed the Notts Junior Cup for good measure, they became the first Realm League club to achieve the feat. The close and competitive nature of the clashes between the top three teams was confirmation that the league contained a few decent sides. Finishing a close second in this field was no disgrace; in fact it was a pretty fair achievement considering it was still only the second year of Rovers' existence.

In the final analysis their valiant efforts to make up for their sluggish start fell just short; for the Rovers it was a case of close, but no cigar. Marys' season on the other hand, abysmal and best forgotten, wasn't even deserving of a nub-end. And despite the nominal difference in the level of standard between the top divisions of the Realm and Spartan leagues, there was little doubt that Rovers had consolidated their position as the team to watch. For now though, there was no change to the honours board. It remained:-

ROVERS : ONE CHAMPIONSHIP

CHAPTER FOUR 1948-49

My mother's earlier comment late in the previous year that things seemed to be picking up on a personal level certainly seemed to be echoed across the country as a whole in 1948. Every child in the land must have been thrilled at the news that bread and jam was taken off rationing whilst their parents' generation were no doubt relieved when furniture joined those foodstuffs in being freely available too. There was a caveat with the latter though. The 'Utility Scheme' remained and priority continued to be given to newlyweds and those whose homes and belongings had been destroyed.

The Utility Scheme for furniture had been introduced in 1943. There was a similar programme for clothing and both carried the distinctive CC41 trademark with the two Cs inadvertently looking like a prototype for the future video game character 'PacMan'. The coalition government had wanted to make available furniture of the best quality possible at prices that were tightly controlled. Whilst top designers were drafted in by the appointed Utility Furniture Advisory Committee, the range was kept to a minimum. It was well made but mostly plain and functional.

Unfortunately, there was a feeling in some quarters that the Advisory Committee were trying to 'educate' the public in matters of 'good taste'. This surreptitious and rather patronising attempt to influence the mass market was doomed to fail, especially once the war was over. Utility furniture proved unpopular, especially as 'utility' was associated with the frugality and drabness of the years of conflict, but it wasn't until 1952 that the scheme finally ended. It is of course quite ironic that the austere, unfussy style that found little favour the first time around is now very much in vogue.

In the corridors of power, the pace of change quickened as the Railways and Gas Industry were nationalised and the National Health Service Act of 1946 was finally implemented, aiming to provide 'free at the point of use' healthcare from 'cradle to grave'. There was initially fierce opposition to the plans to provide for the country's medical wellbeing, and there are still those, nearly sixty years later, who doubt its effectiveness. As for the other attempts by government to burden the country with the monopolistic and monolithic, both the Gas and Railway industries have subsequently been deregulated along with most everything else that was once state controlled.

In the world at large there were a number of events across the spectrum of life that would have deep and lasting consequences of their own; ones that couldn't so easily be reversed despite each of them attracting varying degrees of conflict and a resultant loss of life. January had seen the first stirrings of 'youth culture' and its challenge to the status quo when the first chapter of the Hells Angels motorcycle club was formed in California. Then in May the state of Israel was founded and a month later HMS Windrush docked at Tilbury with Britain's first economic immigrants from the Caribbean; momentous times indeed.

A pretty significant event took place in the country's sporting calendar too when London hosted the Olympic Games in July, the first since Hitler and his National Socialist party had hijacked the Berlin games twelve years earlier. It was no surprise when Germany and Japan weren't invited to participate, but it had been when it was announced that the Olympics were being resumed so soon after the war. Many people argued that with large swathes of Europe in ruins and the people near starvation it was inappropriate to put on a festival of this nature.

A compromise of sorts was reached whereby all the participants would bring their own food, with any surpluses being given to British hospitals. The budget for the Games was nowhere near the obscene level it has reached now. Even if there had been money to do so, which is extremely doubtful, no new facilities were needed as, amazingly, Wembley Stadium had survived the Luftwaffe and the doodlebugs and was to be the centrepiece of the action. Athletes were billeted locally; males at an army camp at Uxbridge and the fairer sex in dormitories at Southlands College. Not quite the Olympic Villages of the modern era.

A Dutch mother-of-two, Fanny Blankers-Koen, was the undoubted star of the show, winning four gold medals on the track. Her fantastic achievements earned her the soubriquet "The Flying Housewife" and in 1999 the much more important title of "Female Athlete of the Century". Despite the original misgivings, the Games proved to be a great success, giving everyone just the kind of fillip that the country had needed.

Whether it was a direct result of the popularity of the London Olympics or not, the following month the football season opened with an even greater air of optimism than ever. Crowds attended the opening Saturday's Football League programme on 21 August in very large numbers, an occurrence that would be repeated with pleasing regularity throughout the season. As was mentioned earlier, the sporting public's continuing love affair with the game would eventually mean the season would attract an all-time high audience of over forty one million spectators.

However, if all the professional clubs and the majority of the local teams managed to kick off on time, both Marys and Rovers were noticeable by their absence. Not that they had packed in; they hadn't. But whatever changes, if any, both teams might have made in gearing up for the challenges ahead, they were keeping them well under wraps. It was another three weeks before Marys opened their season, against opponents whose fourth game it was, whilst Rovers hid their talent under a bushel even longer, not appearing until a week later on 18 September. By then, it was already their opponents' sixth outing of the season.

Whatever the reasons for the delay, it was always advisable, and indeed encouraged by the various local league administrators, to play as many fixtures as possible on schedule at the start of the season. The logic behind this was based on many years' practical experience. Once the first few weeks of the season had passed the various county and league cup competitions began. Any success in these, or even a future opponent's success, could play havoc with arrangements for league games, and once the winter months arrived, adverse weather might always lend its disruptive hand. It remained to be seen whether Marys' and Rovers' late start might prove costly later on.

The initial games brought mixed fortunes to the two clubs, Marys going down three-two but Rovers prevailing four-one. When they both produced good wins in their next outing, the prospect of late season fixture congestion appeared less of a concern. Rovers dispatched Realm League new boys Gotham United by ten goals to nil whilst Marys had a much harder ninety minutes against Spartan newcomers East Kirkby Welfare, edging a fine game four-two. Debutant Stan French scored twice from outside-left and picked up the vote as the game's outstanding player. Albert Allcock was still featuring on the score sheet too but from the inside-left position where he'd moved to accommodate Cyril Middleton at centre-forward.

Seven days later an under strength Marys went down three-one to their previous season's tormentors Stapleford Villa. Having already lost twice in three games there was an urgent need for a kick-start to their season. Most local leagues, with fewer fixtures than their professional counterparts, were won by teams losing no more than three or four matches a season. With the campaign barely underway, Marys had already left themselves with little margin for error.

At the beginning of October, they strengthened their pool of players by signing Ron Hinson, a right-half who'd been a professional at Lincoln City. Amateur sides were allowed to sign ex-professionals like Ron on what was known as a 'permit'. Teams could usually sign any number of 'permit' players, in fact Marys already had another in Arnold 'Arnie' Wilkinson, but they were generally only allowed to field two in any one particular game. Ron's additional presence certainly didn't do Marys' cause any harm. They rattled off five straight victories in the month, including safely negotiating the first rounds of both the Notts Intermediate Cup and the Spartan League Cup.

Rovers on the other hand fell at the first hurdle in the Realm League, again failing to get the better of their biggest rivals, Keyworth United, who they had the misfortune to be drawn against so early in the competition. They also disappointingly lost their unbeaten record in the league when they went down four-one to newcomers Dakeyne Street Old Boys, a team they'd beaten by the same score just three weeks earlier. However, these early October lapses seemed just that as they closed out the month with three high scoring victories and eased into the second round of the Notts Junior Cup in the process. Not surprisingly, Rovers' forward line was reckoned to be one of the best in the league, diminutive and fast, with Jack Surgey and 'Nobby' Clarke both being given good press.

A number of players in Marys' camp had been receiving glowing praise too, courtesy of the attention their good run had attracted. Cyril Middleton had picked up the mantle of goal scoring centre-forward from Albert Allcock with three consecutive hat-tricks whilst 'Arnie' Wilkinson's tireless work as a creator of goals was fully acknowledged also. Commendations for the three inside forwards were completed when everyone was reminded that it was Albert Allcock's eighteenth season with the club. Admittedly disrupted by the war years, Albert's loyalty and longevity were still fine achievements.

The two regular flank men were mentioned in despatches too; right winger Jacky Pearson was reckoned to be one of the best in his position in the Spartan League and to even have few equals in the Nottingham district, although he was currently out following an injury sustained at work, whilst newcomer Stan French had already settled in comfortably on the left wing. The eulogies continued with praise for Ron Hinson's 'professional' touches as well as support for goalkeeper Billy North and fellow defenders Jim Atkinson and Ray Dawes. Expectations had certainly been raised by October's fine run, and it was even suggested that the current team was capable of restoring the great name the 'Saints' had in past years.

If such an idea might have seemed a little premature, nothing that Marys did in November dissuaded the believers from their convictions. A record of four games, four wins, and twenty-six goals was a confirmation of the confidence spreading throughout the club. Two of the matches were in the league, the third was a comfortable success in the second round of the Intermediate Cup, but it was the last game of the month that really sent out a message to the rest of the Spartan League that Marys were on the up. It was a second round League Cup tie against newcomers Balderton Old Boys.

This was only the Newark side's second season in the league, but they'd already begun to emulate the success of their near neighbours Worthington Simpson who'd move to pastures new following their domination of the previous two seasons. Balderton had won the second division championship in their very first season and had also added the Spartan League Cup, a competition open to sides from the top division, a feat never before achieved. Not only that, they had maintained that level of form in the current campaign and were top of the league when they met Marys for the very first time. Such was the anticipation of this initial clash that it was not only expected to prove a classic encounter but to draw a record 'gate' to the Top Rec as a consequence.

When the boys from Newark arrived at Church Lane, they did so boasting a free-scoring attack and one of the meanest defences in local football. Since their debut in the league they'd only conceded thirty two goals in thirty three outings for points, less than one a game and very decent going at any level. Ninety minutes later, they were probably all looking around at each other thinking 'what the hell happened there?' With Jock Neville leading the way with four, Marys overwhelmed the opposition, running out easy winners by an amazing ten goals to two. The bandwagon was well and truly rolling.

Things were a little more subdued at the other end of town where November saw Rovers have little difficulty in reaching the third round of the Junior Cup but drop two valuable points in the league when going down two-one to a strong Newthorpe United side. When the first

Saturday in December pitted Rovers and Keyworth together for the fifth time in a year the game was predictably a keen and exciting affair, much befitting their previous clashes. Sadly, the result had a degree of inevitability about it too, with the South Notts side edging the game by the odd goal in three. As a consequence of these two admittedly close defeats, Rovers were down in sixth place in the league with just twelve points from their nine games. Not quite the end of the world, but there was a lot of ground to catch up if they were to keep the pressure on Keyworth and the rest.

One blank Saturday and two more cup matches saw Rovers slide down to eighth position in the final table of 1948, although they did sign the year off in style with a seven-nil Boxing Day thrashing of Notts Regent with centre-forward Jack Brace accounting for five of the goals. They'd also played a morning cup game against Hendon Rise on Christmas Day, easing past their opponents three-nil in the first round of the newly reconstituted Arnold and District Benevolent Cup competition.

Similar charitable concerns had been prevalent in the years before the war, with most districts having their own competition. Indeed, there had been one such example in Arnold itself since 1926, and various Marys' sides had been victorious, getting their hands on the cup no fewer than five times. Unfortunately, in the long hiatus between the last pre-war competition and its revival in the current season, the trophy had somehow been separated from its base, necessitating the purchase of a replacement.

Mr Jim Kirk, who had been a secretary of the competition before the war and who was at the forefront of the revival movement, approached the various clubs in the district and received such a positive response that a sum of eighty-five pounds was raised in double quick time. The money didn't linger long in the new treasurer's cash box but was used in full to purchase a handsome new silver trophy. All teams within a three and a half mile radius of Arnold were invited to play, and twelve applications were accepted. It had previously been the norm for as many matches as possible to be played on or around holiday dates in order to maximise the charitable contributions that bigger crowds would generate and it was hoped this trend would continue. The two local sides did their bit, but whilst Rovers had managed to fit in their first round tie at Christmas, it would be Easter before Marys could follow suit.

In fact Marys' players could relax over the holidays because they were without a fixture of any kind and they'd also gone into the break on the back of a very decent win in the third round of the Intermediate Cup against Christ Church. The Notts Alliance club were the undefeated leaders of Division Two and even though they played their part in a thrilling game that was reckoned to be the best seen on The Forest recreation ground all season, Marys ran out deserving winners three-two. They'd also taken three points from December's two league games and ended the year holding down third place. The fact that they'd now extended their unbeaten run to twelve games and had already beaten both the teams above them, Balderton Old Boys and fellow newcomers East Kirkby Welfare, meant that Marys entered the New Year with a genuine belief that they might be in with a decent chance of picking up some silverware come the end of the season.

At the beginning of 1949, the people of Nottingham, like those in the rest of the country, were still having to put up with even greater levels of hardship and restrictions than during the war itself as the pace of Britain's recovery was proceeding much more slowly than had at first been anticipated. The coincidence of the year being the five hundredth anniversary of the granting of Nottingham's Charter by Henry VI at least gave its good citizens the opportunity to celebrate something tangible. Though the week of celebrations wasn't scheduled to take place until June, much civic planning was necessary. Schools even engaged pupils in the preparation of projects related to the quincentenary, the importance of which was confirmed when it was announced that the future queen, Princess Elizabeth, would be gracing the celebrations with a personal visit.

When the government withdrew rationing of clothing from the beginning of February, the timing couldn't have been better. Looking at photographs of the brightly garbed crowds thronging the Old Market Square straining to get a view of the next monarch, it seems that one of the first things that many of the city's females did when both bits of good news coincided was to go out and treat themselves to a new frock. When rationing had been in place, there was little chance of that kind of retail therapy happening too often. The annual allowance had been set at just forty-eight coupons and a woman's dress accounted for eleven of those by itself. To make matters worse, fashion in clothing, especially female, had suffered from the dead hand of the 'Utility Mark', so it was doubly delightful for half the population when it too went the way of the dreaded coupons.

Back on the football pitches of Arnold, its teams could hardly have wished for a better start to the year. In the first month, Rovers rattled up four wins out of four, three of which were for league points with a goals tally of eighteen against nil and the other a victory in round four of the Junior Cup. If that was impressive then Marys went one better. They ran up five straight wins and scored twenty seven goals in the process whilst progressing through to the semi-final stage of two knock-out competitions, the Intermediate and Spartan League Cups. Tommy Dickinson went nap in the league game against Netherfield Rovers, scoring all Marys' goals in their five-one win, whilst goal-maker 'Arnie' Wilkinson turned 'goal-taker' with five in two consecutive matches.

THREE SAINTS

(l to r); J Atkinson, K Hoskins, A Wilkinson

(Alec Casterton Collection)

For the first time in the three seasons that the two sides had co-existed, they were both doing extremely well at exactly the same time. Of course, the only competition mutual to them both was the local Charity Cup, but nonetheless even this arm's length rivalry had given the town's football followers something to get excited about. Rovers had quietly put together a seven match unbeaten run and conceded just three goals in that spell, whilst Marys fantastic sequence now stood at seventeen matches, sixteen of which had resulted in victory.

Rovers record wasn't threatened on the opening Saturday of February as they were without a fixture but Marys on the other hand had a very difficult hurdle to overcome to maintain their own unbeaten run. They travelled to Balderton to play the Old Boys and although they'd trounced the Newark side in the League Cup back in November, no one who made the journey across the Trent had any delusions about the task ahead. Their opponents had been stirred but not shaken by their earlier hammering and were leading Marys by a point, both teams having played the same number of matches. In fact it was very tight at the top of the league with only two points separating the first four teams. There was also the added interest provided by a quirk of the fixture list that had the leaders East Kirkby Welfare entertaining fourth placed Stapleford Brookhill that same day.

Ninety minutes later, the two home sides had seen off the opposition and put a bit of daylight between themselves and the beaten clubs. For Marys it was a big disappointment. They had been without centre-half Jim Atkinson but had little cause for complaint as their long run of success finally came to an end. There were ten league games still to go though and as these included the return fixtures against both the top sides, it wasn't as if Marys' hopes of claiming the league title were over just yet. And as if to prove the point, they bounced straight back the next week with a five-two win and followed that up with an impressive ten-two victory with 'Arnie' Wilkinson continuing his rich vein of form with another four goals. Not to be outdone, Cyril Middleton weighed in with four of his own.

Seven days later, Marys had the chance of quick redemption when Balderton returned to Church Lane for the decisive rematch. A couple of weeks earlier the Old Boys had travelled to East Kirkby for another in the recent spate of top of the table clashes and gone down three-one. It had been a bit of a rough house with their centre half ending up in hospital and the centre forward reduced to a limping passenger out on the wing. The talk in the press on the eve of the game with Marys had been that the Newark club were hampered by a heavy casualty list, but no one in the home camp thought that the job in hand would be any the easier for it.

And so it proved. In the kind of contest that had been expected earlier in the season on Balderton's first visit, Marys won a close, exciting battle by the odd goal in five to leapfrog their visitors and move up into second place in the league. It was hoped that Marys might also have drawn nearer to the leaders who were again facing Stapleford Brookhill the very same afternoon but the Welfare side squeezed a one-nil victory to remain top by three points. Reports of the two matches concluded with the opinion that East Kirkby were now almost certain to claim the championship, although with the caveat that they had to do well in the return games against both Balderton and Marys before they could be sure of the title.

ROVERS 1948-49 : Back Row (l to r); B Rodmell, F Hill, L Peck, W Whitt, W Horton, K Atherley, G Tutin, D Thorlby, - -, H Redgate, P Dean. Front Row; E Barber, H Clarke, J Brace, J Surgey, K Crombie, J Turton (Martin Dermody Collection)

Over at Nottingham Road, Rovers' quiet success continued unabated. Their excellent run in the Notts Junior Cup continued with a fifth round three-nil victory over Broxtowe, courtesy of a Jack Brace hat-trick, and February ended with them handily placed in fourth position in the table, albeit eight points behind leaders Keyworth with just three games in hand. The only surprise was when they actually conceded two goals in a drawn league match in the last game of the month, the first time since the beginning of December that the defence had been breached when playing for points. It also brought to an end the streak of nine straight wins and five consecutive games where they had kept the opposition goalless. In fact, their parsimony had meant that the ball had only needed retrieving from their own net just once in eight games.

Rovers' first game in March was the sixth round Junior Cup tie against another Realm League side Newthorpe United. It was a tough prospect as their opponents were no mugs. They were in fact one place higher in the league than Rovers and in with a decent chance of making a push for the title themselves. The two teams had already met twice in the league this season and with the home side winning on each occasion honours were even. After ninety minutes of tough football in atrocious conditions the situation hadn't changed. A one-all draw meant the tie would need to be replayed the following Saturday, but when a further two hours of action couldn't split the sides a second replay was scheduled for the following month.

Rovers' other two games in March, both for points, saw them keep the pressure on the leaders. It was very much business as usual at the Bottom Rec as the red and whites comfortably overcame their visitors, four-nil and six-nil, with Jack Brace claiming another hat-trick in the second of the two matches. Rovers had now gone fourteen games without having their colours lowered, a run that was edging closer to Marys' earlier purple patch of seventeen undefeated matches.

As to the maroon and golds' own performances in March, it was pretty much business as usual for them too. Two comfortable league wins followed a six-one hammering of another Marys' side, this one from Southwell, in the semi-final of the Spartan League Cup. The match had been played in a snowstorm at the Gatehouse Ground of Linby Colliery but, with Cyril Middleton notching another hat-trick, the awful weather couldn't stop Marys' comfortable progress into the final. The day got even better with the news that Balderton had suffered a surprise setback at home the same day, their first defeat at Newark in two seasons.

By the last Saturday of the month, results had gone in such a way that the race for the Spartan League championship had realistically been narrowed down to just two teams. With just six games to go and only three points separating them, the title looked set to end up with either Marys or East Kirkby Welfare. There was the distinct possibility that the league match between the two clubs, scheduled for the very last day of the season, could prove to be the championship decider. Not only that, the luck of the draw in the knock-out competitions had them facing each other in the semi-final of the Intermediate Cup whilst it wouldn't be that long before the Welfare side joined Marys in the final of the League Cup as well. Of the two clubs, East Kirkby appeared to have the easier run-in. They still had to play the bottom side twice, followed by two matches against Burton Joyce, just three places higher. Their form as they moved into the closing stages seemed pretty ominous too when they whipped a mid-table side thirteen-one with their centre-forward really dipping his bread and smashing a triple hat-trick. All in all, the last few weeks of Marys' season were beginning to look very interesting indeed.

Football though is full of surprises and it was rather apt when the Spartan League's other St Marys' side, the Southwell one, pulled off the shock result of the season so far in holding the leaders to a three-all draw at Kirkby, the first point the Welfare side had dropped at home. When Burton Joyce repeated Southwell's feat a couple of weeks later on Easter Saturday, East Kirkby's lead was down to just a single point. Whilst the North Notts side's push for the title was stuttering, Marys in the meantime hadn't put a foot wrong. Four consecutive league wins, each by convincing score lines, had made it a maximum sixteen points from the last eight matches, leaving the top of the Spartan League looking like this:-

	P	W	D	L	F	A	P
East Kirkby Welfare	22	18	2	2	103	37	38
Arnold St Marys	22	18	1	3	99	40	37

For good measure Marys had also qualified for the quarter-final stage of the Charity Cup too. With just three weeks of the season remaining, and despite getting off to a less than impressive start, Marys could quite conceivably finish up by laying their hands on four pieces of silverware.

However, Rovers weren't letting Marys hog the spotlight; far from it. They'd begun April pretty much where they'd left off the previous month by overwhelming Gotham United eleven-nil, Jack Brace scoring his customary hat-trick, his second in consecutive weeks. It was Rovers' third double figure win of the season and their second against Gotham, and the following week their marathon tie against Newthorpe United finally drew to a successful conclusion with a three-two victory and a place in the semi-final of the Notts Junior Cup. When Rovers racked up back to back wins over Easter with a four-two win on the Saturday, Jack Surgey being the hat-trick hero on that occasion, they'd extended their unbeaten run to a tremendous eighteen games, one better than Marys' own fantastic run. To be fair to the town's senior side though, their run had contained sixteen victories to Rovers' fifteen, but that was splitting hairs. Both sides had established themselves as leading lights at their different levels and in their respective leagues and the main beneficiaries of their success were not only their own supporters but football fans in the town at large. Everything was set for a great climax to the season.

A large crowd gathered at Linby's Gatehouse Ground on Easter Monday morning for Marys' eagerly awaited Intermediate Cup semi-final clash with their arch rivals from East Kirkby, the first of the three crucial matches between the two clubs; three games in less than three weeks that could effectively make or break the season of either side. Tension seemed to affect both teams and the importance of the occasion, as is often the case at all levels of the game, led to neither of them playing their best football. With exchanges pretty even the game remained tight, but a solitary goal from Cyril Middleton and a decisive penalty save by keeper Billy North saw Marys safely through into the final.

The Welfare team had no fixture the following Saturday whilst Marys racked up their twelfth straight win in seeing off their namesakes from Southwell. The Saints of Arnold had now lost just once in their last thirty matches, drawing another and winning the rest; an amazing twenty eight victories. These latest two points took them to the top of the table, and as East Kirkby were due to travel to Newark to play Balderton the following Saturday, not an easy task at any time but even more difficult considering that the Welfare side weren't exactly at the top of their game, optimism in Marys' camp couldn't be higher.

However, whilst the maroon and golds had just that single league fixture against East Kirby remaining, Rovers were faced with the daunting prospect of having to cram in nine matches for points in just three weeks. Not only that, they were still contesting the Notts Junior Cup and the Arnold and District Benevolent Cup, and success in those two competitions could add up to five additional fixtures, excluding the possibility of replays. Something had to give, so Rovers reluctantly pulled out of the charity event. There was an inevitability about the decision given that they were only at the quarter final stage, but even so their withdrawal was a big disappointment to the organisers of the competition and, no doubt, to the fans of both Arnold teams, as their opponents would have been none other than Marys themselves. The charity cup was the only competition that offered the possibility of a direct head to head clash between the town's two top sides. It would have been the first time they would have met in a competitive match and the tie would have given everyone a great opportunity to assess which of them was the stronger. That particular argument would have to wait until another day, but in the meantime Rovers began their attempt to close the gap on old rivals Keyworth who had assumed their customary place at the head of the table.

Just four points off top spot and a game in hand, Rovers first game in the run-in was against Cotgrave who, whilst being a decent outfit, weren't in with a shout of the title. Unfortunately, Rovers had one of those days when nothing went right and their long unbeaten run came to a dramatic end. Ken Atherley was one of the side looking forward to the game with no little optimism.

KA : We'd been doing so well up to then that when we travelled to Cotgrave we never even thought about losing. Before we'd even warmed up, we found ourselves two goals down. That was a real shock but things got even worse and we ended up getting thrashed. In the changing room after the match we looked around at each other, totally disgusted with ourselves. I sometimes find it difficult to recall individual games from those days but I certainly haven't forgotten that particular match.

Ken's memory of the occasion was spot on. A defence that had up till then only let in eighteen goals in nineteen league games was breached no less than six times in just ninety minutes. Three consolation goals in the last fifteen minutes couldn't disguise the fact that Rovers had suffered a hiding and that their hopes of league success had taken a severe jolt in the process.

The wisdom of having four blank Saturdays and no midweek games at the start of the season was now looking extremely suspect. Kicking off nearer October than August wasn't the greatest of ideas even back then, but with the benefit of hindsight the decision was beginning to look positively bizarre. An additional eight matches in the successful Junior Cup run had only worsened the unenviable fixture backlog and with games coming up thick and fast the stamina and resilience of Rovers' players would be severely tested. Tiredness and fatigue weren't the only enemy. The state of the pitch at the Bottom Rec was euphemistically referred to as 'leaving a lot of room for improvement'; the reality was that it was in a terrible state and hardly conducive to the type of football Rovers preferred to play.

Notwithstanding these obstacles, the red and whites pursued the title with great resolve, winning six of their last eight matches as they strove to narrow the gap on the leaders. Just as they had been the previous year, Keyworth were late, late visitors to Nottingham Road and at the sixth time of asking, Rovers finally got the better of them, running out winners of a close contest three-two. Unfortunately, it wasn't quite enough to bring the trophy to Arnold as Rovers' other two matches for points were both lost. In the final analysis the league table was a repeat of twelve months earlier with Keyworth taking the championship and Rovers having to settle for the runners-up spot. The margin between the clubs was ultimately just two points, and Rovers had by far the superior goal average, but the handicap of the late start to the season, three defeats in the first nine matches, and a fixture pile up at the fag end of proceedings eventually proved too burdensome to overcome. There had also been the distraction of the Junior Cup to be taken into account.

The long drawn out sixth round tie against Newthorpe United, which had needed a second replay to split the teams, had caused the playing of the semi-final to be delayed until late in April. Thankfully Rovers, meeting a team who'd played eight games of their own in seventeen days, needed just a single attempt to beat Notts Amateur League side St Patricks and line up an all-Realm League final at Meadow Lane against the prominent second division outfit Ferry Rangers. Their quest for silverware would go right down to the wire.

On the other side of town, Marys were free from the hassle of fixture congestion, but their run-in was no less intense as a consequence. Their last four games of the season could hardly have been more demanding: a semi-final, a final, a championship decider, and another final, in that order. It was no time for faint hearts.

First up was the quarter-final tie in the Arnold and District Benevolent Cup against the strongest team invited to participate in the competition, Bestwood Colliery. The miners' side were more than holding their own in the top division of the Notts Alliance and had been the pre-tournament favourites to lift the cup. Even though Marys had the ground advantage, it wasn't enough to stop the colliers from advancing through to the final. Five days later, Bestwood confirmed their superiority as they became the first side to win the new trophy when they returned to the Top Rec and hammered fellow Alliance outfit Mapperley Villa by seven goals to three in front of a crowd of over two thousand. The receipts generated from this and all the other ties would no doubt have pleased Mr Jim Kirk and the various beneficiaries of the spectators' munificence, but there would be little or no charity involved in Marys' next clash, the final of the Spartan League Cup.

Having managed to avoid each other in the earlier rounds, Marys and East Kirkby Welfare, the two best teams in the Spartan League, found themselves lining up against each other for the first of two matches that would determine the outcome of their season. The final took place at the Gatehouse Ground, Linby, just forty eight hours after Marys defeat against Bestwood. The Welfare side hadn't fared too well in their Saturday game either, so both teams carried a bit of a hangover into the match, but as the Saints had already beaten their opponents twice, it was they who carried the greater weight of expectation of success. Even so, the two teams had been well matched in the earlier encounters and this third game was no exception. With so much at stake, there was a certain degree of unwelcome inevitabity about the outcome. As dusk drew in, the teams couldn't be separated, and they'd have to do it all over again three days later.

So, whilst Marys own ground was hosting the Benevolent Cup Final, the maroon and gold half of the town set off to Linby to see whether their side could go one better in the replay. Another close fought game ensued, but first blood was drawn by the Welfare side and they took the trophy by the closest of margins, the odd goal in five. It was a big blow to the Saints and their followers, but at least there was no time to mope about the result. Less than forty eight hours later, the two teams lined up against each other for the third time in just six days, giving Marys the perfect opportunity for swift revenge.

East Kirkby's last match before the series of clashes with Marys had been the crucial trip to Balderton for their penultimate league match of the season. The Newark team were in no mood to be generous and sent the Welfare side home with their tails between their legs, soundly beaten by three goals to one. As a result, the Kirkby side remained a point behind Marys going into the last game. The table at kick-off, with the Saints needing just a draw to clinch the championship, now looked like this:-

	P	W	D	L	F	A	P
Arnold St Marys	23	19	1	3	103	40	39
East Kirkby Welfare	23	18	2	3	103	40	38

Once the game was underway, any disappointment that Marys felt as a result of the cup defeat was soon dispelled. Urged on by a large and enthusiastic Arnold presence in the big crowd, they secured an early advantage. As always, Eric and Roy Thompson were numbered amongst Marys' travelling contingent, and their recall of the game is vivid.

E&RT : There was quite a slope on the ground, in fact there were a lot of pitches like that then. Even though we were kicking up hill we were three-none up by half time, but when we turned round they whipped two or three in pretty quick. They had a couple of blokes who were with Forest, they were a good side, it was dead close.

Indeed it was, and with only just over ten minutes remaining and the teams locked at three goals apiece, Marys appeared to have one hand already on the championship trophy; then came the defining moment of the game.

E&RT : Before the game had started the referee asked the two teams whether they'd mind his lad running the line because he wanted him to get some experience as he wanted to be a referee. The two teams agreed. We'd taken five coach loads of supporters over for the match and the crowd was all packed solid around the pitch. There were over two thousand there, shoulder to shoulder, not just two men and a dog. These weren't even senior sides, they were two Intermediate sides, but the ground was packed. People were stacked behind Marys' goal when the ball went into the net and came flying back out straight into Billy North's arms. He caught it and kicked it straight back upfield. Play carried on but the supporters at the back of the goal had seen it go in so they got the ref's kid who was running the line and told him. The lad waved his flag to tell his old man that it was a goal. As soon as he blew his whistle and said "Goal, goal" everybody swarmed onto the pitch. The referee headed straight for a building down by the entrance to the ground and locked himself in the toilet. The police were called and escorted him and his kid off.

As a consequence of this unruliness and the self-imposed incarceration of the referee, the game was abandoned on the eighty minute mark with the score officially four-three to the home side. The powers that be decided that although it appeared that Marys' supporters were to blame for the initial pitch invasion, such was the willingness of the East Kirkby fans to add their own brand of indiscipline to the general mayhem, the only solution would be to have the game re-staged.

RT : The referee was a bloke called Bernard Maltby. He lived down the Meadows and when he hadn't got a match to referee he used to stand the gate for Notts County. I used to work with him and about a week after the game he came to me and said "Hey Roy, look at this." He'd got a letter and it said: 'You have been chosen to referee the replay[ed match] at Bentinck Miners Welfare'. He said "They were after me to bloody lynch me and now they want me referee the next match. I'm going nowhere near them."

Of course, whether the ball ever actually crossed the line remained a moot point. Whilst East Kirkby's fans, especially those closest to the action, insisted that the ball had bounced back out of the goal having struck one of the spectators packed tightly together directly behind the netting, Marys' followers thought differently. Even the referee admitted to being unsure of the actual sequence of events.

RT : He said: "That ball never went in you know, it never went in." He swore when I saw him again some time later that the ball had never gone in and crikey me he'll have been dead many years now and he'd still swear that ball never went in.

What Roy's recounting of the contents of the letter received by Mr Maltby didn't include was the date that had been set for the re-run of the game. As the abandoned encounter had taken place on the very last day of the season, it had been decided that the championship decider would have to be held over to the beginning of the next season. Whilst this was a most unsatisfactory outcome, there really hadn't been much scope for an alternative. The only matches that were normally scheduled to be played after the first Saturday in May were the finals of the various county cups, two of which Rovers and Marys had an active interest in of course.

The first of them to be played was the Notts Intermediate Cup, with Marys meeting Notts Alliance side Mapperley at the City Ground on the Monday night. The senior outfit had already finished runners-up for the second season in a row in Division Two of the Alliance as well as landing the divisional cup, so Marys obviously had their task cut out. Having just played probably their four hardest games of the season in just over a week, it was probably no surprise when Marys eventually succumbed to their higher ranking opponents by four goals to two. The defeat was no disgrace, but it meant that they'd failed to win in five straight matches, been eliminated from three cup competitions, two at the ultimate stage, and would have to wait four months before they could redeem themselves and rescue a result in their return match against East Kirkby that would leave them with something tangible to show for a season that, at least during its middle period, promised so, so much.

Every season deserves a fitting climax, and the best time for it is at the end of that season. A third of a year is a pretty long delay for anything and when the Spartan League management committee decreed that the date for the rearranged championship decider would be the second Friday of September, a day of the week not noted for its staging of a match of any sort, let alone one of some relative importance, it appeared that the race for the previous season's title had become something of an irrelevance. If the scheduling of the game hadn't offered some clue as to the idiosyncrasy of playing the last game of the 1948-49 season almost four weeks into the 1949-50 version, then the fact that one of the participants wasn't by now even in the league they were trying to win probably gave the game away.

East Kirkby had left the Spartan League for the delights of the Central Alliance, but in an attempt to retain some integrity for their flagship trophy, the league's management committee had insisted that they could only use players who were registered to play during the previous season. It was scant consolation for Marys, and especially the players, many of whom had to make their way to East Kirkby for a six thirty kick-off following a full day at work. Players in colliery affiliated sides would often find their work patterns beneficially rearranged to fit in with their football commitments, rather than the other way round as was the norm for most other local footballers. Suffice to say that even the Football Post was moved to comment on the difficulties encountered by Marys' players that particular Friday evening: "Praise is due to the Saints' players who made superhuman efforts to reach Kirkby, some travelling in taxis straight from work, not having time for a wash and a meal." If sympathy won matches, the maroon and golds would have won with something to spare. As it was, it was a game too far in more sense than one. They succumbed by six goals to three and belatedly wound up the third season of the post war period much as they had done the previous two: empty-handed.

It was an anti-climax in every sense. Four trophies had been well within their grasp. Not having a game for the first three weeks of the season and then losing two of the first three they played certainly wasn't a good start, but the six month purple patch which dominated the entirety of all but the beginning and end of the campaign had consigned that stuttering start to the waste bin of history. Ultimately it wasn't even end of season fatigue that did for Marys, although the very last game at the Bentinck Colliery ground wasn't without its own degree of tiredness. Actually, and it was no disgrace, the Saints had effectively fallen at the final hurdle to teams from the Notts Alliance and Central Alliance: Bestwood, Mapperley, and twice to East Kirkby. Eric Thompson summed it up perfectly.
ET : Marys were a good side at the time, a very good side, but it was at their level. When they played teams from higher leagues, they struggled. Later on it changed, but that's how it was then.

MARYS 1948-49 : Back Row (l to r); - -, A Evans, - Wood, R Hinson, - -, W North, F Walker, J Atkinson, R Dawes, C Peck, R Rockley, J Cunningham, A Wilkinson. Front Row; H Elliott, J Pearson, T Dickinson, H Portas, A Allcock, C Middleton, S French, W Parr (Geoff Parr Collection)

Two days after Marys were defeated by Mapperley in the Notts Intermediate Cup Final, Rovers lined up in the Junior version against Ferry Rangers at Meadow Lane. Runners-up in the second division of the Realm League, Rangers would join Rovers in the top section the following season. The two teams' records were remarkably similar, and whilst they both had no difficulty in finding the net, the performances of their defences were just as notable. At a time when it was not quite the art that it became twenty or more years later, Rovers had managed to shut out the opposition on almost twenty occasions. With Rangers conceding an average of just a goal a game too, the prospects for a high scoring final seemed unlikely.

With the scoreline remaining goalless with only twenty five minutes to go and with Jack Surgey having already missed from the penalty spot, pre-match predictions regarding the closeness of the game were proving correct. Then Jack Brace conjured a chance for himself and with the keen eye for goal he'd been demonstrating all season put Rovers ahead just when they most needed it. With the defence again showing just why teams had found it so hard to break them down, Rovers protected their lead with no great alarm. Thankfully, spectators stayed on the terraces and in the stands, at least until the actual presentation of the cup, when Rovers deservedly put their hands on their second piece of silverware in only the third year of their existence.

Ultimately Rovers had succeeded despite their own delayed and less than exhilarating start to the campaign. Whereas Marys' gallant efforts had come badly undone at the final hurdle, Rovers had hung on to the very end and in securing the narrowest of victories at Meadow Lane rubbed a little salt into their neighbours' wounds. Distinctions would inevitably be drawn as to the relative merits of Rovers' achievement but, despite the gainsayers, a trophy is still a trophy. The amended honours board now read:-

ROVERS : ONE CHAMPIONSHIP, ONE CUP

CHAPTER FIVE 1949-50

As the tumultuous years of the 1940s drew to a close, the face of Arnold was beginning to alter quite noticeably. Restrictions on the building of new houses were being relaxed as the demand amongst the baby boomers for homes of their own quickly increased. It was the beginning of the transformation of the area from being effectively little more than a large village to what it is today, a contiguous suburb of the City of Nottingham in everything other than legal status. As far back as 1919 the powers that be had sought to extend the city boundary to include Beeston, West Bridgford, Wollaton and Arnold but on that occasion the attempt had failed. Whilst formal legal procedures couldn't produce the required outcome at that time, the situation was eventually resolved by an increase in the desire for home ownership and a natural migration away from the cramped conditions of inner cities. Even then, in 1949 the urban sprawl which would eventually affect almost all satellite settlements around towns and cities was still a long way off, but the seeds of expansion were sown with the proposal of the massive Clifton Estate to the south of the city and Arnold's own public housing projects such as the Killisick Estate, where the author happily spent the early years of his childhood.

I'd been delivered into the world in the front bedroom of my maternal grandparents' house on James Street, a traditional two-up, two-down terrace with open fires, no bathroom, and an outside privy. For the first year or so after my arrival, the house was occupied by no less than seven of us. Sleeping arrangements were cramped to put it mildly, but at least the overcrowded conditions meant that the authorities looked favourably upon my parents' request for one of the brand new three bedroom semis at Killisick. I was probably too young to have paid much attention at the time but for my mother and father it was idyllic. Not only did it have ample accommodation but we also had a choice of loos, one upstairs adjacent to the bathroom, and another downstairs next to the 'coal hole' and laundry room. Throw in a view across open fields that stretched right up to the Travellers' Rest pub on Mapperley Plains and they could have been forgiven for thinking that they'd died and gone to heaven. My great uncle used to work on Seagraves' farm in the fields that abutted the back of our garden and I can remember waving to him from my bedroom window. That view has gone now too, itself a victim of the seemingly never ending urbanisation of the countryside, with a school and even more houses having taken the place of the farm.

The town centre itself, whilst more or less recognisable as the earlier version of its modern day counterpart, was home to a far different set of uses for its buildings. There were no supermarkets but it did have a cinema, the Bonington; two if you count the Roxy in Daybrook. Most of today's pubs were around then, together with far more privately owned shops too, but national chains were conspicuous by their absence. So too were charity shops, building societies and thrift stores, better known when they were around as 'cheap' shops. The western end of Front Street wasn't pedestrianised because it didn't need to be. The pleasures of mass private motoring were yet to come so as long as you avoided an altercation with any of the numbers 20, 20A, and 52 corporation buses that trundled through every so often, you could walk the length of the street with impunity.

For the ordinary guy, transport was usually by bus or train, which still served the town via the station in Daybrook, named obviously for its location although it had actually started out life in 1875 as 'Arnold and Sherwood'. And it wasn't just the ordinary guy who mingled with his fellow citizens in such a way. If one is to believe all the claims made by the football stars of their day, such as Nat Lofthouse, Sir Tom Finney, and Nottingham's own Tommy Lawton, none of these sporting heroes was averse to hopping on the local bus and chatting to fans on the way to the match.

Whether apocryphal or not, it was certainly true that Tommy's arrival at Meadow Lane by whatever means had started to show signs of reaping dividends. 1948-49 finished with County having to settle for a mid-table spot in the Third Division (South) despite being the only team in the whole of the Football League to score a century of goals that season. Two nines and an eleven certainly helped boost the final tally. Tommy, Jackie Sewell, and Tommy Johnston all contributed twenty or more of them and such high scoring feats brought the crowds flocking to The Lane. Notts' average attendance was over thirty one thousand and the chance to see Lawton and Sewell in particular, the former having just come to the end of his England career and the latter soon to start his, drew large crowds wherever Notts played. No less a place than Anfield, home of Liverpool, was packed to the rafters for a fourth round FA Cup tie. Over sixty one thousand fans, just thirty three short of the then ground record saw the home side squeeze through to the fifth round with the only goal of the game.

Going into the 1949-50 season, optimism was high amongst County fans that the team would finally get promoted. On the other side of the Trent, emotions were mixed. Forest had just suffered the ignominy of being relegated from the second division and would be in direct competition with the Magpies for the first time since 1935. A quick return to the higher sphere was considered essential, but there were no guarantees that this might be achieved at the first attempt.

Optimism was certainly high back in Arnold, especially at the top end of town where it was reasonable to assume that the departure for pastures new of the previous season's arch rivals East Kirkby would offer Marys a fair chance of going one better than runners-up spot this time around. Rovers, remaining in the Realm League, had similar aspirations, if only they could find a way to depose Keyworth from their customary position at the head of the table. They wouldn't be able to defend the Notts Junior Cup though; victims of their own success in a way, they would be joining Marys in the hat for the first round draw of the Notts Intermediate Cup. With this promotion of sorts, the chances of the long awaited initial competitive clash of the two town teams had been improved distinctly. Now they might be drawn together in the county cup as well as the district one which so nearly saw the first showdown the previous season. Unfortunately there was one large cloud on the horizon for Rovers, although the problem wasn't actually up in the sky but was of a more earthly nature, that of *terra firma*. Or maybe that should read '*terra* not so *firma*'. Even right at the very start of the new season, the pitch at Nottingham Road was visibly and rapidly disintegrating, and drawing unfavourable comment from players, officials, and reporters alike.

Francis 'Franny' Greensmith, who would shortly be making his debut for the club and go on to be a fixture in the side for many years was later quoted as saying:

FG : The pitch at the Bottom Rec was so bad that we said we knew every blade of grass on the ground.

An article that appeared in the Football News the previous season had made a passing reference to the inadequacy of the playing surface and when one of the paper's reporters made a visit to the ground early in September, it would appear that very little, if anything at all, had been done to improve matters. Under a banner headline that read 'MATCH RUINED BY POOR ARNOLD PITCH' the writer did not pull any punches. He began: 'The ... teams had to play ... on a field so rough no words of mine can describe it adequately.' He couldn't resist the temptation to have a go at doing so anyway and continued: 'If I say one half of the pitch is almost devoid of grass, the other half studded with dangerous tussocks of coarse grass, and pot-holes here, there and everywhere, you will have some picture of the scene.' Warming to the task he finished with a flourish: 'The field the Council has placed at the disposal of the Arnold lads is in a dreadful state. [The] only purpose it could serve properly – in its present state – would be an assault course, and it might then be ruled as too much of a good thing.' It wasn't only the players who were at risk either. The referee apparently caught a foot in one of the uglier pot-holes, ricked his knee badly and would spend the next few days limping as a result.

In the actual match itself Rovers, probably more accustomed than their visitors to the difficulties that the parlous state of the pitch presented, ran out six-nil winners over Radcliffe Olympic. The reporter called the last of the six goals '... a freak'. He explained why: '[Bill] Horton despairingly lunged at a bouncing ball. It rolled towards Daniels, hit one of the innumerable pot-holes in front of goal and gently bounced over the goalie's outstretched arms.' As a consequence, the reporter, showing a droll sense of humour, suggested: 'The final score should have read: Arnold Rovers, five goals, Arnold Council, one goal; Radcliffe Olympic nil.' However, the state of the pitch was no laughing matter. A very salient point was raised by the reporter in his last paragraph: 'Arnold Rovers have already lost players to other clubs because of the state of their home ground. Unless something is done they will lose others either for the same reason or through injuries.'

The reporter had clearly done his homework. Players who had left Rovers since, and despite, the Junior Cup Final success of just a few months earlier included Jack Brace and Jack Surgey. The loss of either would have been a blow, so it was doubly so to have both of them leave at the start of the new term. The former had switched allegiance to Marys whilst his cousin would soon join fellow Realm League side Notts Regent just as they had decamped from their regular home ground at Highfields. Now, joining Marys up on the Top Rec, their arrival would herald a spell where there were three genuine rivals for the title of the town's top team. Whilst their name gave no indication as to any connection with Arnold, a glance at the make-up of the side left no-one in any doubt. At a time when travelling any distance for a match was scarcely an option for an amateur player, they drew the majority of their players from the area; nor were they backwards in signing a player from either of the other two Arnold clubs. Former Rovers' goalkeeper 'Duke' Ryan had played for Regent the previous season together with ex-Saint John Cunningham. Not that they were the only club of the three to accept the signatures of their local rivals' players. In an ironic twist, both 'Duke' and John were back in Arnold shirts for the current season, but not those of their original clubs. 'Duke' took over in Marys' goal whilst John was handed the number four shirt for Rovers, becoming the first guys to have played for all three local outfits.

The comings and goings of players between any combination of the three clubs became a feature of the local scene for some while. It wasn't unknown for a guy to start a season with one team, join a rival part way through the season, and then return to his original side during the same campaign. Whether the number of players passing through the exit door at Rovers was totally down to the state of the ground is open to conjecture but whilst the season was still in its infancy, another of the much admired forward line, left winger Ken Crombie, would team up with his former inside-left partner Jack Surgey at Regent. They weren't the only ex-Rovers in the side at the time either as the highly rated Don Hazledine had joined Regent some time earlier. An indication that the loss of so much attacking talent to both their cross-town rivals might tell on Rovers' efforts to improve on their success of previous years was in evidence in only the second game of the season. Regent hosted Rovers and ran out comfortable winners by four goals to two.

To be fair, it was Rovers' only setback of the first few weeks of the new season. Four weeks later Keyworth United, for so long the nemesis of the Nottingham Road outfit, were summarily despatched in the first round of the Realm League Division One Cup. The game, played at Keyworth, ended in a resounding four-one victory, thanks mainly to a hat-trick from the ever reliable Ernie Barber. When, seven days later, Rovers shared the spoils in a one-all draw in the return league game at home to Regent, they were handily placed in second spot. However, a glance at Rovers' fixture list showed that the next few weeks would be critical. The schedule included crucial home and away league matches against Keyworth, two games that even this early in the season would have a significant bearing on the destination of the championship trophy, but before those clashes there was the not so insignificant matter of the club's debut in the Notts Intermediate Cup.

The draw hadn't been kind. Rovers' name had been pulled out of the hat alongside the holders of the trophy Mapperley. The Notts Alliance club had of course been victorious in the previous season's final against none other than Marys, so the task facing Rovers was pretty daunting. So it proved, because even with home advantage, Rovers' run in the Intermediate

Cup was short-lived; Mapperley's hands stayed on the cup a little longer and Rovers' tilt at the trophy would have to wait another year.

ROVERS 1 OCT 1949 : Back Row (l to r); L Peck, D Thorlby, F Johnson, G Tutin, A Wilkinson, J Cunningham, W Whitt, B Rodmell. Front Row; E Barber, P Dean, W Horton, R Staples, J Turton

(Bill Whitt Collection)

Elimination from the county cup wasn't the best of preparation for the following week's top of the table clash with Keyworth, even though Rovers' had prevailed in the two previous meetings between the clubs. The fixture had always produced goals and the latest instalment of the rivalry at the Bottom Rec was no exception. The fans were treated to an eight goal feast, but unfortunately it was the visitors who emerged victorious by five goals to three to register their fifth success in eight meetings between the two sides. The setback saw Rovers slip to sixth in what was turning out already to be a very competitive top end of the table. The following Saturday they faced the prospect of another tough game as they visited third placed Dale Villa, the previous season's second division champions. Villa were unbeaten going into the game and their record was still intact ninety minutes later. Another high scoring and evenly matched contest saw the home side clinch the two points by the odd goal in seven.

Worryingly, Rovers' traditionally miserly defence was beginning to ship goals at a rate not seen before. An uninspiring point was gained the following week at home to mid-table Wilford Road Athletic, and then seven days later it was back to Keyworth for the return league fixture. By now Rovers, though still in sixth place, were running the risk of falling fatally behind the habitual league leaders. Just as Rovers' previous opponents had been, Keyworth were unbeaten at kick-off, and Rovers, without a win now in five games, had all on to get a decent result. It proved a good distance beyond them, their tormentors notching up another five scoring efforts with just two in reply. The South Notts side's revenge for their league cup defeat had been swift and pretty brutal. Rovers were marooned in mid-table with just ten points from ten games, by far the poorest start to a season in the four years of their existence. Without a fixture for the next two weeks, they also had to sit and mull over the worst sequence of results in the club's short life.

As the calendar pages flicked over into December, Rovers reward for their impertinence in knocking Keyworth out of the league cup was a home tie against none other than Notts Regent. Just like Rovers, their opponents had lately had a fairly indifferent run of their own when points were at stake, but league form usually counted for little in a cup-tie, especially one between two local sides. Not that any were needed, but the appearance of Jack Surgey in Regent's line-up was sure to add a little spice to the proceedings. He had re-signed for

Rovers just before the game against Dale Villa but stayed for only three matches, none of which of course were won. Ironically, having then pitched up at Rovers' closest rivals, his debut for Regent would see him return to the Bottom Rec at the very earliest opportunity. It was a happy return. Rovers' defensive miseries continued and Regent went nap, all their five goals coming from Arnold guys too, with one from Jack himself. Ex-Rover Ken Crombie added another, whilst two ex-Marys' players, Geoff Parr and Roy 'Fly' Carter, both got their names on the scoresheet, with Roy netting twice. Bill Horton replied with two for Rovers.

Rovers had now conceded twenty goals in just five matches and had gone seven games without a win. When the next two league fixtures produced just two points they were approaching the half-way mark in the season marooned in sixth place and with just twelve points out of a possible twenty four. Fate dealt them a severe blow too when shortly afterwards Radcliffe Olympic left the league and their results were expunged. As a consequence of having already beaten them twice early in the season, Rovers' far from healthy points total was now reduced by four, leaving them with all on in the second half of the campaign to rescue a degree of respectability from a situation that was hardly promising.

Over on the other side of town, Marys' own position could scarcely have been more of a contrast. They'd added a number of players during the close season including three ex-Rovers in Ken Atherley, Jack Brace and, via Notts Regent, goalkeeper 'Duke' Ryan. Veteran Tommy Dickinson's nephew Billy was signed to form a left-wing partnership with his uncle, whilst Charlie Moore joined his home town club having had a very successful spell with Mapperley Villa. Despite the natural disappointment of not being able to clinch the previous year's championship in the re-arranged fixture with East Kirkby at the start of the current season, Marys had still made the most impressive of starts. After six matches they boasted a hundred percent record and a goals tally of thirty eight, achieved with scores of six, seven, six, six, five and eight. In the last of those games, three of the new boys were on the score sheet, with pride of place going to Billy Dickinson and Charlie Moore with a hat-trick apiece.

The 'old guard' weren't being upstaged though. The half-back line of Ron Hinson, Jim Atkinson and Reg Rockley was very highly regarded and Marys' other 'permit' player, centre forward 'Arnie' Wilkinson, was continuing his excellent form of the previous season. Ron had, as noted previously, been a professional with Lincoln City whilst Arnie had put his name to a paid contract with Notts County. He'd been very prominent at ATC level and his exploits there had attracted the interest of a number of clubs including Middlesborough and Chelsea. Arnie, who lived in Daybrook and was serving in the RAF, had opted to sign for the Meadow Lane club but couldn't quite make the breakthrough into the starting eleven. His task had obviously been made all the harder by the fact that a certain Mr Lawton was blocking his path.

Marys' next two matches saw them ease through the opening round of both the Intermediate and Spartan League Cups, with the first of the two games being the subject of the cartoonist's art as exhibited by Ted Duncan in the Football Post. Marys played host to Brinsley, a team they had last met in a previous incarnation twenty-six years earlier, and Ted, a teacher at Robert Mellors School, was there to capture the action in his own inimitable manner. His artwork was not only topical but it was fast too, as he had the same tight deadline to meet as all those other reporters who filed match information for that evening's edition of the FP. As anyone who ever attended a Forest or Notts home match back then will testify, by the time you'd walked from the City Ground or Meadow Lane to catch the bus back to Arnold from the Market Square, the city's football papers were already on sale. Ted's work took pride of place, too, featuring prominently on the centre pages.

At the start of November Marys returned to league duty with a visit to Southwell and its own St Marys outfit. The shared name was the only thing the two sides had in common as the visitors inflicted a fifteen-one thrashing on their hosts. Every one of the Arnold forward line ended up in the referee's notebook for the right reason; Jack Brace and 'Arnie' scored four apiece, Charlie Moore and Billy Dickinson repeated their hat-trick feat of a few weeks earlier and Billy's uncle Tommy rounded off the scoring. The pattern of the first couple of months of the season was repeated with pleasing consistency right up until Christmas. By the time of the holiday tie against Mapperley in the Arnold and District Benevolent Cup, Marys had maintained their one hundred percent record over sixteen matches including successful negotiation through the next stage of the league and county cup competitions.

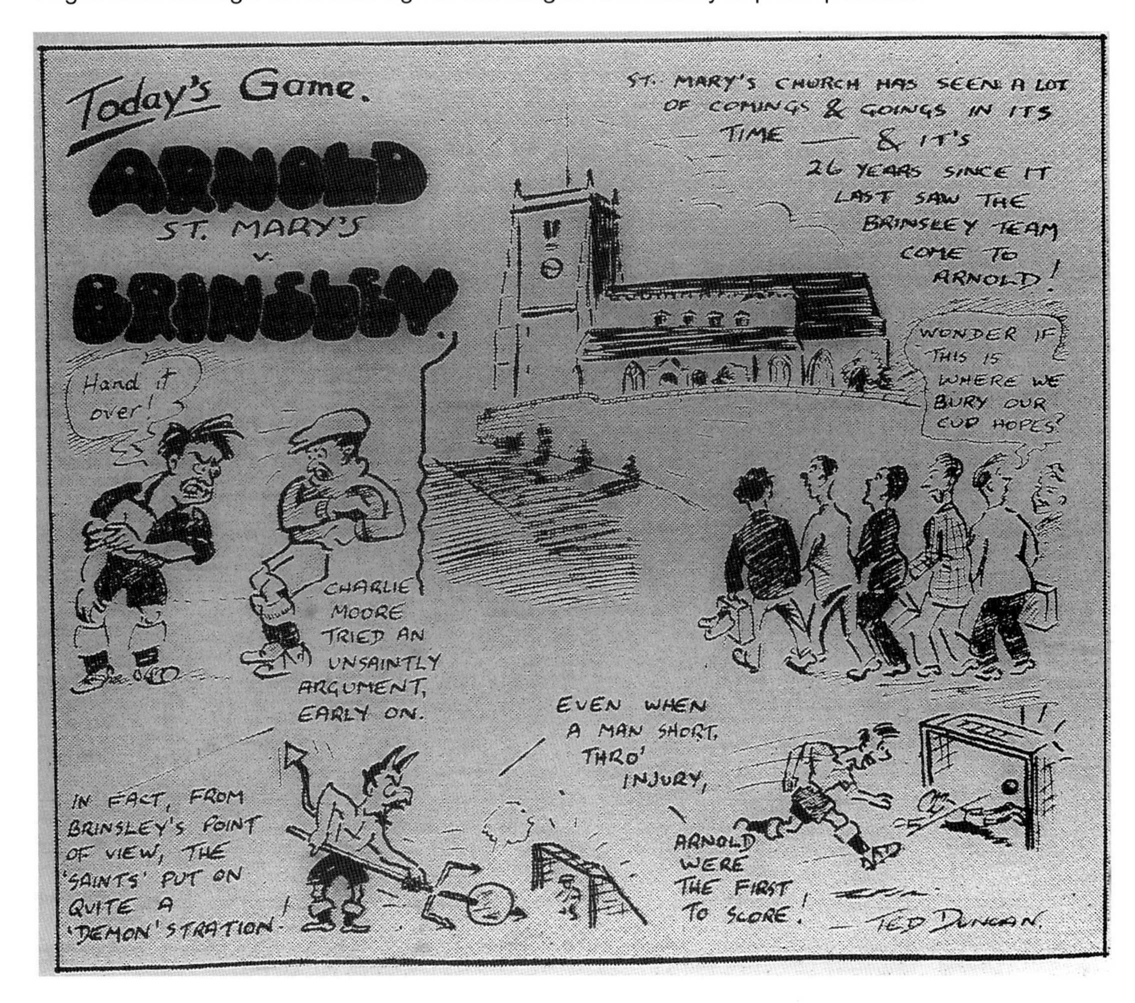

MARYS v BRINSLEY 15 OCT 1949 AS DRAWN BY TED DUNCAN (Courtesy Football Post)

It was a pity for the competition as a whole and for Marys in particular that the draw for the first round of the charity cup had pitted two of the favourites for the trophy together so early. A crowd of over a thousand turned up to see whether the Saints' tremendous run would continue, though with home advantage and having beaten both Marys and Rovers already that year Mapperley were the slight favourites at kick-off. Early in the second half and by then leading three-nil, there was no doubt about their superiority, at least on the scoreboard. According to reports, Marys played much the better football but suffered from a desire to try and walk the ball into the net. Although they pulled a couple back and gave themselves a glimmer of hope, a fourth goal scored from an apparently offside position just five minutes from full time sent Mapperley through and handed Marys their first defeat of the season. The result was a big disappointment for the many Arnold supporters in the crowd but with another important cup match coming up just a few days later, there was no time to dwell on the loss.

More importantly, and not only for followers of local football but the population as a whole, the countdown to a new decade had begun, one which everyone looked forward to optimistically, especially in the shared hope that the depravity and deprivation of the previous ten years would never be repeated. Not that the dawn of the nineteen fifties had everyone on easy street, far from it. Rationing was still in force and the basic working week for most adult men was forty-four hours. Many among the electorate were disappointed that the pace of economic recovery hadn't been as fast as was hoped, and this frustration was a contributory factor in reducing the Labour government's majority to a far from comfortable five seats at the February election.

At least the hopes and dreams of the followers of Marys and Notts County looked like being fulfilled. The Magpies, just like the Saints, had had a fine first half of the season, and at the dawning of the fifties were clear leaders of the Third Division (South); five points ahead and with a game in hand. Their success had drawn crowds to Meadow Lane in unprecedented numbers; the average at the half-way point was almost thirty-six thousand with two gates exceeding forty thousand. A football follower of modern times would scarcely believe that a regular season third division league match in October could attract nearly forty-three thousand spectators, especially when the teams in question were Notts County and Walsall, but it did. Lawton-mania was well and truly at its peak.

If the Magpies were grabbing all the local headlines at professional level, and Marys' exploits were the talk of Arnold as well, Rovers' followers might well have been forgiven for thinking that the season, if it hadn't already, was in danger of passing their own favourites by. However, a reversal in fortune of sorts had begun when the team had seen out the old year on its very last day with a comfortable three-nil win over Cotgrave, only the second time they'd kept the opposition out all season. The revival wouldn't be noticed until some time later, but sure enough results indicated that the start of 1950 pointed to a much better performance than the second half of 1949. Although, with five blank Saturdays out of the next twelve, Rovers had a far from full fixture list, by the end of March they'd dropped just a single point from their seven games. Unfortunately, having only moved up a single place to fifth, the improvement in form hadn't been matched by a similar advance in the standings. Even so, Rovers had claimed the scalps of both Dale Villa and Newthorpe United, two sides who'd beaten them earlier in the campaign and who were still above them in the league. Whilst second place remained an option for any one of five clubs, including Rovers, the title would be heading back to Keyworth for a third consecutive season; four if the 1946-47 championship win by Normanton and Keyworth is included.

Rovers' defence had certainly redeemed itself with its performances in the eight match unbeaten spell, being breached on average just once a game. In particular, regular defensive stalwarts Bill Whitt and John Cunningham picked up good press comment, whilst in attack centre-forward Bill Horton led the line with a goalscoring flourish, notching a couple of hat-tricks in the successful run.

The undefeated spell was extended to over a dozen games and continued to almost the very end of the campaign, but old frailties surfaced once more and Rovers picked up just a couple of points from their closing three matches, succumbing badly by five goals to nil and seven goals to two in the matches lost. The last of these was against Dakeyne Street Old Boys who, just a few days later, would win the Notts Junior Cup; the third season in a row that it would be held by a Realm League side. Their success was of little consolation to Rovers though, especially as the Old Boys side had just become the first team ever to score seven times in a game against them.

However, the heavy defeat against 'Dako' could probably be explained by the fact that just the previous evening Rovers had been involved in what had been their only chance of silverware, the final of the Arnold and District Benevolent Cup played on the Top Rec. They'd already seen off the challenge of Mapperley Villa, Lambley Villa and Hendon Rise in getting to the final, but awaiting them there were the competition's strongest outfit, Bestwood Colliery. The Notts Alliance Division One club were also the current holders of the trophy and despite Rovers' best efforts the miners proved just too strong for them. Given that the red and whites' season as a whole had never really caught fire, this poor finale could scarcely be described as an anti-climax, but it was a big disappointment nevertheless. One that was exacerbated not only by the fine season being experienced by Marys but also by the success that Notts Regent were having with a team liberally sprinkled with ex-Rovers' players.

That Regent were direct Realm League rivals of Rovers made the loss of those key players more acute. Arnold's latest side had generally managed to remain above the town's previous new boys in the table and they eventually finished third to Rovers' sixth, but it was their actual winning of a piece of silverware that was harder to bear in the Nottingham Road camp. When Rovers had knocked mighty Keyworth out of the League Cup at the first time of asking back in October there was the distinct prospect of them adding that particular trophy to the Junior Cup they already held. Sadly, those hopes had been quickly dashed when Regent proved much too strong for Rovers in the very next round. As the Realm League organised its own cup competitions on a divisional basis, the outcome of Regents' victory was a place in the semi-final against Newthorpe United, a similarly decent outfit. Ninety minutes couldn't separate the sides and eventually Regent ran out winners by the narrowest of margins, one-nil. That left only Dale Villa, another top half of the table outfit, standing between them and the cup. Twelve months earlier, Regent had reached the final but gone down quite easily by four goals to nil against Keyworth before a crowd of around two thousand at Meadow Lane.

NOTTS REGENT 1948-49 : Back Row (l to r); H Lord, E Woollacott, D Parr, - Green, W Hardy, H Ryan, - Blasdale, J Cunningham, E Darking. Front Row; - -, - -, F West, D -, G Parr (Geoff Parr Collection)

NOTTS REGENT 1949-50 : Back Row (l to r); L Woollacott, E Darking, J Surgey, W Hardy, F West, J Snowden, B Tomlinson, D Parr, T Price. Front Row; E Woollacott, K Crombie, D Hazledine, W Standen, G Parr, R Carter, E Williamson (Martin Dermody Collection)

This time around, and with the final being staged across the river at the City Ground, the Arnold side made no mistake. Just as the Junior Cup was about to leave the town, a rather pleasant trophy was heading in the opposite direction.

The only question remaining was whether it was the sole piece of silverware claimed by an Arnold club this season, or whether Marys would at last add their own names to the honours board. The Saints' season had seen its first stumble when Mapperley had knocked them out of the district charity cup at Christmas and the previously unhindered run of success had suffered another little hiccup a few days later when they could only manage a four-all draw against Bramcote and Stapleford British Legion in the third round of the Notts Intermediate Cup. The replay took place the next Saturday, the first of the new decade, and before the game it seemed that everything possible was being done to avoid a repeat of the previous week. For some reason the Top Rec had been nicknamed 'Roker Park', better known as the home of Sunderland Football Club, and under the supervision of Syd Grey, a number of players were flattening the pitch with a fifteen hundredweight roller. Not only that, but a new perimeter rope had been acquired and was being put round the ground for the very first time. Questions might have been asked as to the whereabouts of the Arnold Council groundsman at that crucial time but the absence of that particular gentleman would be a recurring conundrum down through the ensuing years. When asked why they were rolling the pitch, the players responded that they were "Getting it ready to show Bramcote how we pop 'em in on Roker Park."

If the reasons behind the adoption of Roker as an alternative moniker for the Top Rec are lost to the mists of time, so apparently are the origins of the many and varied nicknames attributed to the players of the era. Apart from the obvious use of 'Arnie' when referring to Marys' own Arnold Wilkinson, and "Franny" when mentioning Francis Greensmith, newly arrived at Rovers, and the almost obligatory presence of at least one 'Jock' and 'Nobby', there were many others whose source was unknown even to the very person to whom the nickname had been attached. In no particular order, the following were a cross section of alternatives of the time: Walter 'Kegga' Parr; Herbert 'Duke' Ryan; Roy 'Fly' Carter; Jack 'Shonk' Surgey; Charlie 'Wag' Moore; Jack 'Dagger' Brace; Jim 'Blood' Atkinson; and Ken 'Nunk' Atherley. Somewhere in the background was another Marys' committeeman Walter 'Doddem' Archer. Whilst it might not have been confusing for anyone at the clubs themselves, my own research into the times has certainly thrown up at least one instance where the goalkeeper of the day appeared in print as Duke, Herbert's nickname, rather than Ryan as it should have been. Then again maybe 'Kegga' or 'Doddem' had been having a bit of fun with the reporter.

The record books don't show whether 'Wag' or 'Dagger' or 'Nunk' got on the scoresheet that first Saturday of the nineteen fifties, but there was little doubt that on a very flat surface Marys saw off the opposition by five clear goals. Just three weeks later, the outcome of the quarter final away against Lenton Gregory was a much closer call. Gregory, from the second division of the Notts Amateur League, led two-nil at one stage and it was only in the last twenty minutes that the Saints were superior. The ending to the game was quite dramatic and unusual in that forty-two year old Harold Portas, normally a full back but filling in on the left wing, scored direct from a corner kick with the scores level at two apiece with just a few minutes remaining. Harold had been Marys' captain during the previous campaign that had promised so much but had ended disappointingly. Now his crucial goal had put his club in the semi-finals of the county cup and reinforced the belief that this was truly going to be the season when all the promise that the Saints had shown over the last year and a half would finally come to fruition.

Between the two rounds of the Intermediate Cup a couple more league games had been won without too much difficulty and Marys' one hundred percent record atop the table looked fairly invincible. When they beat Wilford Village the following week by a handsome margin of eight goals to two, courtesy of an 'Arnie' Wilkinson hat-trick and another unexpected contribution from Harold Portas, the halfway point of the league season had been reached. The maximum twenty-eight points from fourteen games had been amassed, together with eighty-one goals. When scoring efforts from the various cups were added, Marys were already well through the century mark. Off the pitch, the committee had even begun to produce a monthly programme, issued to coincide with the first home match of each month. It was a very professional looking publication too, properly printed and a forerunner of the match day programme that the Saints would unveil many years later. The club's efforts to establish itself as a force to be reckoned with in local football were also being cemented by a number of complimentary press reports, one of which said they were the best side seen outside the first division of the Notts Alliance.

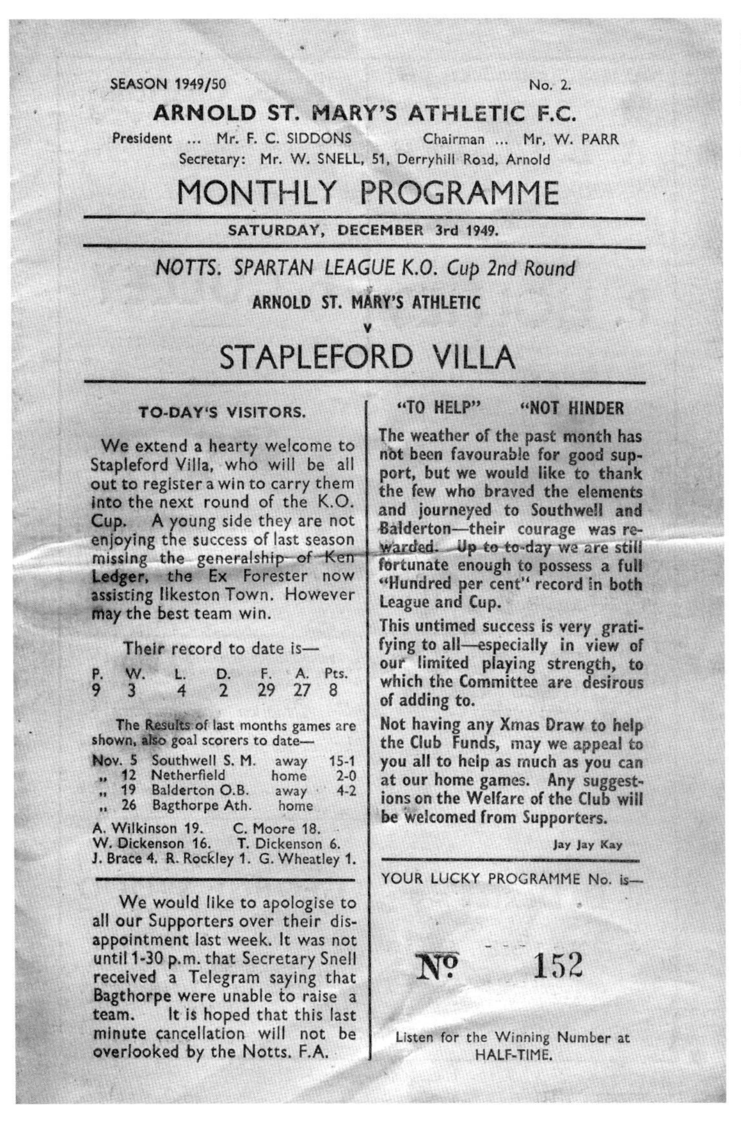

SEASON 1949/50 No. 2.

ARNOLD ST. MARY'S ATHLETIC F.C.

President ... Mr. F. C. SIDDONS Chairman ... Mr. W. PARR
Secretary: Mr. W. SNELL, 51, Derryhill Road, Arnold

MONTHLY PROGRAMME

SATURDAY, DECEMBER 3rd 1949.

NOTTS. SPARTAN LEAGUE K.O. Cup 2nd Round

ARNOLD ST. MARY'S ATHLETIC
v
STAPLEFORD VILLA

TO-DAY'S VISITORS.

We extend a hearty welcome to Stapleford Villa, who will be all out to register a win to carry them into the next round of the K.O. Cup. A young side they are not enjoying the success of last season missing the generalship of Ken Ledger, the Ex Forester now assisting Ilkeston Town. However may the best team win.

Their record to date is—

P.	W.	L.	D.	F.	A.	Pts.
9	3	4	2	29	27	8

The Results of last months games are shown, also goal scorers to date—

Nov. 5	Southwell S. M.	away	15-1
,, 12	Netherfield	home	2-0
,, 19	Balderton O.B.	away	4-2
,, 26	Bagthorpe Ath.	home	

A. Wilkinson 19. C. Moore 18.
W. Dickenson 16. T. Dickenson 6.
J. Brace 4. R. Rockley 1. G. Wheatley 1.

We would like to apologise to all our Supporters over their disappointment last week. It was not until 1-30 p.m. that Secretary Snell received a Telegram saying that Bagthorpe were unable to raise a team. It is hoped that this last minute cancellation will not be overlooked by the Notts. F.A.

"TO HELP" "NOT HINDER

The weather of the past month has not been favourable for good support, but we would like to thank the few who braved the elements and journeyed to Southwell and Balderton—their courage was rewarded. Up to-to-day we are still fortunate enough to possess a full "Hundred per cent" record in both League and Cup.

This untimed success is very gratifying to all—especially in view of our limited playing strength, to which the Committee are desirous of adding to.

Not having any Xmas Draw to help the Club Funds, may we appeal to you all to help as much as you can at our home games. Any suggestions on the Welfare of the Club will be welcomed from Supporters.

Jay Jay Kay

YOUR LUCKY PROGRAMME No. is—

No 152

Listen for the Winning Number at HALF-TIME.

FRONT COVER OF MARYS' GROUNDBREAKING PUBLICATION

(Barry Wildgust Collection)

That claim would be put to the test later in the season in the semi-final of the Intermediate Cup when they would meet Wilford, highly placed in division two of the Alliance, but Marys' biggest immediate challenge was the following week's clash with Aspley Old Boys in the quarter final of the Spartan League Cup. Aspley had emulated Marys' own achievement in reaching the last four of the county cup and were expected to give the Saints a good run for their money in the league version. Marys had twice seen off the Old Boys quite easily early in the season, despatching them pretty smartly by five goals to nil in the league match at Melbourne Road, but Aspley had come on in leaps and bounds since then. Their improvement was quickly noticeable as the game got underway and there was nothing to split the teams. In what was termed 'one of the greatest encounters of the season' on the ground, the sides were tied at three-all at the end of regulation time. Extra time saw no let up in the action but ultimately pressure from the hosts told and they edged victory by five goals to four. 'Arnie' Wilkinson did his utmost for Marys with another hat-trick, his second in a row, but the real star of the show had been the home team's goalkeeper.

Another set of Old Boys were next up with the visit to Church Lane of Balderton. Given the disappointment of going out of the league cup, a competition that Marys' dominance of the league indicated they had been clear favourites to win, the visit of the Newark side was a potential banana skin, especially as the Saints would be without Charlie Moore and Reg Rockley. Happily, even though the absence of such key players meant that Marys' one hundred percent record was lost, the game itself wasn't; it ended in a two-all draw. It was one of only two points that the Saints would drop all season. 'Arnie' Wilkinson's fine campaign continued in the next month with yet another hat-trick and a couple of fours taking him past the fifty goal mark and apart from the odd awkward moment here and there Marys, even with an injury list that was causing some concern, had too much in their locker for the opposition. By the time of the Intermediate Cup Semi-Final on the penultimate Saturday of April, the Saints needed just three points from five matches to clinch the championship.

MARYS 1949-50 : Back Row (l to r); W Parr (Chairman), K Atherley, R Dawes, H Munday, R Hinson, J Atkinson, R Rockley, H Elliott (Trainer). Front Row; W Snell (Secretary), A Murray, C Moore, A Wilkinson, T Dickinson, H Portas

(Courtesy Football Post)

With an almost unassailable position in the league, Marys entered the cup tie with a great belief that they would finally shake off their inability to beat teams from the Notts Alliance. Their opponents Wilford were battling with Christ Church for the championship of the Alliance second division so whilst there was a degree of confidence in the Saints' camp, there was no complacency. The match was staged at the ground of Formans Athletic before what was described as an 'exceptionally large crowd'. After forty five minutes the Marys' contingent amongst them must have been thinking the Alliance Indian sign was still in place as Wilford, with the wind in their favour, had already run up a two-nil scoreline; all the Saints' forwards had been guilty of poor finishing. When the teams turned round and the elements were with the maroon and golds, play was spent almost entirely in the Wilford half, but Marys were impotent in front of goal. Despite only crossing the half way line twice in the second forty five minutes, Wilford managed to add a third. Marys' only consolation came with a forty yard free kick from full back Ken Atherley. Chances had gone begging at just the wrong time and it was inevitable that the game would be remembered by supporters of the Saints as one of many missed opportunities. As it happened, Wilford lost to Marys' own league cup conquerors Aspley Old Boys in the final of the Intermediate Cup, but had the satisfaction of winning the Alliance Division Two championship.

As for the Saints' one remaining chance of silverware themselves, only Sherwood Colliery could mathematically prevent the Spartan League Division One trophy from heading to Arnold, and even then it would also need a complete collapse by Marys for the unthinkable to happen. The miners' side were second in the table and by a quirk of the fixture list still had to play the Saints twice. When the first of those games took place at Arnold in the last week of the season, Marys' target had been reduced to just a single point from their remaining four matches, courtesy of an eight-nil thrashing of Southwell St Marys the previous Saturday. The game against the colliery side was, as expected, a much tougher affair. The Mansfield side hadn't turned up for a coronation, and with Marys' side containing a number of players nearing the veteran stage of their careers and with quite a few of them carrying injuries too, it was no foregone conclusion that the championship would be settled there and then. There was no real advantage in playing at 'Roker Park' either; most colliery club pitches were the equal of many in the Football League. Ultimately though, and unlike twelve months earlier, Marys' faithful following weren't to be disappointed. The Saints edged home by the odd goal in three to bring silverware to the club for the first time since 1939. A few days later they finished the season with a flourish. Visiting the colliery side on the last day of the season they despatched their hosts by four goals to two, and in the process maintained their tremendous unbeaten record in the league, finishing a clear ten points ahead of the runners-up.

For those with an interest in statistics, Marys ran up some pretty impressive numbers too. All fourteen away games in the league were won; the side was unbeaten at home in all matches; and one hundred and seventy nine goals were plundered in the thirty seven games played. Not only that, but no other team in any Nottinghamshire league had produced a better record; quite an achievement.

With Notts Regent's success in the Realm League Cup and Marys' outstanding feat in winning the Spartan League Championship, the top end of town was now the home to two trophies, but in the general scheme of things the most popular of all accomplishments in local football had been the clinching of the Football League Division Three South Championship by the Lawton-inspired Magpies. Tommy had weighed in with thirty-one league goals, the crowds had kept flocking to see the team home and away, and the Meadow Lane derby against Forest attracted forty-six thousand spectators to see Tommy and Jackie Sewell both score in a two-nil victory that completed the double over their neighbours.

All was well in the footballing world at town and city level. Now all that was needed was for England to show that Johnny Foreigner just who was the best in the world too. The 1950 World Cup, due to be played in Brazil and the first one that the country had ever entered, was just a few weeks away.

The amended honours board now read:-

ROVERS : ONE CHAMPIONSHIP, ONE CUP

MARYS : ONE CHAMPIONSHIP

REGENT : ONE CUP

CHAPTER SIX 1950-51

Today the World Cup is such a massive intercontinental sporting occasion, second only in coverage to the Olympics, that it seems almost impossible to believe that once it was hardly more than a footnote, especially in the British media. The competition had first been staged in Uruguay in 1930 and none of the home countries of the British Isles had been bothered to enter. The host nation had gone on to win the inaugural competition, and when it was next contested in 1934 in Italy, the host nation won that one too, giving Mussolini and his Fascist party the victory they craved. Four years later, in France, *Il Duce* was rewarded with a second propaganda gift as the *azzurri* retained the trophy. The England side and those of the rest of Britain were still noticeable by their absence, but of course most citizens of the UK had their eye on something far more significant than football as Europe was already showing signs of the turmoil to come. The dark years of the war, and their deleterious effect, meant that the fourth World Cup was eventually staged a whole twenty years after the first. At least by this time the powers that be at the Football Association hadn't considered it too *infra dig* to send a team across to South America. With a squad that included players who would later be knighted for their services to the game, Alf Ramsey, Tom Finney, and Stanley Matthews, and a couple in Billy Wright and Stan Mortensen who weren't that shabby either, England were amongst the pre-tournament favourites.

When in their first match they saw off the challenge of Chile fairly easily, the prospects of advancing to the final stage of the tournament were high, especially as the next game saw them scheduled to play against one of the competition's make-weights in the form of the USA. The composition of the American side was made up of amateurs and part-time professionals; a pot-pourri of nationalities. Although they'd led Spain in their first game right until the last ten minutes, no one gave them a chance against mighty England. Even the USA's own players didn't expect too much of themselves, many of them indulging in the carnival atmosphere beloved in Brazil even on the eve of the game itself. The only note of caution was concerning the venue for the match, a small stadium in Belo Horizonte with a rutted pitch and dressing rooms so inadequate that the English team changed at a local sports club and were bussed to the ground. Once the game was underway, relentless pressure from England's forwards failed to break down the USA defence with goalkeeper Frank Borghi in particularly inspired form. It was soon obvious that England's opponents weren't just a bunch of 'waiters, taxi drivers and college students', or any other pejorative term used to describe most every small nation, in the footballing sense, that the national side has ever played against both before and since. When the Haitian Joe Gaetjens scored for his adopted country just before half-time, England were staring a major upset straight in the face.

The second half brought no joy to Tom Finney and company, and with more heroics from Frank Borghi, some intentional, some not, and the welcome intervention on a number of occasions from the woodwork, the USA held out for one of the most unlikely World Cup results of all time. So unlikely that when the result was wired back to Britain, quite a few editors took the scoreline to be a misprint, thinking that it should have read 'USA 1 England 10' instead. The consensus was that England would have beaten the Americans nine times out of ten, but this had been that 'one chance in ten' day, and had resulted in a classic one-nil mugging. Once the score had been ratified back home, the backlash inevitably began. One recurring theme that appeared to be accepted by most observers was that the insularity of the British Football Associations in refusing to embrace the competition earlier had cost the team dearly, but it wasn't that England had not played against foreign opposition on a number occasions, they had. Perhaps when all is said and done it's best to remember that sometimes, in the words of England's Rugby World Cup winning coach Clive Woodward, you have a day where you just 'cop it'.

England's historic set-back on the football field wasn't the only piece of bad news in the month of June. The citizens of the USA, as was their wont, had paid little attention to the sporting sideshow in South America; they'd had more on their minds. Four days before the game in Belo Horizonte, the Korean War had started and they'd begun hoarding supplies in case of rationing and shortages. There was an immediate impact in this country too as the period of National Service was amended, an increase from eighteen months to two years. For footballers of a certain age, the last few days of the month had hardly been a barrel of laughs. The national side had been exposed as being not quite the invincible force that people were led to believe and now another compulsory six months in the forces meant even greater interruption to the fledgling footballing careers of any number of local footballers.

Availability of players was at the forefront of the planning for all three Arnold sides just a few weeks later, and for Rovers and Regent it was very much business as usual when the former's highly thought of left-half Bill Whitt joined the cross-town exodus to Arnold's newest side. Bill had been a regular in Rovers' defence since the club's inception so it was a major surprise when he decamped and joined forces again with Jack Surgey, Ken Crombie and the rest. Regent's acquisitions didn't stop there either as Geoff Hazledine left Lambley Villa to join his older brother Don in what was shaping up to be a very decent outfit. Rovers, not to be outdone, adopted a policy of 'do unto others' by making a raid on Marys' squad and signing centre-half Jim Atkinson whilst forward Jack Brace also returned to Nottingham Road after a short spell with the Saints. Marys themselves raided Rovers' ranks for Bill Horton whilst the Nottingham Road outfit also decided to reinstate their second eleven.

When the season finally began Regent sent out an immediate message that they were a side worth keeping an eye on with an eighteen-one thrashing of their hapless opponents, newcomers Group 61 (BRS). It also seemed that they'd done rather better in the player acquisition merry-go-round when Rovers went down five-three in their own opening game against Hendon Rise. The hopes of a successful league campaign were high in the camps of both Regent and Rovers, especially now that Keyworth United had apparently grown tired of winning the Realm League championship year after year and decided to move up the ranks and join Marys in the Spartan League. They wouldn't be the Saints only obstacle either in the latter's attempt to hang onto the championship trophy; old rivals East Kirkby Welfare's stay in the Central Alliance had been short lived and they had rejoined the Spartan League. The prospect of clashes with these two clubs, as well as with the previous season's front runners Sherwood Colliery and Notts Intermediate Cup winners Aspley Old Boys, pointed to a very interesting season ahead, to say the least.

As it happened, the early season fixture list kept Marys away from these particular teams and their form continued where it had left off the previous season. With six games gone the Saints held top spot on goal average, still unbeaten with five wins and eleven points, the same record as Sutton Colliery. The miners' team had held Marys to a two-all draw in the third game, despite the Saints turning round at half time two up. Players among the goals in those opening games had been Cyril Middleton with four against Burton Joyce and Charlie Moore with a hat-trick at Rangers Athletic, but an unusual name on the scoresheet in the former match had been that of Ray Dawes. Ray had been the club's regular left back throughout the championship campaign but against Marys' near neighbours he wore the number ten shirt and helped himself to a hat-trick. It was just as well that everyone was firing on all cylinders because the next three league games would see them play Keyworth, Aspley, and Keyworth again.

Keyworth had been the nemesis of Rovers for the past three years and the concern around town was that their domination of one Arnold side might just develop into a similar ascendancy over another. The first of the tough run of matches was played over at Keyworth on the last Saturday of September and when the home side enjoyed a three-one advantage at the interval Marys' long unbeaten run looked well and truly in jeopardy. However, the Saints put in a great fighting finish to claw back the two goal deficit and pick up a hard earned share of the spoils. No one in Marys' camp was kidding themselves though; they all knew that Keyworth had demonstrated championship credentials of their own and had put down a marker for the rest of the season.

MARYS 50-51 : Back Row (l to r); E Jones, R Hinson, H Ryan, H Munday, H Wharton, R Rockley. Front Row; A Wilkinson, T Dickinson, C Middleton, C Moore, K Atherley

(Courtesy Football News)

The following week the Old Boys of Aspley were the visitors to Church Lane. They'd remained unbeaten so far and of course had knocked Marys out of the Spartan League Cup the previous season at the quarter final stage, but the Saints hadn't lost in two seasons on the Top Rec and there was no great pre-match apprehension that this tremendous record was in any danger. Then again all good runs have to end sometime and records are there to be broken, but even so it was a humbling experience when Marys failed to score in a game for as long as anyone could remember and their 'Roker Park' invincibility was laid bare as the visitors ran in three goals of their own.

It would be a fortnight before the team and its many followers would know whether the defeat had been a one-off, a hiccup, or whether it was an indication that Marys' two year purple patch was coming to a close. The return game with Keyworth would be a perfect opportunity for the Saints to bounce back and silence the doubts. Unfortunately, just as it is said that you can wait for what seems like an age for a corporation bus to come along and then two arrive at the same time, so it was with Marys' home record; two long years undefeated, followed improbably by two losses in consecutive games. This time the Saints at least managed a consolation goal, but the visitors again helped themselves to three at the other end.

If the wheels were starting to look a little shaky, two weeks later they fell off completely with the visit to Colwick Sugar Factory. The 'Sweeties', as they were known, had given Marys no difficulties the previous year, ending the season just two spots above bottom place, and were hardly faring much better this time around, being just one rung higher at kick-off. Ninety minutes later they'd jumped another couple of places with an improbable win by the odd goal in five. The Football Post reported the result as a 'startling event' which, given subsequent events, was the understatement of the year. The Colwick side would have to withdraw from the league and City Transport would, unfortunately from Marys point of view, take over their fixtures. Had Colwick's record been expunged the embarrassing defeat would have been deemed null and void and forgotten, at least in the record books. As it was, the department responsible for corporation buses would come along later and so effectively prolong the Saints' ignominious sequence of losses.

And Marys' agonies didn't end there either. When old rivals East Kirkby became the third visiting team in a row to lower the Saints' colours on their once impregnable home turf, this time by four goals to two, Marys had capitulated for the fourth consecutive league game with a resultant drop from top spot to seventh in double quick time. It hardly seemed feasible that the maroon and golds could be out of the running in the league with only a third of the season gone, but the table didn't lie. Keyworth, East Kirkby, and Aspley were already leaving them trailing in their wake.

Over in the Realm League Rovers had managed to put together a decent run of form and had remained unbeaten in their next seven outings, winning five and drawing the other two. Regent hadn't done too badly either, losing just a single game to the runaway leaders Bulwell Forest Villa who'd won all of their opening ten fixtures. The first couple of months of the season had seen Rovers and Marys both struggle to keep a settled side, a problem that hadn't troubled Regent. Not that they hadn't made one significant switch though. Geoff Parr, who'd helped himself to a hatful of goals from centre forward in Regent's opening game slaughter, had subsequently been handed the goalie's jersey just a couple of games later. That he was equally at home banging them in or keeping them out was a reflection on how versatile players were expected to be back in that era. At a time when team formations were a lot more rigid than they tend to be today players weren't pigeon-holed to the same extent as their modern counterparts. A lot of that was to do with the guys themselves and their 'play anywhere, anytime' attitude. In fact their appetite for action spilled over from their club football into something far less structured but almost as important; the Sunday morning 'kick-abouts' on the two recs.

The choice of which ground an individual chose was loosely based on the guy's Saturday team and which end of Arnold he came from, so as an example Geoff, who lived on Surgeys Lane and played for Regent and Marys, would turn up on a Sunday morning at the Top Rec.

GP : It started when we were lads and carried on until we went into the Forces. There were loads of us there, not just footballers. There was a bloke called Fred, a miner, and he played in his pit boots. Jack Brace's brother Len, who didn't play for anybody, was there as well. Teams were picked on the basis of 'I'll have you, and I'll have you' depending on who showed up. We usually played until twelve o'clock and then nipped to the pub for a football meeting. None of us were big drinkers and so it was back home for Sunday dinner and then we'd meet back at the rec for another kickabout. We'd finish up by walking up to Rylatt's Café on Redhill Ramper for some tea and toast.

Alec Casterton, who in the 1950-51 season and just fifteen years of age was making his first appearances for Rovers in the reserve side along with the equally youthful goalkeeper Sam Archer and Brian Cunningham, younger brother of John, was one of the many enthusiasts who ended up spending his Sabbath on the Bottom Rec.

AC : I just wanted to play football anywhere. Once I was playing in the street with a tennis ball outside the library with Sam Archer and Joe Wilmot. There was no traffic around but I got fined five shillings for breaking the law anyway. I was nicknamed '999' for quite a while until the novelty wore off. When we played on the Bottom Rec on a Sunday we started with coats as goalposts and then later on we used the actual goalposts themselves. There'd be two captains, sides would be picked, maybe fifteen, sixteen, eighteen, even twenty aside. Players came from all over, a lot of them would be there to run off the beer or aches and pains from the previous day. I lived just a few hundred yards away on Church Drive and always took my boots down to the ground. Sometimes, players would arrive in their Sunday best and end up taking part in the game. There'd even be spectators. We'd usually finish at twelve and head off to the pub to chew over the fat of the previous day's game. The only problem was that the Bottom Rec did get well used as a result.

SA : Yes, it's true, we were playing outside the old library across the road from the Co-op. The local copper came round on his bike and told us to clear off, but once he'd disappeared we came back and carried on playing. The problem was he realised that's what we'd do and so he showed up again and then we were in trouble. He took all our names and addresses and the next thing we heard was that we were going to court. I'd only started work just before the day of the hearing so I couldn't get time off. I was still fined five bob though. It would have been better if the copper had just given us all a clip round the ear like they usually did. Sunday mornings on the Bottom Rec were great, usually about thirty of us, playing all morning and then popping over to the Greyhound for a pint of shandy. It went down in one go.

Francis 'Franny' Greensmith, who was a bit older than Alec and Sam and who had made his debut for Rovers the previous season, had a similar recollection of events at Nottingham Road.

FG : There could be up to fifty players at any time. It was a great way to learn the game. On one occasion I went in for a tackle and didn't make a very good job of it. I wasn't very good at tackling at the time. The player I'd tried to win the ball from suddenly stopped and said to me that if I didn't go into a tackle one hundred per cent then I'd end up getting injured. I'll never forget what he said and I became a better tackler after that.

Regarding tackling, the Football Post ran an article around this time with the headline 'Is the Football Nowadays Namby Pamby?' The columnist, using the *nom-de-plume* Alan-A-Dale, went on to suggest that the contemporary player was inclined to need the trainer even after the slightest of knocks. Personally I had always imagined that that the game was rougher back in the nineteen fifties than it has become in recent years, but then again maybe the Post writer was of the same opinion, but located in a different era. His reckoning implied that football in the thirties was a tougher proposition than twenty years later; maybe it was just the passing of time with each generation of the opinion that things were harder or more physical 'back then'. Funnily enough, this article wasn't the only occasion on which the robustness of current players had been questioned during this particular season. Earlier, in a small match report, there appeared the following prophetic words: 'Spectators commented on the long hair players seem to have today, quite a lot of time being wasted pulling it out of the eyes! One spectator suggested that hair-nets look like being part of football equipment in future.' Of course the hair-nets became hair-bands, but the idea was spot on. It just seemed that the young player of 1950 drew as much censure for his appearance and character as would all his successors in the decades to follow.

In that early part of the season, and on the official Saturday match day, the three Arnold sides had experienced the same mixed fortunes in the opening rounds of their various cup competitions as they had in league games. Regent had emphatically cleared the first hurdle in both the Realm League Senior Cup and Notts Junior Cup, beating league leaders Bulwell Forest Villa by four goals to one in the former and thus avenging somewhat the league defeat to the same side a couple of weeks earlier. In the county competition they had been just as convincing, travelling to Bingham and handing the home team an eleven-one thrashing. Marys put their league troubles to one side in emulating Regent's success in their own Spartan League Cup and Notts Intermediate Cup matches, whilst Rovers were the only one of the three to suffer a reverse, losing in the very first round of the Intermediate Cup for the second year running, this time to the second string of Notts Alliance side Boots Athletic.

As the winter set in, Rovers' league form began to stutter too and they lost back-to-back games against Bulwell Forest Villa and Dakeyne Street Old Boys though they had more luck in the league cup when Dale Villa withdrew and Rovers' subsequent walkover took them straight through to the semi-final. The cup match had been scheduled for the first Saturday in December, but had it taken place there was a distinct probability that it wouldn't have reached its conclusion. As most of the games in the local programme entered the second half, the skies darkened suddenly in almost biblical proportions. Eye witness reports referred to 'the extraordinary darkness which came over the city and county' and the 'blackness over the land'. As it happened the imminent snowstorms and villainous-looking black clouds didn't exactly herald the apocalypse, but they did blot out the light over a large area and cause considerable and sudden havoc across almost all local football fields. The majority of matches had to be called off early, some with as little as ten minutes remaining. The Notts Alliance in particular was badly hit, every one of its fixtures over two divisions failing to last the full ninety minutes. Luckily, Marys' home league cup tie against Sherwood Colliery, which they won two-nil, was one of the few games to survive. Perhaps they'd played with one of those new fangled white balls that had been used earlier in the season in a Notts FA Benevolent Cup match. The game saw the representative sides of the Newark League and the Sutton and Skegby League facing each other and when the light began to fade towards the end, a white ball was introduced. Seen by an official who'd spotted it on a visit to Holland, It was believed to have been the first time that one had been used in competitive football in this country. The hope was that its use would prevent games being abandoned as a result of bad light, but it was pretty plain to see that on that first December Saturday its widespread acceptance was still some way off.

Two weeks later, the weather turned particularly nasty again and severe snowstorms disrupted the sporting calendar once more. Even then Rovers managed to dodge the worst of it but in losing their game probably wished they hadn't bothered. In fact the Nottingham Road outfit suffered the least from December's seasonal blast, being fixtureless only on the last playing day of the year. Arnold's other two sides weren't so fortunate; Regent didn't manage a league game for five straight weeks whilst Marys had no game of any kind for a similar period. Even at this stage of the campaign, another cramped run-in looked to be inevitable, especially for the Saints who had a thirty game league season to fit in for starters. As the old year closed out they had eighteen league games yet to play in the same number of weeks, not forgetting that they also had to fit in ties from three cup competitions.

When Marys finally played their next match in the middle of January at least they kicked-off the new year in style, beating Newstead Miners Welfare five-two in the Intermediate Cup. A couple of emphatic wins in the league followed with Ken Atherley and Charlie Moore both registering hat-tricks, but on the first Saturday in February they were brought down to earth with a crash. Proving that their victory over the Saints earlier in the season was no one-off, Aspley Old Boys virtually ended the maroon and golds' limited championship challenge by a convincing five-two score line. With just eighteen points at the halfway stage of the campaign it was obvious that any success would have to come via the cups.

The same day that Aspley completed the double over Marys, Rovers and Regent were engaged in a head to head league clash on the Top Rec. A glance at the table seemed to indicate that both sides would have all on to meaningfully challenge the leaders, although Regent had five games in hand of most other sides. They had only dropped five points but unfortunately the last of those two came as a result of an eight-five reversal at home to second place Wilford Road Athletic, a bizarre score even by the standards of local football in what was a relatively high scoring era. Early exchanges in the Arnold derby were pretty even and when Roy 'Fly' Carter opened the scoring for Regent, Rovers hit back just a minute later with the equaliser from Jack Brace. Most neutrals, if any could be found of course, would have expected it that way; no quarter asked, no quarter given. What no-one truly anticipated however was that Regent's array of ex-Rovers would then proceed to use the remainder of the match to remind their old club just exactly what it was that they were missing. At the end of the ninety minutes, the home side had dismantled their closest rivals in the most comprehensive and humiliating manner, adding a further nine goals without reply to finish the game ten-one winners. If consolation were needed, Rovers would have to rely on the passing of the years to confirm that whilst it was the very first time that they had conceded double figures, it would thankfully be the last time as well, certainly during the period covered by this book.

To their credit Rovers' season did not subsequently implode. Whilst they now had no chance of anything more than a top half of the table finish they pulled themselves together sufficiently enough seven days later to roar into a three-nil half-time lead against Wilford Road Athletic. Ultimately they had to settle for a creditable share of the spoils as their opponents fought back in the second period with three replies of their own, but at least there would be no further capitulation. From then until the end of March Rovers picked up five points in five outings but more importantly overcame Newthorpe United in the semi-final of the league cup by the odd goal in three. In a season that was otherwise disappointing, they were just ninety minutes from adding some silverware to their trophy cupboard.

TED DUNCAN'S VIEW OF ROVERS v REGENT 3 FEB 1951 (Courtesy Football Post)

At the top end of town Marys' only realistic hopes of silverware were much like Rovers' own; the Saints though had reasonable aspirations in both league and county cups. The week after falling to Aspley for the second time, they met and easily defeated Burton Joyce in the quarter final of the Spartan League Cup, and seven days later travelled to Cossall to play the colliery side at the same stage of the Intermediate Cup. The miners' side were unbeaten in the Ilkeston League and had obviously weathered the coal crisis of January better than most. Increased demand for coal production had led to Saturday shift working and a resultant disruption to colliery teams. At the same time a flu epidemic had been sweeping the country, so they were nothing if not hardy over in the border country; a mite too tough for Marys, unfortunately, who were sent packing following a four-two loss.

Following Marys' untimely exit, only Regent remained to carry the flag for the locality in the county cups, and a fine job they were doing of it too. Given that the secretary of the club, Mr Len Woollacott, seemed reluctant to provide Nottingham's two football publications with information regarding his side's exploits, Regent's progress through the various rounds of the Junior Cup had passed almost unnoticed. Fortunately their cup success was being mirrored in their league form and that was far easier to monitor. Since being turned over by Wilford Road in their high scoring encounter on the last Saturday of December, Regent had remained unbeaten in all competitions through to the end of March. Their league record was an impressive eight wins in eight matches and a staggering goals tally of sixty one with just five conceded. It was the purplest of purple patches; a spell where the result against Rovers looked almost run-of-the-mill. Regent's victories included scores of eight, nine, two tens, and a thirteen against hapless Lodge Colliery. The Hazledine brothers had a field day against this particular set of miners, a team who obviously lacked a certain *je ne sais quoi* present in their Cossall colleagues; Don notched four times whilst younger brother Geoff added another seven to make the family's contribution eleven out of the bakers' dozen total.

Despite the defeat in the Nottinghamshire coalfields, Marys managed to put together a decent run of league form, picking up eleven points out of a possible twelve despite only playing five times. This apparent anomaly is explained by the sensible decision of the powers that be at the Spartan League to allow teams to play each other for four points wherever applicable. Under this arrangement, the Saints entertained another colliery side, this one from Sherwood, and with the benefit of home advantage succeeded in effectively beating them twice; two-one, two-one, as it were.

Notwithstanding the vagaries of the season as a whole, all three local sides were in with a very good chance of actually winning something as the season entered its last full month. Because of the adverse climatic conditions before Christmas the programme had been officially extended to the second Saturday in May but, as was usually the case, April would prove to be the month when most outstanding issues would be decided.

The month started with a bang with each of the Arnold sides not only winning but managing the unusual feat of scoring seven goals apiece in their respective matches. Rovers had the easiest of the three opponents when facing Home Brewery in the Arnold and District Benevolent Cup, Marys despatched old rivals Balderton Old Boys in another four-pointer, but the result of the day was Regent's demolition of Ferry Rangers in the Realm League Cup Semi-Final. One of the Hazledines went nap but the match report neglected to mention which of the two brothers it was. Still, the upshot of the convincing victory meant of course that the Realm League's Senior Cup would definitely be heading to Arnold in a couple of weeks time, Rovers having already booked their place the previous month.

The following Saturday saw all three sides not only win again, but do it with a great flourish. Marys took their unbeaten league run to ten games with a six-nil hammering of Stapleford Town whilst Regent hit another seven, this time against Avro. This victory extended Regent's own run of consecutive league wins to nine, and including the previous week's league cup tie meant that they'd scored an amazing seventy five times in their last ten Realm competition matches. The result of the day, however, belonged to Rovers. Entertaining league leaders Bulwell Forest Villa, they ripped up the form book and chalked up an excellent victory by the odd goal in five. Whilst the unexpected win couldn't do much for Rovers in terms of league position, it certainly did no harm to Regent's chances of catching the Villa. As the Arnold side had only dropped five points all season compared with the Bulwell outfit's six, in theory the title was theirs to lose. The reality of the situation though was that Regent had seven games to make up on the leaders and were fast running out of time in which to cram their remaining fixtures, a situation exacerbated by their cup successes.

Fixture congestion was a bugbear for Marys too. Before they could play their next Saturday game they had the slight inconvenience of having to meet Ruddington in the Spartan League Cup Semi Final on the Friday. The match, an evening kick-off played at Formans Athletic ground, was a very close run affair, so much so that extra time was needed to try and split the teams. Unfortunately that additional period of play was brought to a premature close by the old curse of bad light with the Saints leading three-two at the time. Less than twenty four hours later Marys were involved in another high scoring thriller that went the distance, a four-three win at home to Sutton Colliery.

All Arnold sides were in extremely good form and unbeaten in April but of course there had to be a loss for one of them on that third Saturday of the month as it was the date of the Realm League Cup Final. The match was an evening kick-off for the very good reason that the venue, Meadow Lane, was also host to Notts County's second division match against Swansea that same afternoon. The Magpies had consolidated their position following promotion, and with nothing on the game and Tommy Lawton absent it was hardly surprising that the attendance, at just under eighteen thousand, was the lowest of the season so far.

Also missing was Jackie Sewell who had recently been transferred to Sheffield Wednesday for the highest sum then known in football, thirty five thousand pounds.

Just how many of the afternoon's crowd stayed on for the evening's entertainment isn't known, but the attendance for the final was given as around fourteen hundred, a pretty decent turn out for two sides from the Realm League. The first thing that the spectators would have noticed was the bone hardness of the pitch. Ninety minutes of use only an hour or so earlier had hardly helped the condition of a playing surface that had needed to be liberally sprinkled before the Notts game. The state of the ground was probably the last thing on the mind of the Rovers' players as pre-eminent in their thoughts was the overriding need to avoid being humiliated on the big stage. A final on a Football League ground was no place to let yourself down badly as had been the case back in February.

Rovers' followers were probably of the same mind, but as the game got underway it soon became apparent that their team would be no pushovers on this occasion. Both sides contrived to produce a close and exciting game, one that could have gone either way. With the scores at one apiece though, an unfortunate incident settled the tie in favour of Regent. In the days when a backpass could be handled by the goalkeeper, defenders were more inclined to use this facility. Some observers were of the opinion that the practice was becoming somewhat overdone so when Rovers' left-back misjudged such an attempt and placed the ball wide of his keeper and straight into an empty net it was reckoned to be a case of just desserts. That's probably not quite how the miscreant saw it however. The player with the red face was none other than Ray Dawes, the ex-Saint who'd scored a hat-trick at the right end earlier in the season when drafted in to help the forward line. Unable to gain a regular place in his preferred position at full-back, he'd switched allegiance from the Top to the Bottom Rec, little knowing that he would unwittingly assist the third Arnold side to the first trophy of the season.

For Rovers, in with a real chance of salvaging something from a less than thrilling season, it was a big disappointment. So too was the news that came from the League that the late season withdrawals of no less than three sides had cost them nine points. Their league standings went from

P	W	D	L	F	A	P
25	12	7	6	74	52	31

to

P	W	D	L	F	A	P
20	8	6	6	47	48	22

at the stroke of an official's pen. When Rovers made an early exit from the district charity cup their season ended in quiet anti-climax.

On the Wednesday following the Realm League Final, Marys had a tough league game away to old rivals East Kirkby. Almost two years had passed since the infamous pitch invasion that had caused the abandonment of the match between the two sides but there was still a lot of 'needle' involved in the fixture. The miners were lying second in the table with the Saints just two spots below whilst Marys were also out to avenge the early season home defeat that had more or less ended their championship hopes. This particular evening revenge was sweet as Marys ripped into the home side and saw them off easily by four goals to one. It was perfect preparation too for their next game the following Tuesday, the rearranged League Cup Semi-Final against Ruddington. Close as the first tie had been, there was only one team in it the second time around. The Saints showed no compassion as they ran up six goals without reply and booked their place in the final, scheduled to take place four days later at Meadow Lane against the Spartan League's outstanding side Keyworth United.

The South Notts side had enjoyed an unprecedented run of success since local football resumed after the war, dominating first the Realm League and now the Spartan one too. By the time of the final they'd already clinched the league title and were still in the Intermediate

Cup as well, so a treble was clearly in their sights. Unfortunately, as a direct consequence of being without a game for a whole month in the middle of the season, Marys were paying the price of severe fixture congestion. So severe that on the very afternoon of the final they had the unenviable task of fitting in a league match; hardly the ideal preparation for one of the season's showcase occasions. The Saints would have had all on to overcome Keyworth without that particular handicap, but the physical effort required proved just beyond them and they went down by four goals to two.

It was hardly a disgrace; Keyworth did in fact go on to annexe the Intermediate Cup to prove their total dominance at this level. Nor was it a disgrace to lose to Gedling Colliery just forty eight hours later in the semi final of the district Benevolent Cup. The Plains Road side, who would go on to win the charity cup, were just beginning their own period of total domination, in their case in the Notts Alliance. This season they would successfully defend their title with an amazing one hundred percent record; twenty six wins from twenty six games, the only occasion in the long history of the Alliance that the feat had been achieved. They would then become one of Nottinghamshire's leading clubs over the next ten years, winning the Alliance another eight times as well as clinching the Notts Senior Cup in 1952-53. They would also feature prominently in the FA Amateur Cup, with Plains Road playing host to large crowds packed on temporary seating to see such famous visitors as Pegasus and Bishop Auckland.

Marys' season, much like Rovers', fizzled out quietly after the Keyworth defeat. A final position of fourth was hardly a failure, but after the success of the previous season it didn't seem like much of an achievement either. Once again there'd be no silverware coming their way; which only leaves Regent.

REGENT 1950-51 : Back Row (l to r); F West, B Tomlinson, G Parr, E Woollacott, D Parr, W Whitt. Front Row; K Crombie, D Hazledine, G Hazledine, J Surgey, R Carter.

(Courtesy Football Post)

Arnold's third side had of course already been getting out the silver polish but their season was far from over. With the club's unusual reluctance to blow its own trumpet, their arrival in the Notts Junior Cup Final had been accompanied by little or no fanfare. But arrive they had, and the only other side left in the competition were Rampton Prison Service. Given the nature of that particular institution it was probably no surprise that information was a bit thin on the ground. News blackout or no, an avid following from the town made their way along the A60 to Field Mill, home of Mansfield Town, for the final and they weren't disappointed with the outcome. This time Regent needed no help from any of the opposition defenders as they ran out comfortable winners by three goals to one and laid their hands on another handsome trophy.

Unsurprisingly, given their almost impossible fixture backlog, they couldn't achieve a treble of their own, finishing just four points behind champions Bulwell Forest Villa in third place. Still, it had been a tremendous season with free-scoring attacking play balanced by tight defending. The only cloud on the horizon was the interest being shown by senior clubs in the more prominent members of the side. In particular the overall ability and goalscoring achievements of the Hazledine brothers had attracted the attention of Forest, who had just clinched the championship of the Third Division South. They say that success brings success, but often at local level, it brings its problems too. Still, all that could wait a few months until the start of the next campaign. For now, all that remained was to add Regent's double to the honours board.

REGENT : THREE CUPS

ROVERS : ONE CHAMPIONSHIP, ONE CUP

MARYS : ONE CHAMPIONSHIP

CHAPTER SEVEN 1951-52

The close season of 1951 saw an important development in the provision of leisure facilities for the masses, and it didn't involve either of the two traditional heavyweights of football or the cinema. In fact, the designation of the Peak District as a National Park had actually occurred right at the end of the previous season, but the selection of the Lake District as the second such area came only three days before the new football campaign was due to get underway. The demand for 'the right to roam' had been gathering momentum for many years. Back in 1932 there had been a mass trespass on Kinder Scout in the Peak District, resulting in the arrest and imprisonment of five people. Despite the interruption of the war, pressure had been maintained by various groups such as the Ramblers Association and the Youth Hostels Association to persuade the government to introduce measures to both protect and allow access to the countryside for the benefit of everyone. A White Paper was introduced in 1945 and four years later an Act of Parliament was finally passed to establish the Parks in order to preserve and enhance their natural beauty and provide recreational opportunities for the public.

ROVERS (AND OTHERS) OUTING TO THE EAST COAST : JULY 1951 (Sam Archer Collection)

The effect of designating these areas of natural beauty, and there would ultimately be eight more, would naturally take time to change leisure patterns, especially for the pleasure seekers of the East Midlands. Back in 1951 a time honoured trip to the East Coast was more likely than not to be the preferred holiday break for many in Arnold, whether a week in a caravan or boarding house or just a day's outing to Skegness, Ingoldmells or Mablethorpe. In fact Rovers organised one such event in July and pretty much every member of the team and quite a few others besides met up early outside the Cross Keys pub in the middle of town for the luxury coach trip to the coast. If one or two of the travelling party fancied themselves as footballers, there was no doubt that more than a few had a high opinion of their fashion sense too. A contemporary photograph of the party shows some pretty snappy dressers ready to strut their stuff along the seafront, a clear sign if one were needed that the drabness and conformity of years past was just beginning to change.

In fact a major event that took place during the summer reinforced that view; the Festival of Britain. Trailed as a 'tonic for the nation' it was a large scale exhibition, both static and touring, designed with the aim of reinforcing the country's tentative signs of recovery and progress following the post-war struggle to escape the clutches of austerity. Though based mainly in London, the Festival also travelled around the country and called in at Nottingham in the middle of September for a three week stay. Trowell, just a few miles from the city, was also chosen as the Festival Village of Britain and like the Broadmarsh site that was the temporary home of the travelling exhibition found itself the centre of attraction for many thousands of people. Whilst the exhibits stressed pride in the history of the country, many had one eye on the future, and one in particular brought the magic of television to a large part of the population for the very first time. By its conclusion, over eight million people had visited the exhibition's main centre at London's South Bank with probably the same number catching the touring version. The Festival, which had also incorporated many sports events including a large number of football tournaments, as well as the first ever Miss World competition under the title of 'Festival Bikini Contest', had been an overwhelming success, adding a dash of colour and excitement at just the right time whilst providing a serious look at innovations that would shape the future. The Festival was never designed to be permanent although elements do remain, in particular the Royal Festival Hall in London built specifically for the exhibition. There are also references like the Festival Inn at Trowell as reminders of the events of the time, but by late summer, dismantling was underway.

Nearer to home and back in the world of local football, something else was being deconstructed too, except unlike the taking down of the exhibition structures, this particular exercise was never part of the plan. Indeed it was a shock, deserving of its bold banner headline in the Football Post: '**Notts Realm Sensation**'. At a time when the word wasn't anywhere near as overused as it is today, the reference to a sensation was even more eye-catching. After twenty six years in existence, and current double cup holders to boot, Notts Regent were calling it a day even before a ball was kicked in anger in the new campaign.

Resignations at this level were hardly a new thing of course. Just the previous season three teams had had their records expunged from Regent's own division in the Realm League. There was even a case to be had for one of those clubs' demise being precipitated by Regent themselves. When Group 61 (BRS) were blitzed by the Arnold side to the tune of eighteen goals to one on the opening day of the campaign, they were already odds on favourites to fold before the season's end. When even middle of the table teams began racking up twelve a game against them, all bets were off. No player likes to be on the receiving end of a pasting week in, week out, and given human nature, there normally follows a predictable sequence of events; defeat after defeat leads to disaffection, disaffection precipitates defections, and the poor old secretary is then faced with the hopeless prospect of scratching round for eleven players, any eleven, to fulfil the next fixture.

Trouble was, the cause of Regent's resignation didn't even remotely fit this pattern; except the last bit of course, when Mr Woollacott was apparently left with only four players. The press report actually suggested that it was the very success of the previous year that was to some degree responsible for the club's downfall, with most of the players being snapped up by teams operating at a higher level, but every piece of anecdotal evidence points to this only being true in the case of the Hazledine brothers. Don, the elder of the two, had been attracting the attention and interest of professional clubs ever since he first burst on the scene as a seventeen year old with Rovers in the very first post-war season. Geoff, three years his junior, had joined him in the sights of a number of league scouts with his own goalscoring exploits for Regent. When Derby County finally showed the keenest interest in their signatures, there was never any doubt that the brothers would put pen to professional forms and take a shot at making the grade. In fact their emergence was also a tribute to the type of football that both Rovers and Regent had always tried to produce; neat, fast, and with the emphasis on attack. Both the brothers broke through into the Derby first team and played for other league clubs too, but it was their exploits with Boston United that they are probably best remembered for, especially the day they helped the Lincolnshire side whip their old club by six-goals to one in the FA Cup at the Baseball Ground in front of nearly twenty four thousand spectators, with Geoff notching a memorable hat-trick.

The Hazledine brothers apart, any interest being shown by league clubs in other Regent players had not to all intents and purposes led to any exodus. Overtures from professional clubs had been made on more than one occasion to Jack Surgey but, and more of this particular player later, he had stayed put. Geoff Parr was another whose performances had warranted the attention of the pro's, in his case Peter Doherty's Doncaster Rovers. In early 1950, the season before last, Geoff, then still at centre-forward, had rattled in five goals against Everton; not the giants of Goodison Park obviously, but the local team of the village of the same name situated at the northernmost tip of the Nottinghamshire border. Much nearer Doncaster than Nottingham, the Junior Cup game had been attended by one of the Yorkshire club's scouts who, impressed by what he'd seen, invited Geoff for a trial.

GP : It was a midweek game and I had the day off work. Mr Woollacott, Regent's secretary, took me up in his Austin Eight and I was paid four pounds ten shillings expenses, more than I was earning in a week. I'd tried to go up before but each time for three weeks in a row it was too foggy to make the trip. The match was played behind closed doors, the first eleven against the reserves. I played centre-forward and the centre-half marking me was Syd Bycroft. He'd played over three hundred games for Doncaster and by now he was thirty eight. He was one of those 'Thou shalt not pass' defenders. He said to me "I shan't go easy on you, kid. It's like a league match to me." Charlie Williams, who became a TV comedian, played too. It went well and they wanted me to play again on the Saturday but Regent were playing Ransome and Marles 'A' in the quarter final of the Junior Cup and I didn't want to miss that game. Unfortunately we lost and I never heard from Doncaster again.

Thinking that there might be more to the situation than was being reported, I asked both Geoff and Bill Whitt whether something had gone off, an incident maybe, a bit of bad blood that might have precipitated the club's termination. Neither of them could recollect any such skulduggery, both saying independently of each other that it was 'just one of those things'. In a move that in the circumstances could hardly be classed as moving up into higher circles Bill, Jack Surgey and Ken Crombie all returned to Rovers following their spells of differing lengths with Regent, along with ex-Saint Roy 'Fly' Carter. Unfortunately Roy wouldn't take much part in proceedings for the best part of the next two years. In the middle Saturday of September he was best man at Geoff Parr's wedding and on the following Monday he took poorly and was soon found to be suffering from TB. When defender Fred West made the same move he brought to five the number of ex-Regents in the Rovers side. Whether there had been an element of 'poaching' taking place would have been hard to identify even at the time, and impossible more than fifty years later. There had always been a history of players tooing and froing between Arnold's various teams since football was first played in the town so this latest episode would hardly have warranted a mention had it not been for the shock of Regent's resignation. One thing is certain; there were no financial inducements promised or made for these changes of loyalty. One day there would be, but this wasn't it.

Of the 'four players' referred to in the Football Post report, Geoff was adamant that he and his brother Dennis were two of them, with Mr Woollacott's younger brother Eric a certainty too. Eric's own take on the situation his brother faced was not dissimilar to the official line.

EW : It had become very hard work for my brother. It had always been a labour of love as he spent all his spare time running around for the club. He often had to fetch and carry players to make sure they got to the game. The Hazledine brothers left, one or two others went as well, and he was left with about five players. I was thirty five at the time and had almost finished playing too. Geoff Parr and his brother were still there but Len decided to call it a day. He'd been running the club for many years, well before we moved to Arnold and shared the ground behind the church with Marys, playing on the second pitch, the one with the slope. In the end it was sad but we lost too many players and he really didn't have a choice.

With Eric's reference to the hard work that his brother had to put in, one aspect that shouldn't be overlooked was how the three sides were set up at the time off the field. Marys, probably as befitted their status as nominally the most senior of the Arnold clubs, not only had Walter 'Kegga' Parr, Syd Gray, and a Secretary, but also a committee consisting of a further seven people. Rovers, even in putting out two teams, couldn't call on as much administrative support as the Saints, whilst Regent's non-playing duties had to be borne in the main by just Mr Woollacott, with assistance from trainer Mr Ted Darking and a Mr Tom Price. Ironically, there was for Len a little twist at the end of the tale. He'd indicated that with Regent having folded he had been asked to take up refereeing, but his brother Eric is of the firm opinion that he never followed the invitation up. What was not in doubt though was his love of the game and he couldn't stay away too long from the dubious pleasures of helping to run a football club. Not long afterwards he joined Marys and proceeded to spend many years on the Saints' committee, including a spell assisting the reserve teams of the time following their introduction in this current season. He wasn't the only former Regent to make the move either, as Geoff and Dennis, effectively clubless, elected to stay on the Top Rec and join their father 'Kegga' in Marys' quest to reclaim the role of the dominant team in town. At least with Regent now just a footnote in history, it had become, all of a sudden, strictly a two-horse race.

At twenty to five on the first Saturday in September, it appeared that Marys had made the stronger start, despatching Newark newcomers Castle Brewery by eight goals to two whilst Rovers had to be content with a share of the spoils in a three-all draw with Oakdale Rangers, but being first away at the tape is no guarantee of assuming the same position at the post. As the scoreline might have indicated, Rovers' opening day visitors would prove to be dogged opponents all season long whilst by the same token the brewery side would find very little to celebrate during their first Spartan League season.

In the previous campaign a criticism that could be fairly levelled at the Saints was that of a lack of consistency, and in only the third game of the new season it seemed that they might still be suffering from the same failing. Playing away against Chilwell United, who prior to the match had picked up just two points from a single win in four attempts, the old problem of being able to knock them in with ease at one end whilst giving a passable imitation of a colander at the other was in evidence once more; the hosts won by the odd goal in nine.

Nine goals per game was par for the course for Marys over the next seven matches, all of them won. With sixty three goals going in at either end, most of them in the Saints' favour, watching the maroon and golds at the time certainly wasn't dull. They rattled up maximum points in the league against what must be said was rather modest opposition, and safely negotiated the first rounds of the Intermediate and Spartan League Cups, with revenge of sorts being achieved in the latter with the thrashing of Chilwell by the improbable score of twelve goals to five. Stand-in centre forward 'Dickie' Roberts hammered in six whilst ex-Rover Ernie Barber added a hat-trick from the right wing. The seventh game of the sequence was a home tie in the Intermediate Cup second round against the unbeaten Notts Amateur League side Bridgford Rovers, and although it ended in a more than emphatic ten-two victory for Marys, this match marked the beginning of the unravelling of the Saints' season.

For some unexplained reason, certainly in the newspapers that I have scoured for exact details of the misdemeanour, the Saints had fielded an ineligible player. This was not a rare occurrence in local football; it normally led to a points deduction if the incorrectly signed player or players had featured in a league match, and could also lead to immediate expulsion from a cup competition if the fielding of such a person had led to the winning of a tie. Marys seemed to get off lightly when the Notts Football Association ruled that they could remain in the cup but that the game would need to be restaged on Bridgford Rovers ground. The rematch wasn't scheduled until four weeks hence, but the uncertainty seemed to trigger a collective loss of nerve.

A week after the original game the Saints played host to Grove Celtic who were at the time the league's joint leaders. To all intents and purposes, this game was entirely winnable despite the opposition's good start to the season. After all, in Marys' second game of the season they had picked up a useful point in a one-all draw on the Victoria Embankment against the same side and whilst Celtic had dropped just an additional two points in the season's opening skirmishes, so too had the Saints. Having rattled up scores of eight, seven, twelve and ten in their first four home games, their supporters might have been forgiven for thinking that an air of invincibility was developing around the Top Rec too. Unfortunately, any pre-match hopes for the continuation of this high scoring run began to look decidedly shaky early on in the game when Marys' centre-half succumbed to injury. Back in those pre-substitution days, the normal course of action was to put the stricken incumbent out on one of the wings and then reshuffle the remaining players accordingly. This day, however, a decision was taken that quite probably appeared pretty risky even at the time; with the benefit of hindsight it was verging on the suicidal. The cunning plan saw the crocked number five pull on the goalie's jumper and the original custodian take up position in the outfield. No doubt the sight of the Saints' stand-in keeper hopping about on one good leg was as good an invitation to the opposition to euphemistically 'put him under pressure' as they could get without actually receiving it in writing. Unsurprisingly taking advantage of Marys' unexpected benevolence, Celtic's thank-you came in the shape of six goals, promptly stuck past the home team's token last line of defence.

It wasn't the greatest of results to take into the next two matches, away to East Kirkby in the second round of the league cup and then back at the Top Rec to receive Keyworth with points at stake. The long standing rivalry between Marys and the miners was still greatly in evidence, although the Welfare side were only having a fairly average season so far. The 'you attack, we attack' mentality of the football the Saints currently seemed to be involved in was to the fore once more, only on one of the occasions that it was Marys' turn to threaten the opposition goal they missed their go at scoring, and from the penalty spot too. This chance spurned proved decisive and the home side held on for a four-three victory.

To have Keyworth as your next opponents following two defeats wasn't the most encouraging of prospects even if they too, by their own high standards, had only made what could be called a steady start to the campaign. Despite the blustery conditions, Charlie Moore scored a fine second-half hat-trick. Unfortunately for the Saints' inside-right his one-man efforts were all in vain. His team had turned round six goals down at the interval and the deficit had proven insurmountable as the visitors held on to win seven-five.

Marys were in a state of disarray, certainly in defence where they'd now conceded seventeen goals in just three matches, with thirteen of those being given up on their own ground. At least they had the chance of getting their season back on track with the re-run of the Intermediate Cup tie they'd 'won' so handsomely just a few weeks back. Their opponents were unbeaten in the Amateur League and its sister cup competition, in fact the only time they'd had their colours lowered was in the original tie against the Saints, but most neutrals would have backed Marys to repeat their victory, if not by quite such a convincing margin. So much for punditry; the Saints managed to lose the rematch seven-nil. Considering that Marys' had run up an eight goal margin in the original tie, Bridgford Rovers' convincing demolition in the re-match meant there had been a fifteen goal swing over the two games. It might sound flippant, but whoever the ineligible guy was in the first match, it would appear that he was one hell of a player to have been missed so much second time around.

In four short weeks, the Saints had been ousted from two cup competitions and given a thorough going over from a couple of their main rivals in the league. A season that had promised much was effectively over, even though Christmas was more than a week away. A crystal ball would have shown that the eventual champions Ruddington would only drop six points all season and Marys had already exceeded that in just nine outings.

A month before the Saints' slide, the country's governing Labour Party was heading towards a decline of its own. They'd been hanging on to power since the previous year with a slim majority of just five seats and a series of setbacks at home and abroad had put them under even more pressure and an election became inevitable. When the cost of supporting the USA in the Korean War had impacted on the country's economy, one particular measure of raising funds had blown a gaping hole in the fundamental principle underpinning the party's own greatest claim to improving the lot of Britain's citizens, the 'free at point of use' National Health Service; prescription charges were to be imposed on NHS glasses and false teeth. This hardly went down well with the electorate and considering also that rationing was still around whilst enough new houses weren't, facts naturally picked up on by the Conservatives as part of their election campaign strategy, it was no great surprise when the Tories finished with a comfortable majority and Winston Churchill became Prime Minister.

One way or another 1952 would prove to be an interesting year. The chances of the Saints joining the Labour Party in the margins of power, relatively speaking, looked ominously high, but first things first. Rovers, just like the Conservatives, had spent the latter part of the current year promising better things. They'd started steadily, picking up nine points from their first seven matches with just a single loss, a home defeat by the odd goal in three to early league leaders Wilford Road Athletic on the last Saturday of September. Significantly, the first and last of those seven fixtures had also produced hard-fought draws against Oakdale Rangers, three-all and one-all. Before October was out, these two opponents were holding down the two top spots, the only sides who remained unbeaten.

Rovers' progress in cup competitions had been a bit of a mixed bag. They'd safely negotiated the first two rounds of the league cup and in doing so landed themselves an early semi-final berth but had been less successful in the Intermediate Cup, going out in the second round to Notts Alliance outfit Lenton Gregory. The following week poor weather had caused the abandonment of their local derby with Home Brewery with Rovers leading six-two at the time. New signing Les Peel had been hitting the back of the net from the centre-forward position since the beginning of the season, but unfortunately his contribution of four more on this occasion was destined to remain outside the record books.

Les Peel's success wasn't the only high spot either. The reintegration of all the ex-Regent players had gone pretty smoothly and two youngsters, goalkeeper Sam Archer and right winger Brian Cunningham, had made the step up from the reserves so successfully that they were already attracting the interest of Notts County. By the turn of the year there was a quiet confidence forming down at Nottingham Road.

Optimism was high amongst the population as a whole too as January saw another austerity measure consigned to the history books as the generally unloved utility furniture scheme was brought to an end. If it appeared that change was in the air then the death of King George VI five weeks into the year provided another golden opportunity to move into a new era. His eldest daughter Elizabeth was touring Kenya when the news came through of her father's demise. Popular history has it that she was dining on an upper floor of a hotel at the time and so 'went up a princess and came down a queen'. Apocryphal or not, the King's passing did leave many commentators heralding in the 'New Elizabethan Age', although in truth it would be the Queen's coronation the following year that would prove to be the true focus for this attempt to throw off the post-war shroud still clinging doggedly to the nation. Winston Churchill did his best to accelerate the process too when later in February he scrapped compulsory ID cards, another unwanted left-over from the dark days of war.

Whether any of these changes had any direct impact on the young footballers of the town is doubtful but in the case of Marys in particular, something or someone triggered a change in fortune because following the Intermediate Cup debacle they rattled up four straight wins. In one of the matches Geoff Parr scored what was described in the football press as a 'beautiful goal' from a free-kick. Given Geoff's scoring prowess from both the left wing and centre forward positions this feat might not have seemed that newsworthy, except for the fact that he was playing in goal at the time. With him seemingly able to shuttle from one position to another with equal facility, I ventured the question as to which position he preferred, number one, nine or eleven. "Left half" he replied, his answer completely throwing me in the process. Anyone old enough to know which position attracted which shirt in those long ago days of the WM formation, prehistoric times when compared with modern 4-4-2 and 4-5-1 line-ups and squad numbers that see players with anything up to ninety-nine on their backs, will sympathise with me: the left-half always wore number six. Sensing that he'd not given me the answer I was angling for, Geoff at least had the decency to add the reason for his preference; "I always felt that you're more involved in the game there."

The chairman's son wasn't the only player with a family connection to make his mark at this time either. Keith Moore, younger brother of Charlie, scored three times in the first game of the New Year against no less an opponent than East Kirkby Welfare. With Charlie occupying the inside-right berth, number eight whilst on the subject of such identification, Keith took up a similar role on the other flank, inside-left, number ten, and at just seventeen years of age announced his promotion from the second eleven with a decisive hat-trick. Not to be outdone, a couple of weeks later Ernie Barber and 'Dickie' Roberts reprised their nine goal performance from earlier in the season in a twelve-two trouncing of Wilford Village. This time though Ernie edged ahead with five from the right-wing; he was wearing the number seven for those in doubt.

Despite racking up fourteen goals against Sutton Colliery, Marys would eventually have to settle for fifth place in the league, a distant eight points behind champions Ruddington, if only four away from runners-up Keyworth. They even managed to beat the top side in the very last match of the season by four goals to one, but it was a dead rubber. Ruddington had clinched the title some time before the game, and in any case also had one eye on the upcoming Notts Intermediate Cup Final. Just to emphasise their superiority this season the south Notts side won the county trophy in style, recording a resounding seven-nil victory. The Saints only lost three games in the second half of the season, but they all showed that Marys had a long way to go to recover the position they held just a couple of years earlier. The Old Boys of Aspley visited the Top Rec in February and took both points in a comfortable three-one win, their fourth in a row against the maroon and golds. Early in April, with the title not yet secured, Ruddington had again let in four goals against the Saints. On this occasion, however, they had countered with a mere nine of their own. Later in the month, Notts Alliance superpower Gedling Colliery had seen off Marys in the semi-final of the Arnold and District Benevolent Cup to round off a disappointing campaign. One bright spot was the general consensus that Notts Regent's unfortunate and abrupt termination had been to the benefit of the Saints. The only two players to make the short journey from second to main pitch on the Top Rec, brothers Geoff and Dennis Parr, had received good press in both the Football News and the Football Post. The former praised their consistency and versatility whilst the latter called them the club's 'best find of the season'. It was a pity that their efforts hadn't been matched by the side as a whole.

Rovers on the other hand were proving to be a team in every sense of the word. Their first three matches in January, all away and all for league points, saw them extend their winning run to five games with Sam Archer singled out for a 'magnificent display of goalkeeping' in the two-one victory over Dakeyne Street Old Boys. February saw no let up in Rovers' advance; three matches, three more wins, including a convincing four-one victory in the league cup semi final against the only Realm League side to beat them this season, Wilford Road Athletic. Les Peel had carried on scoring for fun, adding another nine goals in those three games, whilst the forward line as a whole was also hitting top gear.

March, however, was to prove a pivotal time in Rovers' season. The league table at the start of the month was:

	P	W	D	L	F	A	P
Bulwell Forest Villa	16	12	1	3	63	28	25
Oakdale Rangers	13	8	5	0	48	11	21
Arnold Rovers	13	9	3	1	41	25	21

The fixture list had thrown up the intriguing prospect of Villa, the previous season's champions, having to play both Rangers and Rovers before the month was out, and when Oakdale got the better of the Bulwell outfit by four goals to two, their superior goal average compared with Rovers meant that the championship had effectively become theirs to lose. Rovers though continued in a rich vein of form and scored twenty goals in the month's four matches with Les Peel and Jack Surgey both grabbing hat-tricks as the Nottingham Road side racked up four more victories to stretch their run of wins to twelve. The last of the four games, all for league points, was the top of the table clash on the Bottom Rec against Bulwell Forest Villa, who were clinging onto the top spot although they had no better than a slim chance of retaining their title. Rovers put the final nail in the coffin of their aspirations as they ran out clear winners by five goals to two. Oakdale had gained another easy win since their own clash with Villa and were still holding the upper hand over Rovers. With a home game against Arnold's own Home Brewery, struggling at the wrong end of the table for most of the season, Oakdale looked certain to improve their goal average and maintain pole position but in one of the shock results of the year contrived not to score against a side who'd already conceded eighty goals in just seventeen games. Having to settle for a point, Oakdale surrendered the lead and the advantage to Rovers. The table now looked much healthier:

	P	W	D	L	F	A	P
Arnold Rovers	17	13	3	1	61	29	29
Oakdale Rangers	16	10	6	0	56	13	26

It was a difficult task, but if Rovers were to win their last five matches, the title would be theirs. Oakdale's more impressive goal average would not be a factor.

As if to rub salt into Rangers' wounds, Rovers' next match, the first in April, saw them line up against Home Brewery. Rovers' near neighbours were indistinguishable from the side that had nicked a point on the other side of Carlton Hill just a couple of weeks earlier as Jack Brace led the way with five goals in a nine-one hammering. The following week, Easter Saturday, Rovers were hosts to Dakeyne Street Old Boys and found themselves behind at half-time to the only goal. Happily, the home side made a strong comeback after the turn round. Les Peel notched a couple as Rovers pulled away to win four-one. Ironically it was a missing Rover who attracted most attention that afternoon. With a large holiday crowd watching the action, a collection was taken for left-winger Roy Carter who'd been very ill with TB for some seven months and was, even now, facing an uncertain future.

Rovers' own prospects though remained very favourable, especially when they visited East Leake on Easter Monday and took both points in a five-two win. Six points from three games was as good an outcome as there could be. Unfortunately Oakdale hadn't given up the chase and succeeded in emulating Rovers' performance, scoring heavily in the process with an eight and a nine thrown in for good measure. Rovers couldn't afford the slightest slip. With just three games remaining they continued to hold a single point advantage, but Oakdale's goal average was now five compared to their own two and a bit. Back then, final placings in all competitions including the Football League could often be decided by a fraction of a goal. Quite why the much simpler method of superior goal difference, that is the number of goals scored minus the number of goals conceded, hadn't already been introduced is beyond me, but suffice to say that in those pre-calculator days you often had to be pretty good at long division or adept with a slide rule to see who finished higher or lower in a close call situation. In this particular season and at this particular time, Oakdale would have ranked higher by both methods but goal average, calculated by dividing the number of goals scored by the number of goals conceded put them well ahead of Rovers, assuming that it might come down to level points at the season's end.

To avoid this scenario, Rovers had merely to pick up three wins from their last three matches; which is easier said than done of course. Fortunately, two of the games were against RAF Newton and Basford Hall Old Boys, destined to join Home Brewery in the contest for the bottom three places. A six-one win against the RAF side was no more than was expected. The penultimate fixture however was the home clash with Ferry Rangers, the very same team that Rovers were scheduled to meet in the Realm League Cup Final. Rovers had already seen them off comfortably in their first league meeting back in January, but this Rangers side were a bit of a dark horse; their mid-table position belying the fact that they would end the season as the only team in the league to achieve a century of goals. With Oakdale still winning, it came as an enormous relief when Rovers saw off the other Rangers team by three goals to one. They were now just one match away from the Realm League championship and just to keep them on their toes, Oakdale had finished their own season in another flurry of goals, nineteen in total. If Rovers were to win the title, they would have to do it the hard way. They needed no less than a win against the Old Boys from Basford Hall and if they got it, it would be their sixteenth straight league victory, a run stretching right back to October.

Rovers' had already beaten their final league opponents four-nil back in March, and even with one eye on the League Cup Final they proved just as superior the second time around. Six-nil was the score line this time, a fitting end to what had been an amazing run of results. A sequence such as that would have been an accomplishment at any time, but considering their less than impressive start to the campaign and the fact that Oakdale were constantly breathing down their necks, it was a remarkable achievement. Their closest rivals went on to confirm their own credentials by winning the Notts Junior Cup, becoming in the process the fifth Realm League club in a row to capture the trophy. Now all that remained in this excellent Rovers' campaign was the opportunity to add to their league title a cup trophy of their own, or maybe two as there was also the small matter of the district charity cup to contest.

First up was the chance of completing the league and cup double at Meadow Lane against Ferry Rangers. All the caveats mentioned above remained relevant, even though by now Rovers had completed the double over their cup final opponents, but Rangers could probably beat any team in the Realm League on any given day; their problem was that they just hadn't done it in a consistent manner. Cup games were different though and Rovers' biggest problem would be to ponder just which Rangers' side would show up on that first Friday evening in May. As it happened, it was the one they didn't really want. Before most of their players had even had a feel of the ball other than in the warm up the favourites found themselves a goal down. If the old 'Ivor Thirst' clock was in place on the scoreboard at the Spion Kop end of the ground back then it would have shown the time as around six forty-six and the referee's whistle would still have been wet considering that he'd blown it for the start of the game less than a minute earlier. Rovers had of course recovered from similar setbacks during the season, but this night wasn't to be one of them. Rangers consolidated their early advantage and eventually ran out comfortable winners by three goals to nil. Whilst it was a disappointment, the defeat didn't diminish the team's efforts in the league. What's more, there was also the prospect of claiming the local bragging rights in the Arnold and District Benevolent Cup.

ROVERS 51-52 : Back Row (l to r); F Greensmith, J Atkinson, S Gretton, S Archer, W Whitt, J Cunningham, J Passey (Secretary). Front Row; L Peel, A Casterton, J Brace, J Surgey, K Crombie.

(Alec Casterton Collection)

Even in the usual mad rush to fit in games at the end of the season Rovers' tremendous run of form hadn't faltered. They'd successfully navigated their way through the quarter- and semi-finals, admittedly helped by the luck of the draw that saw them face lesser lights Sherwood Rangers and Lambley Villa, and were due to meet the competition's true heavyweights, Gedling Colliery, in the final. The miners' side had enjoyed another fantastic year of their own, dropping just three points all season and establishing a Notts Alliance League record of sixty seven consecutive victories before losing their only game for points in two seasons to Rufford Colliery. Gedling, the current holders of the trophy, had also comfortably seen off Marys in the other semi-final so Rovers had it all on by any measure to bring the silver cup back to the town whose name it bore. Given the success of the two sides the match was shaping up to provide a fitting climax to the season, a game guaranteed to attract a large crowd, one that would give generously to the collecting tins carried round the perimeter of the pitch for the benefit of district charities. Except it didn't happen; well, not in May that is. No mutually convenient date could be found for the game and it was decided that the final would have to be held over until later in August, the beginning of the next season.

ROVERS : 29 AUG 1952 v GEDLING COLLIERY : ARNOLD & DISTRICT BENEVOLENT CUP FINAL
Back Row (l to r); S Gretton, K Dove, W Whitt, S Archer, F Greensmith, J Cunningham. Front Row; L Peel, T Hatfield, E Crofts, J Surgey, T Hardwidge.

(Courtesy Football Post)

Now this was decidedly a big let down at the time, especially for followers of football in the locality, but the delay of four months changed the complexion of the game in a manner that was certainly unforeseen back in May. It wasn't just that both sets of players might have a bit of a sun tan following the summer holidays or that the make up of the two teams would inevitably be slightly different from the respective elevens that ended the previous campaign. The biggest difference was that a fund set up in response to a tragedy that had made headlines across the nation would now be the beneficiary of all monies raised at the match.

The picturesque North Devon village of Lynmouth, situated in a deep cleft between cliffs below its neighbouring village of Lynton, had become known countrywide for all the wrong reasons. Two weeks earlier an intense storm had swept over south-west England. Nine inches of rain fell in just twenty four hours on an already waterlogged Exmoor. Ninety million tons of swollen flood waters swept down through the narrow valley, dislodging tree trunks and sending them hurtling down towards the village along with forty thousand tons of mud and boulders. Many of Lynmouth's inhabitants were caught by surprise and thirty-four people lost their lives. Roads and bridges were destroyed and over four hundred villagers made homeless. As a result of the tragedy, many communities both at home and abroad contributed generously to the disaster appeal, and the movers and shakers behind the Arnold and District Benevolent Cup responded accordingly. When the collecting buckets went round the Top Rec on that last Friday evening in August, all contributions were directed towards helping to rebuild the stricken Devon community.

As to the match itself, and unlike the situation that Marys and East Kirkby found themselves in three years previously in their own match held over until the following season, there were no restrictions regarding eligibility of players. The two Spartan League sides could only field those guys who had been signed on during the previous season but in the charity event Rovers, for instance, were allowed to play newcomers such as centre-half Ken Dove, inside-right Terry Hatfield, and centre-forward Ernie Crofts. Even faced with these additions, Gedling were still the odds-on favourites at kick-off time to retain the trophy. Then again, the history of football at all levels is littered with tales of giant-killing and 'against-all-odds' victories, and ninety minutes later the ABC, as it was referred to on the winners' medals, had witnessed another; Realm League Rovers had toppled the mighty Notts Alliance Gedling Colliery. The two-one win was variously reported as, modestly, 'a surprise result' or, more in keeping with current day parlance, 'their sensational victory'. Either way, Rovers had brought distinction upon themselves and the Realm League by association.

In many respects it was a pity that the game had been deferred to the beginning of the 1952-53 calendar, because had the result been achieved at the climax of the season in which it was meant to be played, the accomplishment would have assumed an even greater relevance. It would have provided a crowning moment to an already successful campaign; one which, at its end, could support the reasonable claim that Rovers had stolen a march in the race to be called Arnold's premier side. However, the fact that it was tagged onto the chronology of the next season didn't alter the fact that Rovers had won the 1951-52 version of the trophy, their second of a season which showed them to be a club on the move, and not just on the honours board.

ROVERS : TWO CHAMPIONSHIPS, TWO CUPS

REGENT : THREE CUPS

MARYS : ONE CHAMPIONSHIP

CHAPTER EIGHT 1952-53

A week after Rovers' great win over Gedling Colliery, the new season proper got underway with both town sides recording resounding victories, each winning by an eight goal margin. Rovers ran up ten against Bestwood whilst Marys kept their goal intact for the first time in many a month. Unusually, given that Spartan League games didn't normally merit such attention, Marys' first game was the subject of a live match report on the centre pages of the Football Post. The fact that the Saints were four up at half time down at the Trent Lane ground of Burton Joyce wasn't the reason I had paid particular notice. What had really caught my eye was the appearance of Rockley (L) in the line-up.

Now Len Rockley was a goalkeeper of some promise, a regular in the reserve side that had won the Division Six championship of the Notts Amateur League the previous season, but the accepted order that all football teams were printed in the press at the time was in numerical order, one to eleven; goalkeeper first, outside-left last. Rockley (L) was definitely in last place and not first on this particular occasion. The reason for the (L) was to distinguish this Rockley from Rockley (R), a namesake but no relative lined up at number six, left-half. To complicate matters a Rockley (F) would also turn out for Marys this season and he wasn't related to the other two either. So here we have a Len, a Reg, and a Fred, all with the same surname, a nightmare for a researcher especially on those days when only one of them might play in any particular game and their identifying initial wasn't given. Or worse when, as appears in this case, the wrong initial was used. Or worse still, when the wrong initial might have been used deliberately.

For the record, Rockley (L) did not play in this game. The giveaway was that the report had him scoring the third goal after forty minutes. The real Len Rockley assured me that he had never ever scored a goal in his life.

LR : I took three penalties and missed them all. Each time the ball ended up nearer the corner flag than the goal. Once I raced the whole length of the field to take a penalty when we were leading nine-one and it still went in the same direction.

So what exactly was the situation on the banks of the Trent that first Saturday in September? If the left winger hadn't been Rockley (L), had a genuine mistake been made? Or were Marys fielding a 'ringer', an unregistered player, and using Len, a registered one, as cover? If they were, then it wouldn't have been the first time that the ploy had been used, by them or many other sides in local football, but given Marys' problems over ineligibility the previous season, surely they wouldn't have risked being penalised again?

LR : I seem to remember something about what had happened. I'm sure that it was Fred Rockley who played because left-wing was his position, but I'm pretty certain that he hadn't officially joined the club yet either. It doesn't surprise me because that kind of thing happened a lot.

Len's official debut in his favoured position between the sticks was a few months away yet, but whatever Marys did or didn't do, there was to be no deduction of points this time. Even so, for those of a suspicious nature, an 'L' and an 'F' don't sound as though they might easily be mistaken for each other no matter how bad the telephone line and they are certainly quite a distance apart on a standard keyboard too.

Fred Rockley wasn't the only new face in the Saints' line-up. Harry Marshall had taken over between the posts and Brian Cunningham had crossed the town from Rovers. However, even with the youthful addition of the latter, the average age of Marys' side on the opening day was uncomfortably high, with a number of players already at the veteran stage of their careers. If the Saints weren't to finish outside the honours yet again, sterling performances would be needed from the old guard whilst the club's search for younger talent continued.

MARYS : OPENING DAY OF 1952-53 SEASON, 6 SEPTEMBER 1952 v BURTON JOYCE
Back Row (l to r); W Parr, D Parr, R Hinson, W Franks, H Marshall, A Evans, H Wharton, R Rockley, D -, K Atherley, S Gray. Front Row; E Barber, B Cunningham, C Middleton, C Moore, F Rockley.

(Martin Dermody Collection)

Their next league game, home against Aspley's own Old Boys, would be a good pointer for the season as a whole especially as the Melbourne Road outfit had held the Indian sign over Marys in recent times. Of the last five meetings, the Old Boys had won all but one of them with the other ending in a draw, and had beaten the Saints comfortably on their last two visits to the Top Rec. At the start of the match Aspley headed the table with seven points from their four games and had, as one the strong favourites, already set a fast pace in the race for the championship trophy. Marys on the other hand had been without a fixture on three of the four Saturdays that opened the campaign and had so far played just the single game against Burton Joyce. This lack of matches proved too big a handicap for the Saints and despite Harry Wharton scoring from the penalty spot they went down by the same scoreline, three-one, that they'd suffered on the Old Boys' previous visit. It was a disappointing defeat, one that might even prove crucial to Marys' own chances of winning the Spartan League title for the second time, but at least it had come early in the season; there was every chance to recover over the next seven or eight months.

The Saints had another tough game scheduled for the following week, an away trip to Keyworth. A quirk of the fixture list saw Marys, for the third season in a row, facing one of the league's strongest sides early in the campaign immediately following a bad result. Two years ago they'd played the South Notts side straight after losing against Aspley, last season they'd met them after losing to East Kirkby, and now there was to be a repeat of the back-to-back games from 1950-51. The omens weren't good considering that Keyworth had taken advantage of the Saints' low morale on both previous occasions and had beaten them with something to spare. Thankfully, it was third time lucky from Marys' point of view; they avoided defeat. This latest contest between the two teams ended in that most unusual of scorelines in matches where the Saints were involved; nil-nil. In fact, and certainly in local football as a whole, goalless games were as rare as hen's teeth back then, but the Football Post managed to wax lyrical about the result, saying that it was a goalless classic, the outcome of both sides' brilliant defence rather than inept attacking, with Marys' new keeper Harry Marshall being singled out for particular praise. A point against Keyworth was always a point gained rather than one lost, but the league table after the game still made uncomfortable viewing. The South Notts side remained in second place, unbeaten, tucked in behind Aspley who'd now picked up eleven points out of a possible twelve. It was early days, but Marys' eighth place with just a point a game from three outings wasn't quite the start everyone at the club had hoped for.

Rovers on the other hand were sitting at the top of the Realm League, despite having just lost their first league game almost a year to the day after their previous defeat for points. Following a fantastic run of nineteen straight league victories, they finally succumbed on the last Saturday in September to Dakeyne Street Old Boys, who took advantage of a lacklustre Rovers' performance and ran out deserved winners by four goals to two. In fact, Dako and Rovers had been pretty evenly matched for each of the last four seasons and it had only been in the previous campaign that Rovers had held the upper hand. Even now the Old Boys were only second to Rovers on goal average.

Disappointingly, neither of the two town sides had a game the first Saturday in October, but it could hardly be called a quiet weekend. The day before, Britain had exploded its first atomic bomb off the Australian coast. The government had obviously decided that we must join the nuclear arms race, for better or for worse, but just in case the population might grasp the implications of this decision and scare themselves witless, they announced a far more reassuring news item; tea would finally be taken off rationing with effect from Sunday. That was alright then. At least when the four minute warning sounded, Her Majesty's subjects would now have plenty of Rosie Lee from which to make their last cuppa on Earth before being vaporised to eternity.

Whether it was the extra availability of the nation's favourite non-alcoholic beverage, or the acknowledgment that from now on every game might be their last, Arnold's footballers swept all before them in the three months to the end of the year; seventeen games played, seventeen games won. The rivalry between the two clubs was well and truly met. Both of them safely negotiated the first three rounds of the Notts Intermediate Cup, their first games in their respective league cup competitions, and picked up maximum points in their leagues; Rovers claimed ten points from five matches, with Marys earning eight from four. The sports press praised Rovers' keeper Sam Archer in the kind of language not seen these days, referring to him as a 'grand custodian'. The same reporter used less archaic terms when confirming that Rovers' forward line was 'one of the fastest in the league'. Other individual highlights were the four goals apiece registered by 'Dickie' Roberts and Geoff Parr in Marys' league cup victory and the similar number scored by Jack Surgey in Rovers' memorable third round tie against Awsworth Villa in the county cup.

Awsworth were top of the Notts Amateur League Division One with a one hundred percent record. Their ground, aided by a formidable slope that the home side had obviously known how to use to their advantage, had been something of a fortress in recent times. Even so, Rovers certainly didn't turn up with an inferiority complex. Slope or no slope, unbeaten or not, Villa had struggled to dispose of Gedling Colliery's second string in the previous round of the competition. In the days before the dreaded penalty shoot out was invented, cup ties were replayed until a victor emerged, and they had needed the original game plus three replays to dispose of the colliery side and even then had needed a little help from the authorities in doing so. Between the third and fourth matches, the Notts Football Association had decided that Gedling had fielded two ineligible players in the previous clashes. The argument wasn't totally convincing so they fudged the issue somewhat and instead of expelling the guilty team from the competition, they ordered another replay to be held. With the colliery side unable to field the two players who were the subject of the dispute, they turned out with just ten men and finally went down by three goals to one. Considering that Rovers had famously disposed of Gedling's first eleven in the held over charity cup final at the start of the season, everyone in the Nottingham Road camp had every reason to believe that they could overcome an Awsworth side that had needed a degree of outside influence to dispose of the colliery club's reserves. After forty five very one sided minutes, Rovers' supporters were already looking forward to the prospect of playing in the next round. Jack Surgey had been in fine form and team-mate Alec Casterton recalled the situation at half-time quite clearly.

AC : Jack had scored a hat-trick in the first half and we turned round three-nil up. The local supporters said that three wasn't enough on this pitch. That was because there was such a slope on the ground that it was like trying to play football up a mountain when were kicking uphill in the second half. They pulled back the three goals but Jack hit the winner late on. It was the first time they'd lost there for two years.

Two key members of Rovers' defence, goalie Sam Archer and right back Franny Greensmith heard the comments of the Villa fans too.

SA : I was down Arnold only last week and I bumped into Franny. He mentioned the Awsworth game and we both got talking about it. Their supporters were saying things like 'Three goals makes no odds, you've been kicking down the slope. Wait until you kick uphill. You've got no chance. You'll get hammered in the second half'.

The Villa fans hadn't reckoned on the resilience of the visitors from Arnold. It was indeed a fine performance by Rovers but at the same stage of the competition Marys made rather heavier weather of beating another Amateur League outfit Gas Sports. The Saints needed a replay of their own before they finally ran out five-one winners, the original tie having unfortunately been abandoned in extra time with Marys in the lead. The match, played on the second Saturday in December, couldn't be completed because of poor visibility caused by the fog that had been hanging around most of the day, playing havoc with a number of other local matches.

Of course, poor climatic conditions were a natural hazard at that time of the year, more so then than now. Just seven days earlier, five London clubs, Arsenal, Brentford, Charlton, Chelsea, and Leyton Orient all had their games called off because of a dense smoke-filled fog that had shrouded the capital the previous day and which would bring the city to a standstill until the following Wednesday. It wasn't only the *hoi polloi* whose entertainment was affected as Sadler's Wells had to call off its production of La Traviata after just the first act because the theatre was full of smog too. Motor vehicles had to be abandoned, buses ground to a halt, trains were disrupted and airports were forced to close. London was of course notorious for its fogs, usually suffering from them for around forty to sixty days each year, but this one, subsequently dubbed the 'Great Smog of London', was estimated to have caused the deaths of over four thousand people. If the weather proved fatal to the old and infirm, it provided a little bit of a welcome and unexpected break at the other end of the generational spectrum; much to the delight of many children, parents were advised to keep them away from school until conditions improved.

Despite this beneficial but temporary chink in the gloom for the kids of London, it was necessary for government action to try and reduce the chances of similar events in the future. In 1952, virtually every living room in the UK had an open fire or a coal-fired stove. Coal was in plentiful supply, pits were working at full capacity, and for the majority of people, especially those in Nottinghamshire sitting on top of a major coalfield, the days of gas, electric or oil-fired central heating were a long way off. However, as a direct consequence of London's problems, wheels were set in motion to introduce measures to control and reduce smoke pollution; the days of the 'pea souper' were numbered.

Meaningful changes were naturally a long way down the line and the fog returned to once more wreak havoc with the fixture list on the last Saturday of the year; London was again badly hit, but this time so were the north-west and eastern regions. Happily, Rovers' game managed to escape the worst of the weather as they continued their winning streak, whilst Marys were without a fixture anyway. The Saints' last game of the year had been a festive friendly against a Nottingham Forest XI just a couple of days earlier; the morning of Christmas

Day. The reds had promised to put out a strong side whilst Marys decided that it would be a good opportunity to hand reserve team keeper Len Rockley his debut.

LR : Jim Kirk, the Secretary, came round to see me a couple of days before the game and said 'you're playing against Forest'. I must admit that I laid awake all night on Christmas Eve. I was still on edge the next morning, especially as it was very frosty. There was a good crowd and things didn't go too badly. I think that we only lost two-nil, maybe two-one.

At least Len had now appeared in the first eleven in the actual flesh, and not just in newsprint.

The league tables at the end of the year showed Rovers in second place in the Realm League, tucked in behind the only side to have beaten them so far this season, Dakeyne Street Old Boys. However, considering that Rovers were only two points behind with three games in hand, the gap between the two sides looked eminently bridgeable. The real danger to the red and whites appeared once again to be third placed Oakdale Rangers. They were unbeaten, just a couple of points behind Rovers with a game in hand, and with the two teams yet to meet. Looking at the Spartan League listings, Marys' fifth spot didn't look that encouraging, but a closer inspection showed that only Aspley Old Boys had dropped fewer points than the Saints. The problem was that the Melbourne Road side had already completed thirteen of their scheduled twenty two league games, whilst Marys had managed just seven. Even so, both Arnold sides had closed out the year on a great run of form and if they could maintain that momentum, the town's football followers could certainly look to the New Year with a great anticipation of exciting times ahead.

On the first Saturday of 1953, the fourth round of the Intermediate Cup was staged. Marys had been drawn at home against Eastwood Collieries, a strong side from the Derbyshire and Notts Alliance whilst Rovers faced Spartan League outfit Netherfield Rovers. Although Len Rockley had handed back the goalie's jumper to Harry Marshall, the Saints had introduced much needed new young blood into the team. Ken Cunningham had joined his brother Brian via the crosstown route, and John Pike had slotted in at inside-right. With Keith Moore at inside-left and the two Parr brothers, Geoff and Dennis, featuring prominently, no one could accuse the committee of not giving youth its chance. Unfortunately, on this particular occasion, the miners' side proved that bit too strong and Marys' hopes of county cup glory had to be shelved for another year. Not so the Rovers. They had very few problems in despatching their namesakes from Netherfield by three goals to nil to take their place in the fifth round.

As January unfolded, the Saints recovered quickly from their setback, getting the monkey that was Keyworth off their back in handing them a six-three defeat, 'Dickie' Roberts grabbing a hat-trick. Next time out it was the turn of Ken Cunningham to grab the headlines with four goals of his own as Marys saw off Manor Farm Old Boys eight-four, and the following week the Saints advanced to the semi-finals of the Spartan League Cup with a best of five win against Hucknall British Legion. On the other side of town, Rovers just kept on winning too, adding three straight league victories to their county cup success whilst scoring twenty one times in the process. Their seemingly unstoppable run had seen them claim the Realm League top spot whilst Marys had edged up to third place in the Spartan version. The only disappointment was that both Oakdale and Aspley had continued their own successful spells and continued to present a tangible threat to the Arnold sides.

Just seventy miles or so away danger of a different and more elemental nature had been building up that very last Saturday of the month. Two days earlier a depression had developed over the North Atlantic but meteorologists had concluded that it appeared to be nothing out of the ordinary. Unfortunately, twenty four hours later the depression had begun to deepen at an alarming rate with winds reaching fifty miles per hour. Scotland was the first to feel the effects as gales lashed its north-east coast but as the depression moved further southwards winds on its western flank dragged vast quantities of surface water into the narrower southern part of the North Sea, driving it towards the coast. Early warning systems back in those pre-satellite, pre-computer days were virtually non-existent and there was no individual agency or organisation responsible for co-ordinating information arising from different parts of the country. With little advanced notice, thousands of people living along the east coast were unaware of the fact that they were soon to be hit by one of the worst storms for hundreds of years. By the time the surge struck land, tides were more than seven feet above expected levels, driven on by gales that had raged at between one hundred and forty and one hundred and seventy five miles per hour. The massive wall of water crashed ashore, smashing what coastal defences there were as it worked its way down from Yorkshire, past Lincolnshire and on to East Anglia.

The disaster affected the Netherlands even more severely than Britain. With waves there reaching fourteen feet above normal levels and shattering more than fifty dams in this low-lying country, eighteen hundred Dutch perished as a result of the subsequent flooding. In the UK three hundred and seven people lost their lives in the disaster whilst many families lost all they had, particularly in Lincolnshire, as the sea moved two miles inland. Shops and businesses at the popular resorts of Skegness and Mablethorpe were severely affected as thousands of tons were washed their way by the advancing waters. Most coastal communities had contingency plans for such emergencies, but many telephone lines had been brought down by the gales and as a consequence no large scale evacuation took place. The government's reaction to the horrific events was, quite rightly, to begin the implementation of a building programme of stronger and better sea defence systems. Rather more bizarrely, just five days later and whilst thousands were still mopping up and hundreds were yet to bury their dead, they also announced that sweets were to be the latest item to come off rationing.

Back on land that, despite the seasonal difficulties of frost and snow, was rather drier than at the coast, Marys managed to fulfil their fixtures on each of February's four match days. Continuing their heavy scoring they dropped just one point out of eight whilst beating the opposition keepers no less than twenty three times. Brian Cunningham almost emulated his brother Ken in the return game against Manor Farm but had to settle for a hat-trick, a feat he shared with one half of another pairs of siblings in the side, Geoff Parr. The Saints had now moved into second spot, having only lost just a single point more than leaders Aspley.

Rovers' success was obviously drawing a good response from their town rivals, but they now had a chance of laying down a really good marker for the title of Arnold's premier team in one of the two matches they played in February. The luck of the draw, or otherwise, had seen them given a fifth round home tie in the Intermediate Cup against the very side who'd knocked Marys out just one round earlier, Eastwood Collieries. Having already claimed the scalps of Gedling Colliery in the charity cup and Spartan League Netherfield Rovers in the county cup, Rovers could rightfully challenge the Saints' traditional position as the superior side in Arnold if they could just achieve what Marys had failed to do; beat the tough pit team. When the result of the game reached the ears of 'Kegga' Parr and the rest of his committee, their reaction wouldn't have been one of great joy. Rovers had triumphed where his beloved Saints had struggled, and triumphed in style, too, comprehensively ejecting the colliers from the competition in a free scoring eight-four victory. In their other game that month, they also saw off the slim challenge of Dakeyne Street by reversing the score of their only defeat of the season when the teams met back in September; four-two. As a result, Rovers remained on course for a grand slam, whilst Marys could, with a little good fortune, claim a treble of their own. For the likes of Eric and Roy Thompson and many others besides, it was a great time to be a fan of football in Arnold.

E&RT : We used to try and see as many matches as we could, especially at the end of the season when we'd watch a game every day of the week if there was one on. We were Marys' fans first but we'd go and watch all the other local sides as well. We once went to see Jack Surgey play in an evening game over near Eastwood when he was playing for another team, not Regent or Rovers. When we went to see Rovers play when they were doing really well, Len Brace, Jack's brother, would come over with a big smile on his face and say "Jack Surgey has told me that you're seeing the best football that's ever been played round here".

If Rovers' inside-left was as good a judge of local football as he was skilful a player, then his opinion carried some weight. Both his own performances and those of his team had been of a most consistently high standard and the arrival of spring did nothing to change that picture. In fact, Rovers' burgeoning reputation was almost having the effect of convincing their prospective opponents that they were nigh on unbeatable which, considering that the red and whites extended their winning run to eighteen with three more victories in March, was being borne out on the field of play where it really mattered. The Old Boys of Dakeyne Street were unceremoniously dumped from the league cup at the semi-final stage five-one, Jack Surgey hit the target four times as neighbours Home Brewery were seen off by six goals to nil, and in the crucial top-of-the-table clash at home to Oakdale Rangers, Rovers ran up a further half dozen, courtesy of another individual four goal haul, this time from Les Peel. Prior to kick-off, Rangers were the only side truly capable of preventing Rovers from retaining their title. They were still unbeaten, having dropped just four points all season. Ninety minutes later the championship was Rovers to lose, and there didn't seem much chance of that happening.

Over at Church Lane, Marys entered March looking forward to a schedule of four straight league matches, the last of which, the return clash with Aspley Old Boys, looked likely to have a decisive influence on the destination of the league title. Unfortunately, after just the first of the four games the Saints' championship hopes took a serious nosedive. Playing against fourth from bottom Hucknall British Legion they somehow managed to lose two-nil to a side that had themselves been thrashed only a week earlier by a team sharing last spot. Seven days later a draw at Ruddington hardly improved Marys' prospects. To make matters worse Geoff Parr, deputising in goal for Harry Marshall, suffered a bad knee injury following an ugly challenge from the home side's centre-forward. Even so, it was mathematically possible for the Saints to catch Aspley, especially when they picked up maximum points in a three-one win over Hucknall Collieries the following Saturday, but it would have needed a freakish combination of results for this to happen. It didn't. The Old Boys secured a four-two advantage and the title was theirs. If Rovers were on course for an *annus mirabilis*, March was definitely Marys' *mensis horribilis.*

In those areas of human endeavour far removed from the playing field, spring of 1953 saw major advances. Jonas Salk, a US physician and researcher, announced the creation of a polio vaccine, whilst Englishman Francis Crick and American James D Watson published what is accepted as the first accurate model of the DNA (Deoxyribonucleic Acid) structure.

On a lighter note, James Bond, Secret Agent 007, made his very first appearance as Ian Fleming's novel 'Casino Royale' hit the bookshelves whilst the early stirrings of disaffection and rebellion amongst adolescents was given increased impetus with the filming of 'The Wild One'. Ostensibly a dramatisation of a true event that had taken place a few years earlier, the film essentially played up a clash of the generations, an 'us versus them' scenario between freedom-seeking youth and the old time conventions of their reactionary elders and betters. In one scene Marlon Brando, in the starring role as Johnny, leader of the motorcycle gang that has descended upon a small quiet town, is asked "What are you rebelling against?" His drawled reply was "Whaddya got?" The film, which in truth now looks quite tame, was deemed too controversial for release in this country for another fourteen years, but Johnny's trademark black leather jacket was adopted as a must have accessory for thousands of American kids wishing to distance themselves from the old order.

Thankfully Arnold was a long way from Wrightsville, USA, both in distance and time; people were still having to mend and make do as a way of life, and making light of such obligations too, whilst the town looked little different in 1953 than it had done ten, maybe twenty years earlier. Any rumblings of discontent were likely to be no more than a gripe about the ale being off in one of the town's numerous hostelries and the worst thing that most youngsters got up to was scrumping apples, unless of course like Rovers' Sam Archer and Alec Casterton you'd committed the heinous crime of playing football in the street and landed yourselves with a criminal record.

By now though, these two were much too busy with their legitimate football pursuits to trouble the local bobby. Rovers' season was now entering its final decisive phase, and their first game in April was no less than the Intermediate Cup Semi-Final against Spartan League outfit Ruddington, winners of the same trophy the previous year. The South Notts side were also vying with Marys for runners-up spot behind Aspley Old Boys and had taken a valuable point off the Saints just a few weeks earlier. A Rovers' win now would really help the argument as to which of the town's two teams was top dog. The game was played at

Meadow Lane on Easter Monday morning and an excellent crowd of some three thousand spectators took advantage of the holiday to view what was expected to be a close contest. Ruddington, as befitted their position as the existing cup holders, were pre-match favourites, but someone had forgotten to tell their opponents, or then again maybe they had. When the game kicked off Rovers were quicker out of the traps than Ruddington and grabbed the ascendancy right from the start. With their forwards causing havoc amongst the opposition defence and with rock solid performances from their own rearguard, Rovers never once looked in danger of losing the tie. Unfortunately, as Marys' Geoff Parr could confirm following his recent injury against Ruddington, Rovers' opponents were hardly genteel and at one time in the second half the red and whites had just nine men on the field. Thankfully, their opponents' robust approach proved no more than an irritant and Rovers ran out comfortable winners by three goals to one. Defenders Ken Dove and Franny Greensmith, together with goalie Sam Archer all received good press, but the star man in this latest county cup triumph was undoubtedly Rovers' hat-trick hero, Jack Surgey. With his exploits in a previous round against Awsworth already well documented, it seemed that Rovers' inside-left was on a one man mission to bring the cup home to the Victory Club in Arnold, a licensed establishment frequented by many of those associated with the football club. The Nottingham Advertiser reported that there had been 'special jubilation' there at mid-day when news of Rovers' victory came through. Given that it was a public holiday and that it had only just turned noon I expect that the 'jubilation' was followed pretty quickly by some serious supping.

However, before players, committee and fans could turn their attention to the final there was the small matter of focusing on the other three trophies Rovers were chasing. The next two Saturdays saw them pick up four points in two comfortable league victories to set themselves up nicely for the return game with Oakdale Rangers seven days later. Mathematically, Rovers might yet be denied the title but it would have needed them to lose both their last games by an aggregate of a dozen or so goals and their current form was such that the destination of the championship trophy was never in any doubt; Rangers were seen off comfortably by four goals to nil. Unsurprisingly, Rovers rounded off their league season with another victory. Their dominance over every opponent since their solitary league defeat to Dakeyne Street back in September was so compelling that a casual observer might be left wondering just how they'd managed to lose that game in the first place.

However, it was the games to come that mattered now. In the Arnold and District Cup Rovers maintained their unexpected superiority over Notts Alliance Division One teams when they knocked Bestwood Colliery out of the competition at the semi-final stage by the odd goal in three to claim a place in the final. Whilst Marys had struggled in the recent past with teams from the second division of the Alliance, Rovers had belied their status as Realm League underdogs and given everyone notice that they could tangle with the big boys from a higher standard. By the end of the month Rovers had not only secured the first leg of the grand slam, they'd extended their winning run to twenty five consecutive games and were relishing the exciting prospect of adding to their trophy cabinet. With three finals in eight days at the start of May to look forward to, the Victory Club was doing good business.

As for Marys' own efforts to remind folk they were still around, they certainly made a more convincing fist of it in April than they'd done the previous month. With only second place to play for they closed their Spartan League season out in style with five wins from five outings, scoring twenty four times in the process. A new name at centre-forward, Ray Bennett, showed that he was one to watch when scoring five of the Saints' six goals against Netherfield Rovers.

Despite having to settle for runners-up spot in the league, Marys did at least continue to have an interest in two cup competitions; the district charity event and their own Spartan League Cup. Their prospects in the latter had looked quite encouraging when they were drawn to meet Ericsson Athletic from the Second Division. The works team from Beeston would one day progress to the Notts Alliance but for now, even though they'd finished runners-up themselves, it wasn't anticipated that they'd present too much of a hurdle for the Saints to overcome. So much for expectations; a two-nil victory was more than sufficient to see the telecommunications side through to the final and Marys embarrassingly licking their wounds. This unexpected setback left the maroon and golds with just one last chance of salvaging something tangible from yet another season that had promised so much but had delivered so little; the Arnold and District Benevolent Cup.

With the holders Rovers having already booked a place in the final, all that remained to be determined was the identity of their opponents. Would it be Notts Alliance Division Two side Mapperley, or would the townspeople of Arnold have their dream final courtesy of a Marys' victory. Considering that the Saints had already thrashed them once this season, seven-two in the opening round of the Intermediate Cup, no one held out much hope that Mapperley would spoil the anticipated party. They didn't; Marys again ran out easy winners by a five goal margin, this time keeping a clean sheet into the bargain. Thankfully the Saints had managed to keep their season alive and provide the town with a climax to it that would be truly that; the very first competitive match between Marys and Rovers since the latter's arrival on the scene almost eight years earlier. It had been a long-awaited contest but there was still a further week to go before the two teams would meet. Arnold's football followers, who were growing in number by the day, could instead content themselves with Rovers' other two finals, conveniently scheduled just either side of this season's FA Cup Final itself.

First up was the Realm League Cup Final against Trent Rangers at Meadow Lane. Played in the evening of the opening day of May, which happened to be a Friday, Rovers, unusually, started the game as strong favourites. Rangers were only a mid-table side and at their last meeting Rovers had unceremoniously handed them a seven-nil hiding, but in cup games, especially finals, there is always the chance of an upset. Happily for the red and whites, Jack Surgey was in no mood for anyone to spoil the party and scored twice early on to calm any nerves his side might have had. Rovers' inside-left had been in mercurial form all season, seemingly raising his game even higher for vital cup matches. In fact the consensus was that Jack was a player who had it all; well almost. Blessed with a great left foot, well balanced, capable of beating an opponent in a number of ways, and with an eye for goal, he was an inside-left with all the technical ability necessary to make a living out of the game. Any number of his contemporaries have confirmed, unprompted and without reference to each other, that he was the best player who Arnold had ever produced, or they'd ever played with or against, or they'd ever seen in local football

The endorsement of his talent was unequivocal. Unfortunately, the damning verdict regarding his temperament was just as indisputable. They say that cream always rises to the top, but the history of sport and football in particular is littered with maverick talents held back by their own wilful predisposition to refuse to marry their natural ability and technical skill to a commensurate degree of application. Jack was such a player. Unfortunately, he is no longer here to give his side of the story, so it falls to those who knew him, saw him and played with him to tell it like it was; from the outside looking in.

GP : Jack was definitely the best player I've ever seen at local level; a completely natural ball player. Unfortunately he had a terrible temperament. If he didn't feel in the mood, or if the condition of the pitch wasn't to his liking, then that was it, he didn't play.

Whilst he was playing for Mapperley Villa they were due to play in a Cup Final and Jack turned up without his boots, saying he'd forgotten them. A Cup Final!

When I was with him at Notts Regent we had a cup game on the Top Rec against Ransome & Marles and he decided that it was too wet for him. Of course this didn't go down too well with the rest of his team mates but he was that good a player that he was straight back in the side for the next game.

Even off the field he could be an awkward character. He was the kind of bloke who'd be talking to you in a group and then the next thing you'd know he'd disappear without a word. You'd look round and he'd be gone. But in later life he was absolutely brilliant, different again. He lived over at Clifton and I bumped into him in a pub. He made a point of coming over to me and bought me a couple of pints too. Whenever he popped back to Arnold, he was always interested in his old footballing mates and asking after them.

BW : A brilliant player but... [taps finger on temple]

FG : The best player I ever played with. One day I was round at his house when there was a knock on the door. It was a scout from Aston Villa. Jack said 'I don't want to talk to him, tell him I'm not in'. That's just what he was like.

KA : A brilliant player.

EW : In my opinion he was the best player around, he could have turned professional, but maybe needed a bit more devil in him. He was an exceptionally good footballer. In those days the game was about getting stuck in but Jack didn't get mucky, he was purely a footballer. I played many times with him and got on well with him but I can't say I ever really got to know him.

AC : The best player I ever saw at local level. He was brilliant, so good that he could have signed for anybody, except he just wasn't interested. He carried us through some games, especially in the Intermediate Cup. In one game, we'd been given a penalty and he'd thought it was the wrong decision, so he took the kick but hit the ball towards the corner flag. I think we were winning ten-one though! But that was his temperament, and sometimes, if he didn't feel like it, he just wouldn't play at all; he'd have a cold. No one could handle him.

Trent Rangers certainly couldn't, well not without a degree of physicality at least. Soon after scoring for the second time, Jack picked up a bad ankle injury that severely limited his influence. He hobbled around for the rest of the half but had to give it up as a bad job during the second period. Despite considerable pressure from their opponents Rovers' remaining ten men hung on to the two goal lead that Jack had given them until, with just a few seconds to go before the final whistle, Rangers grabbed a late, late consolation goal. It was a bittersweet victory because the damage to Jack's ankle meant that his season had been cruelly brought to a premature end. With Alec Casterton having already been ruled out more than a month ago with a similar injury and Les Peel being far from fit too, it was a case of having to send out a patched up team the following Monday in the Intermediate Cup Final. Before then though there was the weekend to get a bit of rest and relaxation and at the same time tune in to the FA Cup Final between Blackpool and Bolton at Wembley Stadium.

This game had garnered just as much attention nationwide as Rovers' and Marys' upcoming clash had done on a local basis, largely because it was seen as being Stanley Matthews last chance to pick up a Cup Winners medal. Now thirty eight, Blackpool's legendary number seven had missed out twice previously, in 1948 and 1951, and there was a genuine desire, not just amongst the football fraternity but across the population as a whole, for this to be third time lucky for him. However, when Bolton went three-one up ten minutes after half-time, it appeared that Stan and the rest of the country were going to be disappointed once again. Blackpool's other Stanley, Mr Mortensen, pulled one back mid-way through the half but Bolton hung onto their lead until a couple of minutes before the end. Mr Matthews then began to weave his magic and created the equaliser for his namesake. With time ticking down he continued to torment the left flank of Bolton and with just a few seconds left on the clock he cut a diagonal pass back from the by-line for Bill Perry to score the winner. The dramatic climax to the game and the crucial part played in it by the veteran winger ensured that even Stan Mortensen's hat-trick was overshadowed; the match was destined to be remembered as 'The Matthews Final'.

With televisions still pretty thin on the ground, a number of Rovers' players, Sam Archer and Alec Casterton among them, had seen the game at someone else's house. Alec, though, couldn't bring himself to watch the Intermediate Cup Final at the City Ground the following Monday night. Unable to play because of his ankle problem, he found it too unbearable to view the game as a mere spectator up in the stands. On the field itself, Les Peel continued to nurse an injury of his own and Roy Carter had only just recently resumed playing after the equivalent of nearly two whole seasons out through his illness. Jack Surgey could play no part in the match either.

Rovers' opponents, Sutton and Skegby League Champions Sheepbridge Steel, had no such problems. Their forward line had rattled in well over six goals a game during the season, a total that the Nottingham Road side, even with a fit Jack Surgey, couldn't match, and their defence was just as parsimonious as that of Rovers. It promised to be a cracking match, one which everyone in the large crowd hoped would rival the previous Saturdays FA Cup Final for drama. What no one present at kick-off could possibly have realised was just how amazingly similar the twists and turns of the two games would turn out to be. Rovers drew first blood with a goal just after the twenty minute mark from Jack Brace, but then could do nothing as Sheepbridge hit back to equalise after thirty three minutes, go one ahead seven minutes before halftime, and take a three-one lead just two minutes before the hour mark. Franny Greensmith decided it was time for a change.

FG : Sammy Gretton had got injured in the first half and had to go up front with Les Peel coming back to right-half. I said that we might as well lose six- or seven-one so we put Peely back up front and brought Sam back.

The switch paid off straightaway as Les Peel narrowed the deficit at just about the same stage of the proceedings as Blackpool's own fightback had started. The question on the lips of every Rovers' supporter now was 'can we go on and do what Matthews' side did?' When Bill Whitt equalised with not long to go, there was a sense of destiny about the outcome. The odds had swung remarkably in Rovers' favour and in an ending that would have seemed far fetched in a Roy of the Rovers storyline, Ernie Crofts, himself a passenger due to yet another injury, somehow managed to clinch the winner with just a couple of minutes to go; comic book stuff indeed.

ROVERS INTERMEDIATE CUP WINNING SIDE : 4 MAY 1953 Back Row; F Greensmith, J Cunningham, S Archer, S Gretton, K Dove, W Whitt. Front Row; K Pritchard, J Brace, E Crofts, R Carter, L Peel

(Courtesy Football Post)

In claiming their third trophy of the season in such a dramatic style, Rovers became the very first Realm League side to win the Intermediate Cup, a fantastic achievement in itself, but it was the uncanny resemblance to the season's FA Cup Final that still remains in the memory of Rovers' players and fans. The obvious comparison was the comeback from three-one down to win four-three right at the death. Not so commonly known was the unlikely correlation between the times of the goals in both matches. At least five of the seven Intermediate Cup scoring efforts went in within a couple of minutes of its corresponding one on the Saturday.

With the Intermediate Cup taking its rightful place on display back at the Victory Club, four sparkling trophies gleamed down on a bar that was naturally doing great business; four trophies because Rovers didn't have to give back the Arnold and District Benevolent Cup which they won back in August until Friday, the day of this year's final. When Franny Greensmith and his men turned up at a photo shoot in the back yard of the Greyhound pub, the four trophies were spread out in front of the players, two either side of a ball inscribed '1952/53'. Strictly speaking, the charity cup, second on the viewer's left of the picture, related to the previous season's competition but no one could dispute the fact that Rovers were the legitimate owners of all four pieces of silverware. In fact if they were to beat Marys a couple of days later, they'd be well within their rights to say that they'd actually won five competitions in one season. They'd have to be satisfied with just the four trophies though.

ROVERS ALL-CONQUERING SIDE OF 1952-53 Back Row (l to r); K Atherley, S Gretton, S Archer, J Cunningham, W Whitt, K Dove. Front Row; L Peel, J Brace, E Crofts, F Greensmith, J Surgey, R Carter.

(Arnold Library Collection)

Just what Marys' committee truly thought of all this success coming Rovers' way can only be guessed at. 'Show us your medals' is a phrase used down the ages when trying to establish the credentials of a player, and Rovers could provide 'Kegga' Parr and his men with proof positive enough of their growing reputations. The Saints, however, had one last chance to burst Rovers' balloon, to remind them that despite all the cups on display it was Marys who were even now regarded by many as the top team in town. Ninety minutes in which to salvage some respect from a disappointing season and keep the upstart Rovers in their place.

By now the town was really buzzing with the anticipation of this showdown, a match that might have taken place at any time during the previous six seasons but never did. As a consequence record receipts were expected to swell the season's contribution to local charities but at the last minute fate, in the shape of the Notts Football Association, dealt everyone concerned with the Cup a severe and unexpected blow. For no reason in particular, other than that it was in their remit to do so, the Notts FA decided that the final couldn't be played as planned and would have to be held over until the beginning of the following season. It was a ruling that made little sense to all those affected and one that was hardly in keeping with the charitable aims of the competition. The rescheduled game would invariably draw a large crowd, but it was thought that it wouldn't generate the same amount of money that the end of season clash would have done had it been allowed to go ahead.

Having fallen foul of officialdom, the cup committee did its best to mitigate the situation by fixing the new date for the final on the August Bank Holiday Monday. It was the best compromise possible, even though many potential spectators would be taking advantage of one last chance for a cheap day excursion to the east coast, slowly rebuilding itself after the pummelling it had taken earlier in the year. Still, come the day of the game, no one who turned up was disappointed. For eighty nine minutes Rovers had displayed the kind of superiority they had enjoyed throughout the previous season, giving every indication to their opponents and all those watching that they were now a force to be reckoned with. Leading three-one at the time, and with their red and white favours ready to be tied to the cup any second, they were about to hand Marys a severe blow to their pride and status. Then, almost as if they were awoken from a bad dream, the Saints seemed to realise the implications of defeat. Stung into retaliation, they scored what looked like no more than a token effort given that there was less than sixty seconds to go but improbably equalised just as the referee was about to call an end to proceedings. With Rovers wondering quite how they'd let the game slip from their grasp and Marys wondering just how they'd managed to retrieve what had looked like a hopeless situation a mere couple of minutes before, the organising committee decided that extra-time would have been inappropriate in the circumstances and declared the trophy shared. It was a pity that the Notts FA hadn't been so sensible a few months earlier.

Even allowing for the fact that the final was unfortunately held over, its outcome in the context of this [project] means that a definitive answer as to who was the better of the two sides at the conclusion of the 1952-53 season couldn't be given. It was clear, as the revised honours board clearly shows, that Rovers had proved to be by far the more successful club in the post-war years so far. However the doubters would say that their achievements, all bar their Intermediate Cup win, had been achieved at Realm League level, and only when the two sides met in direct head to head competition could the argument finally begin to be settled. As it happened, the argument had barely begun.

ROVERS : THREE CHAMPIONSHIPS, FIVE CUPS (INCL ONE SHARED)

REGENT : THREE CUPS

MARYS : ONE CHAMPIONSHIP, ONE CUP (SHARED)

CHAPTER NINE 1953-54

At the end of the previous season, but still some three months before the delayed final against Marys, Rovers were not only a very successful club but a highly ambitious one too. Having dominated the Realm League for two straight seasons it was felt that they should be looking to move up into a higher standard. With this in mind an application was made to the Notts Alliance for a place in their second division. It was turned down. Ken Atherley, acting as spokesman for the club in an interview with the Evening News, expressed the disappointment that was felt by everyone as a result of the Alliance's ruling and confirmed that Nottinghamshire's senior league for amateur sides had refused Rovers admission on the grounds that there were no vacancies available.

As it happened this was patently incorrect. Even before the season had finished Bilsthorpe Colliery had already told the Alliance that it would be withdrawing its second team from the competition and no other club had been lined up to take their place before Rovers' request for entry. Nor did they; by the start of the 1953-54 campaign Bilsthorpe's place hadn't been filled and the division had fourteen teams as opposed to fifteen the year before. It was no consolation to Rovers either that in the season prior to that, 1951-52, there had even been as many as sixteen teams in the division.

Whatever the official line, the biggest single handicap to Rovers' application would have to have been the lack of changing facilities at Nottingham Road. The fact that it was a public recreation ground was immaterial; many Alliance sides rented their playing facilities from various councils around the county. None, though, had to change in the ante-rooms of a public house some two hundred yards from the pitch and which had just a single tap for the twenty-two players to wash at. However, as primitive as these conditions were, they weren't that dissimilar to those once used by Marys themselves even though by now the Saints had the run of the Calverton Road School cloakrooms on match days.

The question for Rovers was simple; whither next? By their own reckoning they'd outgrown the Realm League and the big boys at the Alliance had turned up their noses whilst turning down their application. The only realistic move available was to seek to join Marys in the Spartan League. Ground requirements obviously weren't as restrictive as for the Alliance and Rovers had already given plenty of evidence of their credentials where it really mattered, out on the pitch. It was a shoo-in. The Spartan League welcomed them with open arms, stuck them straight in the top division with the Saints and as a consequence kick started a glorious era of football in Arnold.

From now on there would be a guarantee of at least two local derbies each season in the league, head to head clashes for points, as well as the chance of the two sides meeting each other in various cup competitions, right up to the finals themselves. As mentioned in the introduction, matches between the two would be scheduled on key dates to maximise both the attendance and the amount of money taken as the box, or more likely the bucket, was carried around the ground, usually at half-time. When the fixture list came out and fans eagerly scanned the dates to see when the first historic league derby was scheduled to take place, it was no surprise that the match the whole town wanted to see had been allocated a morning kick-off on Boxing Day. With the held over charity cup final lined up to be played at the start of the new season and the mouth watering prospect of more games like it to come, football followers probably couldn't wait for the close season to come to an end but for the wider public the early summer was notable for two famous events that were entirely unconnected at the outset but became linked almost by coincidence.

During May a British expedition led by John Hunt had been climbing Mount Everest. There had been eight previous attempts by Britons to become the first men to reach the summit and they'd all ended in failure. This ninth group had made the South Peak, just a thousand feet below their ultimate target, but all except two of the party could go no further as a result of exhaustion. Edmund Hillary, a New Zealander, and Tenzing Norgay, a native Nepalese, were the only members able to attempt the final assault. At half past eleven on the morning of May 29 they reached the summit, twenty nine thousand and twenty eight feet above sea level and the highest place on the planet. Everest had finally been conquered.

By the time the news was relayed back to Britain it was the eve of the country's most eagerly awaited event since the announcement of the German and Japanese surrenders back in 1945; the coronation of Queen Elizabeth II. On the day of the great occasion itself, June 2, over thirty million people in this country alone gathered around their radios and televisions to tune into the BBC broadcasts with, for the very first time, viewers outnumbering listeners by almost two to one. Not that there were twenty million television sets around, far from it. Best estimates put the figure at about two and a half million despite the fact that they'd been selling like hot cakes in the couple of months preceding the coronation. This meant that there were roughly eight viewers to each set, with those friends and neighbours who weren't lucky enough to have a TV of their own swelling the numbers. My own family situation was typical.

GR : We didn't have a TV at the time so we popped down the road to our friends Ralph and Audrey. Theirs was one of the first houses to have a television and as sets were very small then we all had to crowd around very closely to get a decent view. We also had to draw the curtains even though it was daytime so that the picture was sharper.

Ironically, if it hadn't been for the Queen herself the coronation wouldn't even have been shown on television in the first place. When Sir Winston Churchill told her that it was the consensus of her Cabinet and numerous advisers that she should not be submitted to the ordeal of live television, she politely reminded him that it was she who was being crowned. She felt that everyone who wished to see it should be given the opportunity and so television cameras made their first ever appearance, but definitely not the last, in Westminster Abbey.

The BBC coverage was met with great acclaim and the broadcast was credited with bringing a new sense of national unity to the country. Just over four weeks earlier the nation had seen Stanley Matthews pick up his FA Cup winners medal, and only twenty fours before the coronation had heard the great news that Everest had been conquered. When England's cricketers regained the Ashes from the Australians in the fifth and final Test just a couple of days before the start of the new football season it put the seal on a splendid summer. These triumphs and accomplishments, combined with the great shared success of the young Queen's inauguration, had given the country a massive boost and it seemed that people's confidence in the future was quickly being restored following a long, long period of wartime hostility and peace-time austerity and shortages. There might still have been rationing of meat and other foodstuffs to endure, but in the twelve months following the coronation over a million TV sets were bought. Irrespective of the amount of food on the plate, the television age had truly begun.

Now whilst it wouldn't attract the interest of outside broadcasters, the new phase in the annals of Arnold football was about to commence, an era of local rivalry not seen since the nineteen twenties when it had been the turn of Arnold Wesleyans to battle it out for supremacy with an earlier version of Marys. Now there were no church connections other than in the Saints' name but the contests would be as keen as when conformists and non-conformists locked horns thirty years earlier.

First off the mark were Rovers, who even before Marys had kicked a ball in anger had picked up four points from their first two league games. The Saints first match of the season was actually the last match of the previous one, the delayed charity cup final against Rovers. This lack of match practice might help explain why it took eighty nine minutes for Marys to find their rhythm. It wasn't as if they were bedding in new players either. Only left back Jack Howe was an addition to the ranks whilst Rovers had been much the busier in the summer and had signed no fewer than four new guys to augment their already successful squad. One, Ken Cunningham, was returning to Nottingham Road after a year with the Saints, but the three others would all be making their first appearances for the club; right-half Ken Renshaw, right-winger Jack Tulley, and inside-right Ron Maddocks.

As September unfolded Rovers' new signings had settled in so well that their long unbeaten run never looked in any danger. Six points were gained from their next three league games as twenty goals rained into their opponents' nets. Jack Tulley was particularly prominent, twice contributing four goals to the impressive total. Marys' own league campaign got off to an impressive start despite the delay as they emulated Rovers' six-point return from three outings. The league table at the end of the month made pleasant viewing as the two clubs' one hundred percent records saw them in first and second place. Both sets of players would also have been pleased to hear that from now on they'd be able to have a bit more sugar in their half-time tea as it became the latest item to be freed from the grip of the rationing book.

The lifting of restrictions came just in time to boost the sales of candy floss at the annual Goose Fair down on The Forest, the traditional early autumn provider of thrills and spills for the people of Nottingham, but on the Saturday, its busiest day, Marys' young centre-forward Ray Bennett was also contributing plenty of excitement for fans of the Saints. The first match of October saw him score seven times in his team's round dozen rout of Hucknall British Legion. Two weeks later he repeated the feat when Marys blitzed Manor Farm Old Boys by sixteen goals to one. He was aided and abetted in his smash and grab raid on the hapless defence of the opposition by the left wing partnership of Keith Moore and Arthur Webb. Inside-left Keith scored four of the goals whilst Arthur, making his debut in the number eleven shirt added a couple himself. Even more impressive than the scoreline itself was the fact that it had been achieved with no member of the forward line being older than nineteen. Senior players like Ron Hinson and Harry Wharton continued to provide stability in defence but 'Kegga' and company had obviously decided to give youth its chance. The policy was clearly reaping an early dividend and they eased through the opening rounds of the league and county cups and picked up another couple of league points to make it five wins out of five in the month.

Rovers weren't being troubled too much by the opposition except on the very last day of October when playing host to Underwood Villa in the first round of the league cup. The visitors, undefeated leaders of the Spartan second division, were holding a two-nil lead with seventy minutes gone when their goalie suffered an unfortunate injury. It was Rovers' 'get out of jail' card. With the home supporters finding their voice, the red and whites ran in six goals without reply in the last quarter of an hour of the game. By contrast they'd had little difficulty in getting over the first hurdle of the county cup and had also registered a win in their only league game during the month. However, Rovers had had two blank Saturdays and this had given Marys the chance to catch up with their own games in hand. With the help of their two double figure wins the Saints had taken Rovers' place at the top of the division on goal average.

As autumn turned to early winter and the prospect of the first ever league meeting of the two Arnold sides drew ever closer, there was no let up in the performances of both teams, save for a little stumble on the first Saturday of November when Rovers surprisingly dropped a point at home to mid-table side Hucknall Collieries. The draw brought to an end Rovers tremendous run of twenty-one straight league victories and there was a bit of a hangover the next week when they struggled to eliminate fellow Spartan Leaguers Linby Colliery Colts from the Intermediate Cup. Having already beaten them eight-two in the league back in September they stuttered slightly the second time around and only just managed to edge through by the odd goal in nine. Happily, normal service was resumed seven days later when they went one better than Marys and thrashed hapless Manor Farm Old Boys by seventeen goals to one, the biggest victory in Rovers' short history. Ron Maddocks didn't quite emulate Ray Bennett's seven goal haul but he did record a double hat-trick whilst wingers Jack Tulley and Roy Carter had to be content with just three apiece. John Cunningham, Rovers' regular left back, missed all the fun as he was away representing the Notts FA in the Northern

Counties Amateur Championship clash against Leicestershire and Rutland at Field Mill, the only Spartan League player in the eleven. Then, just to show what a blip the first game had been, Rovers thrashed Hucknall Collieries in the second round of the Spartan League Cup by nine goals to three with the ever prolific Jack Tulley hitting four of them.

Marys' November on the other hand was a much quieter affair. Without the extremes experienced by their town rivals they still saw off four opponents with relative ease, two for league points and two more in the league and county cups. The league table at the end of the month showed the Saints now ahead of Rovers by a point but neither could afford to relax. Third placed Grove Celtic had an identical record to the red and whites except in the goals scored column whilst the perennially dangerous Aspley Old Boys were hovering ominously in fourth place just two points off top spot. Even so, with both Arnold sides unbeaten all season, and in the case of Rovers for what seemed like forever, followers of football in the town could have been forgiven for thinking that there was an air of invincibility about proceedings. Unfortunately, it was that kind of complacency that had just led the English national side to suffer its most humiliating defeat in its long history. Considering that the good ol' USofA had stuffed us a few years earlier in the 1950 World Cup, then that was really saying something.

The event that had induced what almost amounted to a sense of mourning amongst the footballing fraternity across the country had been the visit of the 'Magical Magyars', the Hungarian national side, to Wembley on the afternoon of the last Wednesday in November. England, previously thought to be unbeatable on home turf, had been well and truly thrashed by six goals to three. Not only that but they had also been given a lesson by their Eastern European visitors in how to play the game into the bargain. Yards faster per man and with far superior ball control the Hungarians had taken the game that England had given to the world and shoved a much improved version right back under their noses. The trouble was that nobody involved in football in this country had noticed what was happening abroad or, worse still, had done nothing about it if they had.

It's never a disgrace in football to be overwhelmed by a better side and Hungary, already favourites to win the World Cup the following year, were just that. Their style was completely different to that of their hosts but that shouldn't have been a surprise. Ever since Dynamo Moscow had unveiled their methods in their post war tour of 1945 it had been obvious that the 'continental' system of play, on the ground, ball to feet, lots of passing, had been adopted by almost every country but the four home nations. The only reason that England had been able to compete with this approach so far was the very fact that their players' strength, robustness, and never say die attitude had compensated for the less technical and skilful aspects of their game. On this particular Wednesday these old attributes came up short when faced with the world class talents of Ferenc Puskas, Nandor Hidegkuti and Jozsef Bozsik.

One of the most abiding memories of the game, courtesy of archive footage that gets run and re-run every time great goals are shown on television, is that of Puskas dragging the ball back with the sole of his left foot and out of the path of Billy Wright's sliding tackle before unleashing a fierce rising shot past England's helpless goalkeeper Gil Merrick. Some unkind reporter likened Wright to a 'fire engine going to the wrong fire'. As it transpired, the nature of the defeat would result in the extinguishing of quite a few of the English players' international careers. For six of the team that fateful afternoon, Alf Ramsey and Stan Mortensen included, it would be their last ever appearance in the England shirt. The fact that they'd both scored counted for little. Indeed, Stan Mortensen had scored in each of his last three games, the previous two against no lesser sides than Argentina and The Rest of the World, so could be forgiven for feeling a little aggrieved. For two of the cast-offs, Ernie Taylor and George Robb, the game had provided them with their one and only cap.

Chastened by their experience the players returned to their clubs and the coaches and administrators went back to the drawing board; in truth, though, very little changed. Billy Wright's Wolverhampton Wanders went on to win the First Division championship with a direct and powerful system of play and it could be said that English football has never truly been comfortable in putting technique before endeavour, silky skills ahead of blood, sweat and tears. However, football is invariably about players and the teams with the best ones usually win out in the end. Essentially, England were not beaten through any revolutionary coaching or by a tactical system that had never before been seen but simply because Hungary's players were far superior to theirs on the day.

Not that this would have been troubling the fans of Rovers and Marys because they knew that at the Spartan League level their sides did contain better players than the majority of the opposition. In a little over three weeks time the more pertinent question of just which of the two clubs could genuinely claim to have more of these 'better players' than the other was to be answered out on the pitch. In the meantime, each side had three matches each to fine tune their game before the Boxing Day showdown.

It really was of little surprise given the level on consistency that they'd shown so far this season that both teams won all their games; two for league points and a victory in the third round of the county cup. The most impressive performance fell to Rovers, who hammered Keyworth United on their own ground by ten goals to two. Jack Tulley, who was having the kind of goalscoring season that a centre-forward would have been proud of, rattled in five of the ten from the right wing. The top of the table on Boxing Day morning looked like this.

	P	W	D	L	F	A	P
Marys	9	9	0	0	52	12	18
Rovers	9	8	1	0	60	12	17

It wasn't just the success of the two sides that had been feeding the enthusiasm for the long awaited contest. Contemporary newspaper reports had been giving the game the big build up too. The popular 'Searchlight on Sport' column in the Nottingham Evening News carried an article that started: 'Of all the holiday games in the junior realm one match stands out a mile. All of Arnold will turn out...' The Football Post also waxed lyrical in describing the eager anticipation of the fans of both clubs: 'Excitement in the town is at fever heat'. And so it was.

Such was the interest that you could, if you were so inclined, also wager a bob or two on the outcome of the game. Betting shops were illegal at the time and would remain so for another eight years but that didn't stop there being at least two or three in Arnold at the time, probably more. My own granddad was an occasional visitor to these dens of iniquity but the most he would ever venture was a few pence 'each way'. One day however, when he was obviously younger and more agile than in his later years, he was picking out a bet when the place was raided by the police. Thinking no doubt that, had he been caught, the wrath of my nan would have been a far worse punishment than any handed out by the strong arm of the law, he dived through a half opened window and made his escape. The betting shop was called 'Dids' and was known to just about everyone in the town, including Rovers' captain Franny Greensmith.

FG : Dids used to lay bets on the derby games. They were up an alley behind a pawnbrokers' on High Street. Of course it was illegal then. If you got caught you were stamped by the police with a blue mark on the back of your hand and were fined. I think it was five bob. One day just before a match with Marys the guy who ran the shop asked me how things were. I suppose when you think about it he might have been trying to get some inside information from me. We were just talking but you'd be in big trouble these days for doing something like that. In fact I could have put a few quid on Marys to win and then scored a couple of own goals but I'd rather have died than do something like that.

With such devotion to the cause shared by all the players on each side and with both sets of fans mingling in the mass of bodies standing three or four deep around the ropes the moment everyone had been waiting for had arrived at last. After just one previous clash in the charity cup Rovers and Marys finally lined up against each other with league points at stake for the very first time, seven and a half years after the Nottingham Road side had first appeared on the scene. Although the game was being played on the Top Rec, it really didn't matter. The atmosphere was that of a cup final with both sides having equal support and there was little or no ground advantage for Marys. The point was proven immediately as Rovers, much the faster of the two sides, sped into a two goal lead inside the first twenty minutes thanks to efforts from, not surprisingly, Jack Tulley and, rather more unusually, left half Bill Whitt. Dids might even have contemplated paying out on Rovers already.

Certainly this poor start would have had many Marys' supporters reaching for the hip flask or drawing more heavily on that cigar they'd been given as a Christmas present the day before. On the half hour mark they could relax a little though as inside-right John Pike, described by the Evening News as 'one of the cleverest forwards in this class of football' and who had already attracted the interest of Aston Villa, reduced the arrears. There was no further score in the first half but the first forty five minutes of action had certainly not been a disappointment to all those watching. Just exactly how many were actually there would have to remain an estimate. Because Church Lane was an open ground there was no possibility of having turnstiles or charging admission. The Football News had the number as two and a half thousand and the Football Post put it another thousand higher. Whatever the actual figure it was a tremendous turn out, one that might just have been bettered by Marys' game against the POW eleven back in 1947 but was still reported as a 'record breaking crowd'. 'Kegga' Parr would have been rubbing his hands with glee as both collecting box and bucket did their half-time parade around the touchlines, entreating his fellow townsfolk to take their hands out of their new gloves and dig deep into their pockets.

He'd have been even happier on the resumption when his team's captain Ron Hinson brought the scores level and positively beaming when Keith Moore put Marys into the lead for the first time in the match soon after. With both sides playing their best football Rovers couldn't find a way to draw level until one final opportunity arose in the very last minute. With memories of the dramatic ending to the earlier charity cup final flooding back, all eyes were focused on Marys' penalty area as Rovers won a corner on the left. Amidst tremendous enthusiasm from their fans, winger Roy Carter took the kick and delivered a perfect cross. Centre-half Ken Dove had gone up for the corner in a last ditch attempt to rescue a point for his team and launched himself full length, meeting the ball perfectly and directing a powerful header into the net. There was no time left on the clock. The referee's whistle went and the second local derby ended in the same score as the first: three-all. This time it had been Rovers' turn to deny Marys a victory right at the death and in doing so had ensured that three hours of play between two finely balanced teams had failed to produce a winner; the question of superiority remained unanswered. As both sets of fans headed off to the town's pubs and clubs for a lunchtime drink, or just back home to the previous day's leftovers, the talk was already turned to the next time the teams were due to meet. Unfortunately, unless the two sides found themselves drawn against each other in one or other of the various cup competitions, supporters would have to wait almost four months, to Easter Saturday in the middle of April, for the third instalment of what had already become a fascinating contest.

All in all, 1953 had been an action packed year, both on and off the field, but it was Rovers' exploits in remaining unbeaten for the whole three hundred and sixty five days that was deserving of special acclaim. It was an achievement unparalleled in Arnold post-war football and one which neither of the clubs would ever repeat. Not that it mattered at the time. As Big Ben chimed in the New Year supporters of both clubs were just hoping for more of the same, thank you very much, and that is exactly what they got.

By a quirk of the fixture list and the luck of the cup draws there were just two games played in Arnold during the whole of January and they were both on the Top Rec. Rovers had to take to the road for the whole of the month and in fact completed a sequence of seven straight matches away from Nottingham Road. Travelling wasn't that onerous in the Spartan League though and Rovers' fans only had to find their way to Woodthorpe, Netherfield, Hucknall, Linby and Beeston to give their team the benefit of their support in those opening five games of 1954. The players responded in their usual fashion with five comprehensive victories including a twelve-nil thrashing of Netherfield Rovers and a couple of four-one wins in the league and county cups.

Marys hadn't let Rovers' last minute Boxing Day comeback affect them and posted four comfortable wins of their own during the month, including a league cup victory over the unusually named second division side Dodgers Athletic. Their moniker wasn't intended to imply that they were a bunch of evasive or shifty characters but was merely a reference to the fact that their main sporting love was baseball and they were just paying homage to the Brooklyn Dodgers, one of America's most famous clubs.

ROVERS v CHURCH WARSOP AS SEEN BY TED DUNCAN (Courtesy Football Post)

Whilst January hadn't proven to be that testing a time for either of the town's sides, a glance at February's schedule indicated that there were going to be tougher times ahead. The first Saturday of the month saw both clubs involved in the quarter finals of the Intermediate Cup and drawn against tough opposition from the Mansfield area. Marys were up against St Aidan's Stags and Rovers played host to Church Warsop Welfare, both members of the North Notts League. The Nottingham Road side had the services of Jim Short as trainer. Jim had been a professional with Birmingham before the war and had started out as a youngster with that version of Marys that was around in the early part of the century, well before 'Kegga' had started his own version in the late twenties. With Rovers making heavy weather of their cup tie Jim was apparently getting through a packet of cigarettes at a fair rate of knots until Les Peel settled everyone's nerves with the opener. This did the trick and the red and whites ran out three-one winners. Marys completed a fine double as they defeated the Stags and joined Lenton Gregory and Thoresby Colliery in the county cup semi finals.

The following week Rovers had no game whilst Marys stuck seven past Netherfield Rovers as they warmed up for their next, crucial, match against third placed Grove Celtic. Whilst the two Arnold teams had been winning almost as a matter of course, both Celtic and Aspley Old Boys had been quietly matching them stride for stride. On the eve of the game the Spartan League table showed how just tight it was at the top.

	P	W	D	L	F	A	P
Marys	13	12	1	0	73	16	25
Rovers	13	11	2	0	86	17	24
Grove Celtic	13	12	0	1	69	30	24
Aspley OB	14	12	0	2	74	20	24

There was very little room for error and Marys made sure there were no slip ups, running out comfortable winners by three goals to nil. Seven days later it was Rovers' turn to visit the Victoria Embankment home of the Celtic and despite going behind twice they fought back strongly and with Jack Tulley scoring an incredible five goals from the wing for the second time this season the red and whites virtually eliminated the home side from the championship race with a six-four victory. Both Arnold sides cemented their position at the top with another couple of league points each that month and reached the end of February with the remarkable combined record for the season of not having been beaten in fifty games.

The standard of the Spartan League at this time had never been higher. Second division side Underwood Villa had reached the sixth round of the Junior Cup whilst Rovers and Marys had of course qualified for the last four of the Intermediate Cup. The most impressive achievement of all though had been the Saints' long-time rivals Aspley Old Boys' elimination of high flying Notts Alliance sides Players Athletic and Gedling Colliery *en route* to the semi finals of the Notts Senior Cup. And it was the Aspley club who still presented a real threat to both Arnold teams in the run-in to the end of the season. With just eight league matches left, the Old Boys had yet to meet either Rovers or Marys this season. The results of these four crucial games would naturally have a great bearing on the outcome of the championship and as the calendar flicked over into March the shake-out would start that very first Saturday of the new month.

Marys at Aspley was the first of the four clashes and Melbourne Road was packed solid. Expectations that the game would be a thriller were realised to the full with the general view being that it was without doubt the most exciting game seen on the ground all season. Matches between the two sides were generally hard fought affairs but for the last three and a bit years the Saints had been unable to get the better of the Old Boys despite seven attempts at trying.

GP : Games between us and Aspley were always enjoyable. They had some very good forwards like Dennis Stainwright, Stan Balchin and Eric Vickerstaff. I saw Eric recently and we got talking about when we played each other. 'Tell you what Geoff' he said, 'they were right ding-dong battles, weren't they?'

This particular day was no exception with both teams at the top of their game and very little to choose between them. After eighty five minutes of entertaining action the scores were tied at one apiece and a draw would have been a fair reflection of the evenness of the exchanges. Then disaster struck. A mix-up deep in Marys' defence led to the Old Boys taking a decisive lead which they held onto as the clock ran down. Rovers took advantage of the Saints' slip up to claim top spot by a point as they won at a canter, nine-nil, against their personal whipping boys Netherfield Rovers.

All of a sudden the championship had become Rovers' to lose. Unfortunately, just seven days later, the red and whites contrived to produce a shock result that might just have done that very thing. Playing away against Linby Colliery Colts, a team they had already beaten twice this season, they ended up on the wrong end of a five-two scoreline despite being ahead at half-time. There were no excuses, no mitigating circumstances. Linby's first team had been playing their Central Alliance match at Loughborough against Brush Sports Reserves the same day and the Colts eleven hadn't apparently been strengthened in any way by one or two of the club's senior players. It didn't help matters much that Linby had been gifted two penalties that they gratefully converted.

Inevitably every good or, in the case of Rovers, great run has to come to an end sometime, but it was hardly expected to be at the hands of a side who were destined to finish in mid table having lost more games than they'd won, but then such is the fascination of football. The statistics of the red and whites' spell of invincibility certainly make impressive reading. The Linby defeat was the Nottingham Road outfit's first in fifty four matches and only their second league loss in seventy six games stretching over a period of two and a half years. There would have been some shaking of heads in amazement back in Arnold that night even amongst Marys' followers. They couldn't have anticipated the result any more than Rovers did but their own team's five-nil victory at home to Hucknall Collieries, with four goals from Ray Bennett, had put them back on top of the table. The destiny of the championship trophy was firmly back in the Saints' hands.

The next week it was Marys' turn to visit Linby and the Saints must have wondered what all the fuss had been about seven days earlier. Almost as if to taunt Rovers they romped to a six-one victory with veteran Charlie Moore inspiring the younger players around him with two excellent goals. At least Rovers could draw some comfort from the knowledge that with just six league games to go the next five of them were on the Bottom Rec. Grove Celtic were the first to visit and although the game never broke out into the end to end thriller that produced ten goals three weeks ago, the home side did enough to make sure there'd be no hangover from the previous week's setback with a comfortable three-one win.

The last Saturday of March saw Marys with no fixture of their own but many of the players and a lot of their fans would no doubt have found it hard to keep away from the Spartan League match of the day at Nottingham Road where Rovers were playing hosts to none other than Aspley Old Boys. The visitors had taken advantage of the red and whites' slip up against Linby and were now just two points behind Rovers with a game in hand. With both teams chasing their own version of a treble a close encounter was expected but with Rovers returning to top form they took the early initiative and at the break were two goals up. Aspley fought back hard in the second half but it was only in the dying moments of the game that they managed a late consolation goal. Marys' day off meant that Rovers leapfrogged them back to the top of the table and put a little bit of distance between themselves and Aspley. With the Old Boys due to return to Arnold the following week, this time to the Top Rec, what had already been a season to remember was beginning to reach its nerve tingling climax.

As April dawned the impressive recovery that Rovers had made following the Linby debacle continued with a dismissive six-one defeat of Ruddington, but with that result not unexpected, most attention that afternoon was centred on the goings on at Church Lane. The last time that Marys had gained the advantage over Aspley was as far back as 1949 and if they were to have any chance of taking the title it was essential that they rid themselves of the Indian sign that the Old Boys had held over them for so long. Amongst the regulars in the crowd was Mrs Amy Moore, mother of Charlie and Keith, and one of the most vociferous of all Marys' fans. Indian sign or not, she was one lady who would definitely be on the warpath.

AC : Mrs Moore and her friend Mrs Wildgust used to follow Marys around all the time. They'd be there with their scarves and rattles making a tremendous noise. They were terrors.

JP : Mrs Moore had a black bonnet, a long black coat, and little black boots with studs up them. I think she had a stick too.

GP : They could both be a bit rowdy, a bit naughty. Mrs Moore would waggle her umbrella and threaten the other team's supporters. It all got a bit serious at times.

LR : Mrs Moore used to go to games with her daughter Margaret. If the referee, or even one of Marys' opponents, did something that she didn't agree with she'd clock him with her umbrella.

SA : They'd both stand behind my goal, at either end, calling me names and trying to put me off. They never let up.

However on this particular day Marys didn't really need much outside help as they saw off what little challenge Aspley had to offer and ran out comfortable four-one winners. Whether or not the visitors had been dispirited by their loss at Rovers the previous week or that they were preoccupied by their forthcoming Notts Senior Cup Semi Final against Linby Colliery, the defeat put them out of the title race. From now on it was just the Saints and Rovers for the championship.

MARYS v ASPLEY AS DRAWN BY TED DUNCAN (Courtesy Football Post)

Marys were a game in hand of Rovers in the league but with the latter having no match the following week the Saints took advantage. Beating Ruddington as easily as their rivals just had, they regained the lead at the top of the table by a single point and then saw off bottom markers Burton Joyce just as matter-of-factly to stretch the margin between them and Rovers to three points. The lead had changed hands a number of times throughout the season but now with just two games to go compared with Rovers' three, Marys were firmly in the driving seat once again.

MARYS v RUDDINGTON
10 APR 1954

(John Pike Collection)

The stage was perfectly set for yet another dramatic instalment of what was proving to be a compelling season and the scheduled clash of the two teams the very next week, Easter Saturday, was expected to attract a record crowd to Nottingham Road for the showdown. Unfortunately, and for the second year in a row, Notts FA rules and regulations prevented Rovers and Marys from meeting as planned. They'd decided that the Easter week-end would provide the dates for the Intermediate Cup Semi Finals and as a result the Spartan League decider was put back to the last week of the season.

As it happened, both sets of fans of Arnold's high flying duo were out in force over the holiday period. First to play were Rovers who had been drawn to meet Thoresby Colliery at the Gatehouse Ground, Linby, on the Saturday. Seven coaches were laid on to take supporters from Arnold with nearly as many making the trip from the mining village, swelling the attendance to just over nine hundred. The Evening News remarked on the atmosphere generated by the 'wildly enthusiastic' fans with their scarves, rosettes and rattles as being 'reminiscent of a minor Wembley affair'. The colliery side had won the Notts Junior Cup the year before but had had to play another cup game just the previous evening, Good Friday. To make matters worse the tie had gone into extra time. If ever there was a good time to play them this seemed like it, but they put up a stubborn resistance and at the break only trailed Rovers by a single goal, scored by John Cunningham. Weariness set in after half time though and with Ron Maddocks scoring a hat trick and Les Peel adding the fifth, all without reply, Thoresby were overwhelmed.

All that remained now to give the whole of Arnold the Intermediate Cup Final they had dreamed of was for Marys to do the business against Notts Alliance side Lenton Gregory up on the Plains Road ground of Gedling Colliery on Easter Monday morning. In the days when shops closed on bank holidays and the pubs didn't open their doors until twelve o'clock, a ten thirty kick-off on Easter Monday always drew a big crowd, no matter who was playing or where the match was being played. Today was no exception as over fifteen hundred people, the great majority from Arnold, strained for a good view of proceedings. Early exchanges were pretty even but Marys' hopes took a severe jolt when Gregory took a first half lead. The dream final looked to be in some danger as the score remained the same at half time but after the break the Saints picked up the tempo, stepped up their standard of play to its usual high level, and responded with two goals of their own to claim a well-deserved victory.

Both sets of fans could now start making arrangements for the final at the City Ground, which all being well would be the very last game of the season, but in the meantime there was another knock-out competition to occupy the thoughts of the two clubs, the Spartan League Cup. The luck of the draw had kept Marys and Rovers apart, adding an extra incentive for the two of them to prevail at this stage and set up what would be a dress rehearsal for the county cup final itself. Unfortunately, the two next best teams in the league, Aspley Old Boys and Grove Celtic, stood in their way and the games would of course be played on neutral grounds. Also, because of the pressure on fixtures, Marys' tie against old foes Aspley would have to be played on the following Friday evening, less than twenty four hours before they were scheduled to play Celtic in their penultimate league game.

Rovers' semi final against Celtic, on the other hand, was at least scheduled for the Wednesday and would give them more chance of getting their breath back before their own Saturday league game. In the event, proceedings on the night of the game conspired to make sure they needed it too. Celtic came prepared to gain revenge for the two defeats that Rovers had recently inflicted upon them and the tie was a much tighter and close run game than the red and whites might have wished for. With play swinging from end to end it was no surprise when the ninety minutes were up with the scores level. Thankfully, Rovers found additional reserves of strength and edged through by the odd goal in seven. When, two nights later, Marys showed that their recent win over Aspley was no flash-in-the-pan by beating them again, this time two-nil, the football followers of Arnold, growing in number by the day, could have been excused for pinching themselves just to make sure that what they thought was happening actually was. They need have had no doubts. When the Saints beat off both their own tiredness and the challenge of their opponents Grove Celtic in convincing style by three goals to nil the next day, and Rovers kept up their own tilt at the title with a two-nil win against Keyworth, the season had reached the tremendous climax that everyone had hoped for.

All the local papers were full of the two clubs' achievements and the impact that it had made on the town. 'FOOTBALL FEVER IN ARNOLD AREA' and 'Arnold Battle Royal' were just a couple of the banner headlines above articles waxing lyrical about both teams' wonderful seasons whilst also looking ahead to the three derby games sandwiched into a six day span that would have supporters turning out in record numbers. There would actually be four games for local fans to savour or fret over because Rovers had still to play their outstanding league game; they were:

We	28-Apr	Rovers	v	Marys	Nottingham Road	Spartan League
Fr	30-Apr	Aspley OB	v	Rovers	Melbourne Road	Spartan League
Sa	01-May	Marys	v	Rovers	Plains Road	League Cup Final
Mo	03-May	Marys	v	Rovers	City Ground	Intermediate Cup Final

It was the kind of schedule that would have had full time professionals squealing, let alone guys who did it for fun and had to do a day's hard work beforehand as well. If they'd just been any old four games too then it might not have been that much of a problem but two of these clashes were cup finals and the other two might just as well have been for all that was, or might be, hanging on their outcome.

The first one of the four was a potential championship decider but with the advantage firmly with Marys. They held a one point lead over Rovers and a draw would be sufficient to bring them the title for the first time since the 1949-50 season. The league table on the eve of the match showed the two sides neck and neck at the top:

	P	W	D	L	F	A	P
Marys	21	19	1	1	93	20	39
Rovers	20	17	2	1	108	28	36

The Bottom Rec was packed with around a couple of thousand spectators desperate to see which of the two teams would come out on top. I was just desperate to see, so I inched my way between the bodies and finally the legs of the adults standing three or more deep around the pitch until I finally ended up right in line with the edge of the penalty box at the Charles Street end of the ground. I was only five at the time but I'd been taken to see my first ever game of professional football just a few days before when Notts County beat West Ham down at Meadow Lane and now my football-mad family, certainly the male members anyway, had decided to take me with them to see what all the fuss was about on our own doorstep. The main difference between the two games for me was my view of it. On the previous Saturday I'd been high up in the County Road stand, perched comfortably on a retaining barrier with my dad's protective arms around me, now I'd been left to my own survival instincts down amongst the foot leather of a crowd kicking every ball. The noise was different too; here on the Bottom Rec the shouts were much earthier than they'd seemed watching Notts. There was this older, flat-capped, guy standing close by and he provided what seemed like a running commentary for the benefit of himself and anyone else within earshot. I think he was a Marys' fan but he had an opinion regarding both sides. An attack down the wing nearest to us had led to a header just clearing the bar. The old lad saw it like this:

"Gerrit aht wide. Goo on, tek 'im on yersen. That's it, nah gerrit ovver. Naah.....call yersen a centuh forrard, ah coulda put tharrin wi' mi 'at."

He turned to a chap next to him and said:

"Well ah nivver. 'E wahrall by issen an' 'e purrit ovver."

I'm sure Mrs Moore and Mrs Wildgust would have been there too but apparently they weren't the only fans on the distaff side with a reputation for high spirits.

GP : Rovers had a couple of fans, Mrs Eileen Fell and another lady, both little, and they used to stand behind my goal calling me blind. They'd try anything to put me off; they even threw stones at me.

FG : My wife told me that Les Peel's mum hit another woman once. I didn't see it because I was too busy with the game.

The match itself was a tense one on the pitch too, not surprising considering what was at stake. Both sides were evenly matched with both having strong defences and fast forward lines. Considering that the two teams had scored in every match so far this season it was highly unusual that neither of their goalkeepers were being overworked. A nil-nil draw would have suited Marys down to the ground but their hopes were dashed when Rovers took the lead with a rare header from left-winger Roy Carter.

FG : When Roy scored, Geoff Parr should have saved it but he said "Well, he's never headed the ball before, he took me by surprise!"

Despite their best efforts the Saints couldn't find the equaliser and the red and whites held on to the final whistle. Rovers' fans were delirious but the championship trophy wasn't in their hands just yet. They still needed to beat Aspley Old Boys two nights later to be sure of the title.

The newspapers billed the Friday night game as the 'Championship Decider', a term which was slightly misleading. A person not familiar with the battle for the Spartan League title, if one could be found, might have thought that either Rovers or the Old Boys would be getting their hands on the silverware when the reality was rather different. A win for the red and whites would indeed give them the title but a defeat would mean the trophy going to Marys. If the match happened to end in a draw then there would need to be a real decider as the two Arnold clubs would have to play off for the championship.

There were plenty of interested Marys' fans amongst the throng at Melbourne Road as Rovers set about dealing their neighbours' lingering hopes a severe blow. To be fair, Aspley's season had effectively ended with their three-nil defeat at the hands of Linby Colliery in the Notts Senior Cup Semi-Final but they put up a genuine fight nevertheless. Rovers however, buoyed by their decisive win over Marys, had a bit more about them than their opponents and two goals from Les Peel and Jack Brace were more than sufficient to gain them a decisive victory. At the very death they'd drawn first blood. They leapfrogged the Saints one final time and the first of the season's three trophies was theirs.

At least, just under twenty four hours later, Marys had the chance of swift revenge. In theory they should also have been the fresher side too but they had been struck a heavy psychological blow as Rovers' late run had pipped them at the post. The Plains Road home of Gedling Colliery was just a pleasant Saturday evening's walk for most of the large crowd that congregated there for the second helping of this three part drama. Anyone expecting a feast of goals was destined to be disappointed and once again the outcome of the game hinged on a solitary goal. The match had still lived up to its pre-match billing though as John Pike, Marys' inside-right, recalls.

JP : We played beautiful football. In fact we played Rovers to death but just couldn't get the ball in the net. Then they broke away at the end and Jack Brace scored the winner.

The red and whites had done it again. Poor old 'Kegga' would no doubt have been putting on a very brave face but it would have hurt him that Marys had just missed out on two golden opportunities to lift a trophy. It would have pained him even more that they'd ended up at the other end of town with Rovers. At least he would have already convinced himself, and most everyone around him, that it would be third time lucky for the Saints when the two sides met in the Intermediate Cup Final on the Monday. It wouldn't have been false confidence either.

Until these last two setbacks against Rovers, Marys had only conceded three goals in eight games and their forward line had been prolific, none more so than centre-forward Ray Bennett who'd already hit the net a phenomenal sixty-one times so far this season. Considering that he suffered from partial deafness this was a tremendous achievement, sufficient to have a number of league scouts monitoring his progress.

MARYS v ROVERS
PLAINS ROAD
1 MAY 1954

(Geoff Parr Collection)

The weather conditions in the build up to the game had been atrocious and the surface of the City Ground pitch was so wet before the kick-off that even the Forest manager himself, Mr Billy Walker, was helping to fork the water away. Despite the heavy conditions and the greasy ball both sides tried to play good football and it was Marys, with wing-halves Ron Hinson and Barry Brace featuring prominently, who struck first, inside-right John Pike firing in a great cross shot that gave Rovers keeper Sam Archer no chance. There was no more scoring in the half but only two minutes after the restart Rovers' left winger Roy Carter grabbed the equaliser, picking up a stray ball just inside the Saints' half, beating the full back and lobbing the ball over Geoff Parr's head.

MARYS GO 1-0 UP IN THE INTERMEDIATE CUP FINAL (John Pike Collection)

Then the heavens opened again and torrential rain turned the pitch into a mud bath. Rovers seemed to have greater difficulty in dealing with the conditions than Marys with Ray Bennett in particular revelling in them. Ten minutes after the break he scored from a tap-in following a mistake in the Rovers' defence to give the Saints a crucial lead. Try as they might Rovers couldn't find a second equaliser and after seventy minutes Marys' centre-forward scored again, this time with a cheeky back-heel. The trophy was tantalisingly close now for the Saints and when, just five minutes later, Ray completed his hat-trick with a close range effort there was no way back for the Rovers.

ROVERS 1953-54 INTERMEDIATE CUP RUNNERS-UP : (l to r) F Bojar, F Greensmith, R Carter, J Surgey, W Whitt, K Renshaw, E Crofts, S Archer, K Cunningham, L Peel, J Cunningham.

(Ken Renshaw Collection)

Despite the awful conditions Marys had turned in a pretty impressive performance and were good value for their win. Ray Bennett had had a game to remember, taking his goal tally to sixty-four and alerting even more Football League scouts as to his potential. 'Kegga' and the rest of the committee would have been relieved at getting their hands on the trophy and even more relieved that they'd finally broken Rovers' monopoly.

It had of course been a fantastic season for the Arnold football fan. The two teams had dominated the Spartan League throughout the year and received extensive coverage in the press. Rovers had almost surpassed their brilliant efforts of twelve months previous only to be denied in the very last game of the season by their closest rivals. There had hardly been a Rizla paper between the two sides all year as the following summary of all games played shows:

	P	W	D	L
Rovers	37	32	3	2
Marys	37	32	2	3

The head to head clashes between the sides had produced four out of five extremely close contests as well but in the final analysis Rovers had just shaded them too, with two wins to Marys one and two games drawn.

MARYS 1953-54 INTERMEDIATE CUP WINNERS : Standing (l to r); A Evans, - -, - -, W Parr, J Cunningham, B Brace, E Williamson, H Wharton, G Parr, D Parr, C Moore, - -, S Gray, W Franks, W Whittaker. Sitting; B Cunningham, R Bennett, R Hinson, J Pike, A Webb. Kneeling; J Moore.

(Geoff Parr Collection)

Luck always plays a part in knock-out competitions but most footballers believe that the best team over a season always wins the league, no matter the level. With the two clubs splitting the cups, it would be difficult to argue against Rovers' claim to be 'the better side' in 1953-54. There could of course be no argument with the honours board as Rovers' trophy haul moved into double figures.

ROVERS : FOUR CHAMPIONSHIPS, SIX CUPS (INCL ONE SHARED)

REGENT : THREE CUPS

MARYS : ONE CHAMPIONSHIP, TWO CUPS (INCL ONE SHARED)

CHAPTER TEN 1954-55

Just three days after Ron Hinson had lifted the Intermediate Cup for Marys a slightly more famous sporting event had taken place. On the evening of 6 May Roger Bannister broke the world record time for the mile, becoming the first man on Earth to ever complete the distance under competitive conditions in less than four minutes. Assisted by two pacemakers at the Iffley Road track in Oxford, Chris Brasher and Christopher Chataway, Bannister's time was clocked at 3 min 59.4 sec. It was a tremendous achievement, the news of which echoed its way rapidly around the sporting world.

It was a pity that just a couple of weeks later news of a much more dismal nature was following the same route; the English national football team had suffered yet another of its 'most humiliating defeats ever' as Hungary had showed that their six-three thrashing of the previous November was no flash in the pan. In front of ninety two thousand fans at the Nepstadion in Budapest, the Magyars had given England the worst possible send off for the upcoming World Cup in Switzerland by humiliating them seven-one. Only four of the players representing their country that day would go on to have a decent international career and the other seven would collect no more than eleven caps between them before the curtain fell on their own appearances on the world stage. It was no surprise that England didn't go on to win the World Cup, exiting at the quarter final stage to Uruguay, but it was certainly one of the greatest shocks in the history of world football when Hungary failed to beat West Germany in the final, going down three-two after having beaten them just two weeks earlier in the group stage of the competition by a more than convincing eight goals to three.

If English football at the highest level seemed to be stuck in a rut then the same couldn't be said about the country at large and the world beyond. Even as the nation's footballers were returning home with their tails between their legs they could at least console themselves with the news that in their absence butter had come off rationing and that the country was in the middle of a house building spree with a record three hundred and fifty thousand new homes sprouting up nationwide.

They were needed to provide a roof over the heads of the expanding population as the effects of the post-war 'baby boom' were making themselves felt. New schools were also needed to cope with the numbers of youngsters about to enter the education system, none more so than in Arnold itself. With the old, mostly Victorian, establishments struggling with a rapidly increasing intake two new schools were built; Kingswell School on Gedling Road and Richard Bonington School, named after the town's world renowned artist, on Calverton Road.

Together with most every other child of primary school age living on the Killisick Estate at the time I became one of the latter's founder pupils. I'd spent the first few months of my academic career at High Street Infants but the new school bore little comparison with the old one; they were both educational establishments but that was where the similarities ended. It seemed that the new County Primary had more glass in the windows of a single classroom than the old Board School had in its entire building, giving the school a lightness and airiness missing from my first port of call. Nor did we have to use the old slate boards that were standard issue at High Street, a throwback to the days when the school had first been erected in 1895 with its high walls and its high inadequate fenestration. Lots of brick and little glass, designed and built to encourage those early beneficiaries of compulsive but free education to focus all their attention and energies on and in the classroom.

If my old school's windows were hard to see out of during the week then I had a similar problem on the weekend, especially Sunday lunchtimes, when my mum's cooking invariably had the kitchen window running in condensation. It was no wonder considering that the sprouts and potatoes were bubbling away merrily on the stove for what seemed like forever and the joint and Yorkshire puddings were in the oven too. Just as memorable as the non-existent view of the garden and the mouth watering smell of the family lunch cooking was the radio programme that provided the soundtrack to this vision of family bliss in the fifties; 'Two-Way Family Favourites'. Even now whenever I hear the programme's signature tune my mind is instantly transported back to the days when the toughest decision I had to make was whether to have my Yorkshire pudding covered in gravy as part of my main meal or to have it as my 'pudding' smothered in jam.

With the country's Armed Forces still scattered around the globe, 'Two-Way Family Favourites' was a request programme that aimed to link them with their families back home. The format was essentially simple; messages such as 'missing you' and 'can't wait to be home' were read out by presenters Cliff Michelmore and Jean Metcalfe, followed by a record chosen by the sender of the greeting. It always seemed that the majority of the UK's troops were stationed in West Germany but the broadcast was also intended for guys like Marys' goalkeeper Len Rockley who was doing his National Service at the time and spent part of his two year stint in Malta.

The BBC, who broadcast the show via their Light Programme, tried to maintain a certain decorum about proceedings by discouraging mentions of fiancées and girlfriends and avoiding playing anything too raucous. The tone of the show had always been set by the sweeping strings and lush melody of its signature tune, an instrumental version of 'With A Song In My Heart' played by Andre Kostelanetz and his Orchestra and, after all, this was only 1954 and the summer had seen the popular music charts dominated first by Doris Day singing 'Secret Love' and then by the light operatic tenor of David Whitfield, ably supported by Mantovani and his Orchestra, captivating the record buying public with 'Cara Mia'. Amazingly, these two recordings held the number one spot from the end of the previous football season until a few weeks into the next, a total of eighteen consecutive weeks.

In the middle of their run of success though, a small studio at 706 Union Avenue, Memphis, Tennessee played host to a cripplingly shy and limited musician who, within a couple of years of cutting his first record on July 6, would personally change the course of popular culture in the western hemisphere. The young man went by the name of Elvis Aaron Presley and his first record was titled 'That's All Right Mama'. When disc jockey Dewey Phillips first played the song on the Memphis radio station WHBQ later that month, the genie was truly out of the bottle and there was no way back in. It wasn't quite the start of rock n' roll as we know it but by 1956 Elvis would be a regular on 'Two-Way Family Favourites'. As meat and bacon had become the very last items to come off rationing in the UK just two days before that historic recording session, albeit a staggering nine years after the end of the war that had caused the shortages in the first place, the population as a whole could content itself in the knowledge that, by the time Elvis was singing about spending time down at the end of Lonely Street at 'Heartbreak Hotel', beseeching all and sundry not to step on his 'Blue Suede Shoes', and causing palpitations amongst the producers of 'Two-Way Family Favourites', the Sunday roast would be as big as the family budget could afford and not limited by the number of coupons left in a ration book at the end of the week.

With the shackles of World War II and the privations it caused apparently cast off once and for all there seemed little to stop the yearning for newer, brighter, better and different ways of going on from gathering pace. However, just to remind the average man in the street, and especially the one taking a day or a week off at the seaside, that the Government was in control, especially when it came to the overseeing of the country's morals, a respectable gentleman by the name of Donald McGill was being prosecuted under an archaic Act of Parliament.

Mr McGill, whose family connections were impeccable and had seen the founding of the world famous McGill University in Montreal, Canada, was an English graphic artist whose name had become synonymous with the saucy seaside postcard. The cards featured an array of attractive young women and fat old ladies, old buffers and cads, honeymooning couples and staid vicars, and relied heavily for their undoubted success on innuendo or a word, courtesy of the richness of the English language, that had two different meanings depending on the way it was spelt.

My personal favourite had an old guy asking a much younger sales assistant a very innocent question:

"Excuse me Miss, do you keep stationery?"

To which her ingenuous reply was:

"Well, sometimes I wriggle around a bit".

The humour of course hinged entirely on the word 'stationery'; intended as nothing more than an enquiry about items such as paper and envelopes but misinterpreted by the naïve or, given her reply, maybe not so naive assistant who'd assumed the word was 'stationary' and had responded honestly in the context of her entirely different interpretation of the question.

Most people would have viewed this as nothing more than a bit of fun; saucy, yes, but nothing more. However, the artist fell foul of several local censorship committees which culminated in his trial at Lincoln in the middle of July. Amazingly he was found guilty of breaching the Obscene Publications Act of 1857 and ordered to pay a fifty pounds fine and twenty five pounds costs. Thankfully in these less censorious times his original artwork sells for large sums and he is recognised for the talented artist and master of observation that he always was.

Maybe one or two of his cards were winging their way from holiday destinations along the coast as the young footballers of Arnold began their preparations for yet another new football season. For two of Marys' young players though it was a case of pastures new with John Pike signing professional forms for Coventry City and Keith Moore leaving to join a colliery side in North Notts. A third member of their youthful forward line, Brian Cunningham, also left the club but this was more a case of returning to the fold as he rejoined his two brothers back at Rovers. To compensate for these losses the Saints signed a new right wing partnership of Jimmy Bembridge and Terry Butler, and brought in goalkeeper Dougie Hodgson to allow Geoff Parr to revert to an outfield position.

Apart from welcoming back Brian Cunningham, Rovers had stuck basically with the players who'd served them so well over the past year and were rewarded with four straight wins for points to open the new league season much as they'd ended the last; winning. The fourteen goals that had been scored were spread pleasingly around the forward line and crucially they'd met and overcome the two teams who'd finished in third and fourth places just a few months previously. Aspley Old Boys were defeated on the very first day of the new campaign by four goals to two and the following week Rovers saw off the challenge of Grove Celtic even more convincingly, winning four-one.

Rovers' four victories saw them heading the league table at the end of September with just one other side still with a one hundred percent record. Happily that was Marys although, having played just the twice, they were only taking up a mid-table position. Their results had been impressive enough though with a seven-nil drubbing of Armorduct Cables and a nine-two thrashing of an admittedly declining Keyworth on their opponents' own ground. Right-back Dennis Parr, given a run out at centre forward in the absence of Ray Bennett, looked like he'd played there all his life and scored four times in the opener. It was straight back in defence for Dennis though as the Saints' regular number nine returned for the next game and helped himself to a hat-trick with new signing Terry Butler adding three of his own.

Even this early in the season it looked as though both clubs would again be in contention for honours, not least because the Spartan League, like a number of others in the district, had been struggling to find new teams of sufficient quality to replace those leaving. Worryingly, and not just in the sporting sense but as a reflection of changing priorities amongst the younger generation as a whole, the most common reason being given by a whole host of hardworking officials of both clubs and the leagues themselves was good old fashioned, plain and unadulterated apathy.

The Spartan League had done its best to try and attract a couple of extra clubs to bring the top division up to its preferred quota of fourteen teams but had only managed to begin the season with the same number that had finished the previous one; twelve. Long Eaton side Armorduct were one of the new sides, having been promoted from the second division, Rovers' old Intermediate Cup Final rivals Sheepbridge Steel another, and a third was the newly formed 'B' team put out by Nottingham Forest. However, the fourth new arrival, Blackburns Athletic, became the league's first casualty even before a ball had been kicked. They would unfortunately be joined by two others before the season ended and the prestige of the Spartan League would suffer as a result. It had already taken a blow when Ericssons Athletic, who only finished in fifth place the previous season, managed to succeed where Rovers had failed twelve months earlier and convince Mr Wragg and the other movers and shakers at the Notts Alliance that they were worthy of a place in their league. They didn't even offer the same lame excuse they'd given Rovers that there were no places available; they just increased the number of teams in the second division from fifteen to sixteen. The fact that the works' team's facilities included an immaculate playing surface and excellent changing facilities was no coincidence. If either or both of Arnold's two sides harboured any thoughts of advancement into a higher standard any time soon, then thought would have to be given to a move away from the Recs that they both called home. For now though it was enough to keep hammering the opposition whilst waiting to lock horns together whenever the call came and in that respect October met all the pre-requisites needed to keep the town's fans very happy.

When the fixture lists had been drawn up at the start of the season it had been unusual to see that the local derbies were down to be played in the middle of October and the second week in February, well away from the traditional dates at Christmas and Easter. It was even more of a surprise to see that Rovers didn't even have a game scheduled for Christmas Day, which actually fell on a Saturday. Still, with both sides continuing their domination in the early part of the month, by the time the big game came around the demand to see the latest clash meant that over two thousand spectators gathered at the Top Rec to see which of the two teams' one hundred percent records would be the first to go.

When, with just twelve minutes gone, a deflected shot from Jack Tulley wrong footed Marys' keeper Dougie Hodgson, it looked like Rovers might gain swift revenge for their Intermediate Cup Final defeat but Marys immediately fought back in style with Charlie Moore and Jimmy Bembridge both seeing shots coming back off the woodwork. The pressure on Rovers' goal finally told and Ray Bennett struck twice in three minutes to put Marys in the lead. Charlie Moore, wearing the shirt vacated by his younger brother Keith, was in fine form and before half time he'd added two more goals, the first from a solo effort and the second with a header. After the break Rovers made a valiant attempt to get back in the game and Ken Cunningham pulled one back, but it was just a consolation as Ray Bennett completed his hat-trick and Ron Hinson let fly from thirty yards to give the Saints a well-deserved and comprehensive six-two victory. Even at the veteran stage of his career Charlie Moore had given the big crowd a treat. The Football News reported that he was 'the outstanding player of the match' and that his 'ball control and distribution were a delight to watch'. If Ray Bennett might have felt that his own contribution had been worthy of the 'man of the match' accolade, he could happily console himself with the knowledge that his performance had earned him an invitation to have a trial with the mighty Tottenham Hotspur.

The defeat had been Rovers' biggest reverse in over four years. They hadn't been helped by the absence of Les Peel at centre-forward though and the experiment of playing veteran centre-half Ken Dove in his place hadn't, with hindsight, been the greatest of decisions. The setback didn't seem to affect the Nottingham Road outfit too much however and they closed out the month with easy victories in both the league and League Cup. It was much as before, with all the forwards in good goal scoring form and Jack Tulley particularly prominent; in the first game of October he scored four times and he finished the month by hitting a hat-trick.

Even left half Bill Whitt contributed six goals in quick succession to leave Rovers in second place in the league and safely through the first rounds of the league and county cups.

Considering that they had thrashed their arch rivals slap bang in the middle, October was an even better month for Marys. They emulated Rovers' success in the two cups but not without a little hiccup along the way. Ray Bennett had scored five times to help the Saints overcome Newark Central in the Intermediate Cup but they'd needed two bites of the cherry to dispose of strong second division side Lenton Gregory Reserves in the league cup. Marys had been drawn at home and having gone into a three nil lead suffered the misfortune of losing two players to injury. This evened up proceedings somewhat and Gregory fought back to force the tie into extra time. Both sides then scored twice more and the game ended improbably at five goals apiece. Restored to full strength the following week, the Saints made no mistake this time and ran out winners by four goals to one.

The slimmed down fixture list meant that in November Marys had one blank Saturday whilst Rovers were inactive twice. Both teams more than made up for this lack of action when they did play though with the red and whites involved in an amazing score line against Worthington Simpson Reserves in the second round of the Intermediate Cup. Les Peel hit a double hat-trick with Jack Tulley and Ron Maddocks also helping themselves to three apiece. Ken Renshaw made it a baker's dozen for Rovers whilst the Newark side, obviously lacking in the defensive arts but not wishing to be outdone up front, put five of their own past Sam Archer.

Marys' cup exploits that month included some high scoring of their own. Ray Bennett hit all four of his team's goals as they eliminated Sherwood Amateurs B from the county cup and then Albert Moore, brother of Charlie and Keith and making a rare appearance for the first eleven, scored five of the Saints' twelve goals that eliminated second division Moorbridge Lane from the league cup. Albert was standing in for Ray as the latter had been called up to play for the Notts FA side against Sheffield and Hallamshire, along with keeper Dougie Hodgson. Rovers and Marys both won their single league game of the month to maintain the status quo at the top of the table with Aspley leading the two Arnold sides courtesy of having played a greater number of matches than them; eleven, in fact, to Rovers' eight and Marys' five.

There had been a significant change off the field though as Marys' long-standing secretary Jim Kirk handed over the reins to fellow committeeman Len Woollacott. The secretary's role for a local team is an unenviable task but at least Len had the right credentials considering that he'd had so much success a few years earlier when he ran Notts Regent almost single-handedly. His counterpart at Rovers, Harry Redgate, knew all about the demands of the job, especially the very difficult matter of actually putting out a team of eleven players each and every match day, but even he couldn't have foreseen the demands that would be made of him on the first Saturday in December.

Rovers were scheduled to meet Nottingham Forest B on the Bottom Rec in the second round of the league cup. With none of the club's three goalkeepers available Harry, who'd been Rovers' first ever custodian but had been retired now for a number of years, volunteered to turn out at the last minute. It had started as a typical match day for the secretary; he'd been working all morning, had then arrived at the ground to mark out the pitch and put up the nets, and then helped to organise the freshly washed kit for the players. Now he was having to don the goalie's jumper that he'd normally be handing out to Sam Archer and contemplating the prospects of being in the firing line of Forest's young guns. He probably wasn't that perturbed though considering that the opposition had had an indifferent season so far and that Rovers had already beaten them in the league. When the red and whites went into a two goal lead early in the game he might even have been considering making a full time comeback but, even if he had, the thought wouldn't have lasted long. In what turned out to be not only the biggest surprise of just this, but many other seasons as well, the Forest youngsters proceeded to score four times in each half with just a solitary response from the home side to record a shock eight-three victory.

Ironically, in the very game in which Harry was making what would probably be his very last appearance between the sticks, a young Arnold lad happened to be the goalkeeper at the other end of the pitch. Fifteen year old David Tiley's career was only just beginning but his ability was of a sufficient level for him to warrant a place in the Forest B team. Not only that but he was also entrusted with taking his side's penalty kicks and even had the impudence to slot one past poor old Harry.

The newspapers were full of the story a week later. In fact the success of his fourth team even moved Forest manager Billy Walker to cover it extensively in his weekly column in the Football News, saying that they'd 'achieved quite a sensation by defeating the Rovers...' In fact it had been over three years and more than fifty games since any side had lowered the red and white's colours on the Bottom Rec and it was by far and away the worst home defeat the club had ever suffered. Not only that but they'd been knocked out of a competition that they'd won for the past two seasons. The Forest manager did award Rovers top points for one aspect of their play, though. Whereas other adult sides might have responded to a bunch of young kids giving them the run around with a bit of physical retribution, Mr Walker went out of his way to 'pay tribute to the Arnold players and officials and say 'Thank you' to them for taking their defeat in a most sportsmanlike manner.' At least these kind words would have been some consolation to Harry Redgate, especially considering that at the final whistle Rovers' secretary had to take down the very nets that he'd been picking the ball out of all afternoon. Then again, it was hard to find anyone who didn't have a good word for Harry.

AC : Harry was the committee man who did all the work. Everyone respected him; you never fell out with him.

Rovers' chairman on the other hand, Ernest 'Nark' Anthony, was an entirely different character altogether.

AC : You could have an argument with 'Nark' anytime. He was a big guy. He used to look after the pit ponies and the story was that he put one under one arm and one under the other.

RW : 'Nark' was very determined. Harry was not a very strong man and 'Nark' would override him. He wanted this, he wanted that. He was a decent man in his ways but he was very bombastic at times, saying "you will do this". He was the one who more or less sat down and said "this is the teamsheet" and that was the end of it; no one else could have a say. A lot of the players didn't care for his attitude at all. Rovers had good committee men but 'Nark' normally had his way.

BC : We never really got on, I don't think he liked me for some reason.

SA : We called him Big 'Nark'; he must have been six foot six tall and as wide as the proverbial brick out-house.

FG : He was a bit of a lad, never got married. He was a big drinker, always in the Greyhound. One Christmas night the players had been round to my house and we'd been drinking till four even though we had a game on Boxing Day morning. Nark blamed me and said "It'll be your fault, your fault if they lose, your fault." That's how he spoke but we still managed to win.

Two weeks later it was Marys' turn to be on the wrong end of a surprise result with the young Foresters when, meeting them in the league, they lost their first game of the season two-one. It had been unlucky thirteen for the Saints as they'd been unbeaten in their opening twelve games of the season prior to this setback, although they did have a bit of a battle on their hands the previous week. They'd just managed to squeeze through the third round of the Intermediate Cup, beating Kimberley YMCA by the only goal of the game, scored in the very last minute by Geoff Parr. Considering that Kimberley were top of the Notts Amateur League at the time with a one hundred percent record and had only conceded four goals in seven games whilst hammering in fifty seven at the other end, it was a more than creditable performance.

Rovers had seen off the challenge of Sheepbridge Steel in the county cup the same day but the following week, just as Marys were slipping up against Forest B, they met Aspley Old Boys for points at Melbourne Road and compounded the gloom amongst Arnold supporters by going down by four goals to two. With there being no traditional Christmas Day or even Boxing Day fixtures for them to look forward to, the year ended in somewhat of an anti-climax. Still, even though Aspley had stolen a march on both clubs by racking up games when their two main rivals had been idle or otherwise engaged, there was much to play for in the remainder of the season, as the top of the table clearly showed.

	P	W	D	L	F	A	P
Aspley OB	13	11	0	2	47	23	22
Rovers	9	7	0	2	39	22	14
Marys	7	6	0	1	36	9	12

The first Saturday of the second half of the decade fell on New Year's Day and despite both teams ending 1954 on a flat note, Rovers and Marys got off to a fine start with convincing victories in the fourth round of the Intermediate Cup. The Saints' achievement in knocking out Notts Alliance side Wilford by five goals to one was particularly commendable and was just another in a long line of successes by both Arnold sides against clubs from that competition. It was a pity that the Arnold and District Benevolent Cup had been put into mothballs since the epic three-all draw between Rovers and Marys that saw them share the trophy back in August 1953. The exact reasons why the competition stalled are not clear although Eric Thompson, Saints' fan and committee man at the time, had his own theory.

ET : The Alliance sides like Gedling and Bestwood didn't mind playing in the Cup at the start because they were better than us then but when they started getting beat it was a different matter. They didn't like it, so they wouldn't take part.

The big losers of course were the Arnold footballing public who were being denied the chance to see the clashes between the best the Alliance and Spartan Leagues could offer, but as the New Year unfolded they would be struggling to see a match of any sort, especially if they were Rovers' fans. Improbably, between New Year's Day and the end of March the red and whites would play just three solitary games, leaving them without a fixture of any sort on nine of the twelve Saturdays available. In the circumstances it was to the players' credit that they didn't let the long lay-offs between games affect their form. They saw off the challenge of the Newark League's unbeaten leaders Ollerton Colliery, conquerors of Forest B in the previous round, by three goals to nil in the quarter-final of the county cup and hammered Sheepbridge Steel and Keyworth United in the league to maintain their title challenge. Inside-right Ron Maddocks hit four of Rovers eight goals as they completed a hat-trick of wins over the steelmen.

Rovers' lack of fixtures hadn't been helped by the basic shortage of teams in the league but it had of course been worsened by their shock exit from the league cup. Then there was the weather. Most people today are convinced, rightly or wrongly, that winters were definitely worse back then than they are now, and the one that started early in November 1954 and finished late in February 1955 certainly belonged in that category. Arnold had been spared the worst of the old year's problems, which had mainly been ones of flooding, but the town suffered much the same discomfort as the rest of the country when snow blanketed everywhere in the middle of January. Ice and outbreaks of fog didn't help matters either but it seemed that the worst of the elements had passed until the white stuff made its reappearance in February and hung around even longer than it had done the month before.

The adverse weather conditions hit football at all levels pretty hard. All football pools coupons were cancelled on the middle Saturday in January as forty-one games out of the fifty-odd scheduled to be played in England and Scotland were lost to the elements, a record in peacetime football and even worse than the mayhem in the winter of 1947. Amazingly, Marys' game against Grove Celtic on the Victoria Embankment went ahead despite the pitch being completely covered in snow. Not long after kick-off it was impossible to make out any pitch markings including the goal lines themselves. The only way to make absolutely sure that the ball had crossed the line for a goal was to bury it deep in the net, which the Saints did seven times just to be on the safe side; Arthur Webb, playing at inside left, helped himself to three of them.

MARYS v GROVE CELTIC 15 JAN 1955

(Courtesy Football Post)

The next week was almost as bad as twenty six top flight games were called off, mostly as a result of dangerously icy and waterlogged pitches caused by the combined effect of thawing snow and overnight frosts. Happily for the legendary snooker player Joe Davis the inclement weather that day didn't stop him from achieving the very first officially ratified 147 maximum break against Willie Smith at London's Leicester Square Hall. Outside though local football was badly hit too and it wasn't until the first week in February that Rovers and Marys were back in action. The Saints emulated Rovers' success against Ollerton Colliery in the Intermediate Cup by knocking out another unbeaten pit team, Nottingham and District outfit Calverton Colliery. Marys, though, had a bit more of a game on their hands than their town counterparts and were trailing two-nil with just a third of the game left until they rallied sufficiently with a goal from Geoff Parr, followed by the equalizer and the winner from Ray Bennett, to just edge the tie by the odd goal in five. As it happened, Ray had just played his last game in the Saints' colours, certainly for the foreseeable future.

His final two goal flourish had made it seven in four games and had probably taken him close to or even beyond the hundred goal mark for the club; a fantastic achievement considering that he'd only been with the Saints for a couple of seasons. Irrespective of just exactly how many times his name had appeared on the scoresheet, it had certainly made any number of appearances on the scouting reports of bigger clubs. Apart from Spurs' earlier invitation to go for a trial with them, his prolific scoring exploits had aroused the interest of Birmingham City, Stoke City, and Queens Park Rangers as well as Midland League club Worksop Town but he eventually opted to sign for the latter's league rivals, Boston United.

The week after Ray's departure Marys met Underwood Villa, yet another unbeaten side, in a crucial league cup quarter final. Even though Villa were in the second division of the Spartan League their record showed that they were a threat and it took three goals from the left wing partnership of Geoff Parr and Arthur Webb, the former scoring twice, to secure a far from comfortable three-one victory. Soon after, the snow came down and stayed awhile and it would be March before the Saints played their next match.

Despite the interruptions Marys were on a good run, and their win over Underwood was their fifth in a row so far this year. Notts County were having a decent spell of their own at the time too, especially in the FA Cup. Even though I was just six years old at the time, I'd been taken to Hillsborough to see the Magpies play Sheffield Wednesday in the Fourth Round. The game was played on the last Saturday in January, just as the bad weather had relented and a couple of weeks before the second cold snap had hit, so the ground was in excellent condition. Not that I could see that much of the pitch when my dad, granddad, uncle and I finally squeezed onto the packed terraces. In fact all I could really see, even when perched on my father's shoulders, was lots of people in front of us. In the circumstances, though, this was probably a better view than that of the poor bloke standing behind us.

It seemed that all roads led to Hillsborough that day. Not that this was a particularly unusual occurrence, especially in those days when it was the FA Cup that attracted the largest attendances to grounds throughout the country, but it had to be said that Wednesday were rock bottom of the First Division at the time. Maybe it was that fact, together with the relative proximity of Sheffield and Nottingham that enticed approximately fifteen thousand Magpies' supporters to make the short trip north. Quite why another thirty eight thousand or so Wednesday fans would want to see their side host Second Division County can only be put down to the allure and magic of the world's oldest cup competition.

Just so that I might be excluded from the crush of fifty three thousand one hundred and thirty seven other fans, who almost to an exception were very much bigger than me, I was handed, in time honoured fashion, over the heads of everyone in front of us until I ended up sitting on a large white retaining wall at the front of the terraces with a few other waifs and strays. I have to say, without a word of a lie, that the day was one of the very best experiences of my whole life, and I knew there and then, if I hadn't already realised it during the handful of games I'd been taken to before, that I'd be a slave to the beautiful game for evermore. I can't remember that much about any individual aspect of the game, but I do recall the sheer enthusiasm and excitement that enveloped the crowd as a whole. I can also recollect that it took us forever to get away from the ground after the match. In fact we were so slow in moving from the area around Hillsborough that we were still there when that evening's local football paper appeared on the streets; it confirmed that the two sides would need a replay following the one-all draw I'd just seen. Unfortunately, because of my tender years, I wasn't allowed to watch the Magpies go through at the second attempt, a feat they just achieved by the narrowest of margins, one-nil. I'm not quite sure at what time of day the rematch took place, afternoon or evening, but I was excluded anyway; either on the grounds that I was at school or that it was way past my bedtime. At least I'd be able to watch County in the Fifth Round though as they'd been drawn at home to mighty Chelsea.

The tie took place three weeks after my trip to Hillsborough and by this time the snow had made its unwelcome return. On the day before the game the call had gone out for volunteers to help make the pitch playable and they'd worked right into the early evening with the floodlights on clearing the snow and then sanding the pitch to prevent ice from forming. Operations had to be ended for the day when another fall of snow came. The efforts to provide a playable surface continued on the morning of the game and all the snow, except at the Meadow Lane end of the ground, had been removed by kick-off.

Chelsea, who would go on to win the First Division Championship this season for the very first time in their history, were lying fifth at the time just three points behind the leaders whilst Notts occupied a similar position in the Second. Nearly forty two thousand spectators turned up despite the doubts about the fixture going ahead. Just across Trent Bridge, another FA Cup tie was about to start as Forest played hosts to Newcastle United. This was another Second versus First Division clash and after they'd eventually been taken to a second replay by the Reds, the Geordie Magpies went on to win the competition, beating Manchester City three-one in the final at Wembley.

The whole concept of being able to play two such cup ties on the same day just a few hundred yards apart belongs to a long-lost era when supporters of rival clubs could be trusted to co-exist and mingle with each other without threats or actual acts of violence, without damage to grounds or neighbouring property, without trashing trains or terrorising other travellers, and certainly without the need to be chaperoned or otherwise controlled by the combined might of the city and county police forces. Over sixty seven thousand fans turned up in total to the two matches and it would have been more had it not been for the weather as snow in the north-east caused the cancellation of five special trains from Newcastle. With the two Arnold sides fixtureless there was every chance that the town's players were drawn to one or other of the matches. Marys' Geoff Parr certainly was and didn't need any prompting to recall that Notts won a famous victory and that the only goal of the game came from left winger Albert Broadbent to set up yet another home tie in the Sixth Round against York City.

Now if the Magpies had earned a reputation as one of the season's giant killers with their wins against the Londoners and Sheffield Wednesday, York's own exploits had been even more impressive. They were only a Third Division (North) outfit but had already claimed the scalps of First Division Blackpool and Spurs. Even though County were pre-match favourites, no-one was taking the visitors lightly and the interest in the game exceeded anything ever seen before down at the Lane. Geoff Parr and the rest of the Marys' and Rovers' players wouldn't be going because they'd got a game, but more importantly from a personal view neither would I. It had been decided that, considering the numbers expected to shoehorn themselves into the old ground, that it might be too much for a six year old. I was quite upset when I found out I'd be left behind but that was nothing compared to how I felt later on.

The adults had been right about the crowd; a new record attendance of forty seven thousand three hundred and one packed the stands and terraces as the two sides battled for a place in the Semi-Final. My seat for the game, well the second half at least, was the fourth step up the stairs at my Nan's house on James Street. The stairwell had a door at the bottom as it led directly off the living room at the back of the terraced house and I sat there listening intently to live second half coverage of the match courtesy of the BBC and a long flex on my Nan and Granddad's bakelite radio. There had been no score but York had been giving the Magpies as good as they got and it was no surprise when the visitors eventually went ahead with little over ten minutes remaining. I feared the worst and, despite County's best efforts to find an equaliser, it happened. My beloved Magpies were out of the Cup and I was inconsolable. Only six weeks after experiencing one of the best days of my life at Hillsborough, I was now suffering one of the worst and, just as Geoff Parr would always remember the scorer of Notts' winning goal against Chelsea, I will never forget York's match winner either. His name was Arthur Bottom; most inappropriate considering that he'd done more than most to help his side end up on top.

Rovers and Marys were both in the ascendancy that day too and in fact the Saints' win was their seventh in a row since the turn of the year. With their town rivals struggling for a game, Marys had caught up with them in the number of games played and overtaken them in the league at the same time, having dropped just two points to Rovers' four. The Nottingham Road outfit were still without a fixture until April and with the Saints down to play two more league games before the end of March, the momentum had most definitely swung in the maroon and golds' favour.

The first of the two matches was against Aspley Old Boys on the Top Rec and like many of the previous clashes between the two teams it turned into the usual tight and enthralling contest with very little to choose between them. Marys lost the services of right winger Jimmy Bembridge with twenty minutes to go but managed to keep the scores level at three apiece until they finally made the game safe with a penalty. The following week the Saints visited Linby Colliery and thrashed their Colts side by seven goals to one with Charlie Moore showing the youngsters the way to goal by scoring a hat-trick. The standings at the end of March showed that Marys were very well placed to overtake Aspley and keep Rovers at bay too.

	P	W	D	L	F	A	P
Aspley OB	17	13	1	3	67	33	27
Marys	13	12	0	1	70	19	24
Rovers	11	9	0	2	52	26	18

Unfortunately, with the season just about to enter its crucial stage, the scourge of clubs withdrawing from the league late in the campaign began to complicate matters at the top of the table, and in this instance Rovers were the main beneficiaries. Long Eaton side Armorduct Cables, by no means the worst side in the division, chucked in their hand and as a result the wins recorded against them by Aspley and Marys were wiped off. Rovers on the other hand hadn't even played them yet and therefore effectively gained on the two clubs above them without even turning out. What's more, a fixture list that would have been a nightmare had been eased considerably. Rovers, prior to Armorduct's demise, would have had to complete nine league games in a month, not forgetting their continuing interest in the Intermediate Cup; now it was just a mere seven.

Despite the implications of these off-field matters, both Rovers and Marys began April with every intention of making this another thrilling end to a season by keeping the pressure firmly on each other with convincing league victories. Jack Tulley scored a couple for Rovers as they visited Hucknall Collieries and came away with a three-one win whilst Dennis Parr, moved from right-back to centre-forward following Ray Bennett's departure, did even better with four for Marys in their seven two stroll over Grove Celtic. The Saints were still well on course for a tilt at the treble and the results of their next three matches would go a long way to determining just how many trophies might come their way. The last of the three games was the League Cup Semi-Final against Sheepbridge Steel but before then there was a little domestic argument that needed sorting out and to the delight of the Arnold public it would be spread over the Easter week-end. Unlike the previous year when the luck of the draw had kept Marys and Rovers apart in the Intermediate Cup until the final itself, this time around they'd been pulled out of the hat together at the semi-fibal stage. The consolation was that the game would be played on Easter Monday at the Plains Road ground of Gedling Colliery, less than forty eight hours after the two teams were due to meet for league points down on the Bottom Rec.

The timing was guaranteed to attract large crowds to both games but unfortunately I wouldn't be amongst them. I'm sure that I would have been taken to at least one of the matches but Easter was the time of year that my family made its annual trip to visit my paternal grandparents down in London. Well it wasn't quite the Capital itself but most people, on learning that we were off to Epping, invariably said "Where's that then?" Back in the nineteen fifties it was a rather sleepy market town in Essex on the Harlow to London road. Now it's bordered by the M11 to the east and the M25 to the south, with the junction of the two no more than a few miles from the town centre, and is home to the rich and famous.

The biggest change I noticed between there and home was obviously the accent, but there were other differences too. These being the days when more or less every adult in the land smoked and even a child of six could buy them, I was asked by my parents to run an errand for some cigarettes from the newsagent just around the corner. "Ten Park Drive please" I asked when it was my turn to be served. At first I thought that it was my own accent that had caused the look of bewilderment on the newsagent's face but then I realised there was more to it than that when he replied "You got the right address?" Now it was my turn to look puzzled as I could see shelves full of cigarettes on the wall behind the counter and I had definitely followed the exact instructions I'd been given in how to get to the shop. He got out a very large book and after what seemed like an eternity of flicking through its pages he finally put it down and said "No, didn't think so, nothing for Park Drive." It was only when he asked the people in the queue behind me whether they'd heard of Park Drive and the best they could come up with was "No, definitely not 'round here, but there might be a Park Road over at Theydon Bois though" that I finally realised that we were talking about two different things. The confusion hadn't been about my midlands accent but his assumption that I'd come in to 'pay the papers'. As it transpired it didn't matter anyway because none of them had ever heard of Park Drive cigarettes either. I had to return empty-handed and exasperated and my mum and dad had to make do with my nan's Player's Weights for the rest of our stay.

Apart from this little misunderstanding the highlight of the trip, for me anyway, was the Easter Monday morning stroll to see the local team, Epping Town, play the Walthamstow League Eleven in their traditional annual holiday fixture. Epping were probably of the same standard as Rovers and Marys then but they did eventually reach the heights of the Athenian and Isthmian Leagues before finally folding as a result of financial difficulties. There was a good turn out for the game too, around three or four hundred, but back home there were even more watching the two Arnold sides clash in the Intermediate Cup; thirteen hundred and fifty six according to the figures released later by the Notts FA.

There had been just as many down at the Bottom Rec a couple of days earlier as Rovers set about trying to upset Marys' championship aspirations and gain revenge for their six-two thrashing back in October. That defeat had left the tally in the clubs' head-to-head clashes at two wins apiece with two drawn and whilst there was nothing to split the teams going into this latest showdown an early injury in the Saints' defence led to them playing the majority of the game with just ten men. Eleven against eleven would have been a tough enough challenge in itself but the numerical advantage swung the odds heavily in the home side's favour. Goals from the ever reliable Jack Tulley and Les Peel set Rovers on their way and with Marys unable to find a way back they ran out comfortable winners by four goals to one. The victory also brought them within two points of the Saints with a game in hand.

On the Monday, with Marys having to re-jig their defence, Rovers were definitely the pre-match favourites. A win would give them a chance of capturing the Intermediate Cup for the second time in three years whilst also avenging the previous season's defeat in the final by the Saints. With the confidence gained from Saturday's result the red and whites again held the upper hand and, whilst it was a much closer affair than the league game, Rovers didn't even allow Marys the consolation of a goal on this occasion. The Saints drew a blank for the first time this season as their rivals eased through to the final with a two-nil victory. In fact the only opponents who'd managed to shut out Marys' much vaunted forward line in the past two seasons were Rovers themselves, and now they'd done it for the third time.

The following Saturday the Saints, unusually given that this was April and there were still so many fixtures to fit in, had no game. Rovers did though and, in hammering Forest B by seven goals to three with a hat-trick from Jack Tulley, not only went some way to redeeming themselves for the earlier shock defeat by the young reds but brought themselves level on points with Marys.

It hadn't been the best of weeks for 'Kegga' and company and the Saints would be fixtureless again the next Saturday whilst Rovers were playing for league points. However, they had a very good chance of picking themselves up off the floor when they faced Sheepbridge Steel in the League Cup Semi-Final on the Friday evening over at Linby. Marys took advantage of every opportunity presented to them and went some way to easing the disappointment of the derby games with a convincing six-one victory.

Despite this success in the cup, further off-field events had conspired to provide another severe setback for Marys' title challenge. This time it had been the turn of Linby Colliery Colts to withdraw from the league when they had just five fixtures left to fulfil and in theory plenty of time to fit them in. Having the use of a private ground they could easily have played into the first week of May but they made the lame excuse that with their senior team being short of players such heavy calls were being made on them as to make it impossible to carry on. It was a severe blow to the prestige and reputation of the Spartan League but it was even more of a knockback for the Saints who had played and beaten the junior miners twice to Rovers' once. So, four points came off Marys' total to just the two from their neighbours and yet again the Nottingham Road outfit had their fixture schedule eased as well. When Rovers thrashed bottom markers Hucknall Collieries twelve-one the day after the Saints' win over Sheepbridge to put themselves four points clear of their rivals, Marys could be forgiven for feeling a little hard done by.

As the season entered its final week it was the maroon and golds who now had the more hectic schedule. Even with games against Aspley and Forest B still to come though they were by no means out of contention for the title. Even if Rovers didn't slip up in their remaining two games the Saints could yet force a play off with four victories of their own. With the first of the matches being away on the Tuesday night against Hucknall there was every likelihood that the run-in would begin with an easy win. The colliery side were rock bottom with no wins and no points to their name, the two that they'd actually picked up from a couple of draws having been taken off them for some misdemeanour or other. This was their last game of the campaign and it looked like the cricket season couldn't come soon enough.

Then something rather strange happened. A side that was powerless to stop one Arnold side from scoring twelve against them just a couple of days earlier suddenly managed to beat the other one and gain their only win of the season in their very last game. The score was two-one but the shock of the result couldn't have been any greater if the margin of victory had been much wider. Not that the Football Post afforded it such a dramatic mention, saying only that Hucknall 'surprised' Marys. They did that alright and I'm sure that Rovers were surprised too when they heard the result. Considering that two point deductions by the Spartan League were normally imposed for fielding ineligible players I asked Geoff Parr whether Hucknall had included any 'ringers' that fateful evening.

GP : I'm not sure but losing like that you'd have thought we were playing Linby Colliery, not Hucknall.

ROVERS 1954-55 : Back Row (l to r); F Scanlon (Treasurer), F Bojar, J Short (Trainer), K Renshaw, K Dove, S Archer, W Whitt, E Anthony (Chairman), J Tulley. Front Row; F Greensmith, R Maddocks, L Peel, K Cunningham, R Carter.

(Sam Archer Collection)

That 'surprise' result handed Rovers the title on a plate. Well, of course, they had two more games to play and win but they did that without breaking too much sweat, seeing off Ruddington four-two before finally sealing the championship with a three-one victory over Grove Celtic. Marys pulled themselves together sufficiently to win their own outstanding league fixtures but inevitably had to settle for second spot behind Rovers for the second season running. The old sports adage, said to have originated in the USA, that 'First is first and second is nowhere' was never more apt than now. Despite a more than impressive start to the season in which they lost just once and won twenty one matches out of twenty three, the Saints paid heavily for losing three out of four games in a seventeen day spell in April including two back to back matches when league points were at stake. Rovers on the other hand, despite hibernating for the best part of three months, had still managed to rack up eleven straight wins since the start of the year to take advantage of Marys' slip ups. Now all that remained of the season was to see whether Marys could get their hands on the Spartan League Cup and if Rovers could do the same with the Intermediate Cup.

The two finals were staged at the City Ground with Rovers meeting Lenton Gregory and the Saints facing Forest B. Rovers had by far the harder task as their opponents had completed the league and cup double in the Notts Alliance Division Two with a formidable record, dropping just five points out of a possible fifty six whilst scoring a massive one hundred and seventy five league goals in the process, an average of more than six a game. It was therefore much to Rovers' credit that they limited the prolific Lenton side to just four on the night of the final, but in only finding the net twice themselves they were unable to regain the trophy they'd won two years earlier. Marys, facing a much less daunting prospect, had no trouble in seeing off the challenge of the young reds and made sure that the Spartan League Cup joined the Championship Trophy in remaining at Arnold.

With two of the three pieces of silverware on offer at the start of the season safely retained and with Rovers having only failed at the very last hurdle to make it a clean sweep for the town's teams it had been another excellent year. In a way though, and because expectations had been raised so high by the successes of the previous two campaigns, there was a strange sense of underachievement this time around. Maybe it was because Rovers' amazing run of invincibility at home had come to an end the way it did or the fact that Marys lost a game at Hucknall that they would have been expected to win ninety nine times out of a hundred. Most likely though was the overriding sense that the two Arnold teams had outgrown the Spartan League and that the double they'd achieved between them had been no more than was anticipated.

When the final tables were drawn up there were only nine teams left in the top division, which was an indictment of the league's management considering that there were as many as fifteen in the second tier. Four withdrawals in one season hadn't helped but that situation could also be laid at the door of the league itself. Rovers, even with their cup success, played just twenty six games in a thirty seven week season and it wasn't just the lack of fixtures that was a problem for the two Arnold sides, it was a lack of credible opposition. Occasional shocks notwithstanding of course, no team other than old rivals Aspley Old Boys had looked remotely capable of challenging Rovers and Marys, especially in the league. Of course both teams were full of excellent players who'd thoroughly deserved their success and there is a saying in football that you can only beat what's put in front of you, but the time had obviously come for change, a move to pastures new that would show that the two clubs were definitely trying to better themselves. By the start of the following they would both have left the Spartan League behind. For now though Rovers, again based on the rationale that ranks league champions above cup winners, could claim to have been the better side for the second year running, whilst the updated honours board read:

ROVERS : FIVE CHAMPIONSHIPS, SIX CUPS (INCL ONE SHARED)

MARYS : ONE CHAMPIONSHIP, THREE CUPS (INCL ONE SHARED)

REGENT : THREE CUPS

CHAPTER ELEVEN 1955-56

Just as the previous season had been nearing its end the film 'Blackboard Jungle' opened in America. As the opening credits started to roll, the first line of a song that was destined to start a whole new musical genre was heard by a mass audience for the very first time. It went "One, two, three o'clock, four o'clock, rock!" and before long Bill Haley and his Comets were credited with kicking off Rock n' Roll as we know it. The song, 'Rock Around The Clock', had originally been written in 1952 and the version used in the film had been recorded a couple of years later. It had had some success in the American Country charts but it was its showcase in 'Blackboard Jungle' that resulted in it becoming one of the seminal recordings in the history of popular music.

Not everybody was thrilled by the development though, especially the USA establishment who quickly linked rock n' roll with juvenile delinquency. The fact that the subject matter of 'Blackboard Jungle' itself was that of a decent, principled teacher trying to carry on his vocation in a tough inner city school only helped to reinforce the connection. It also introduced adolescent slang to a wider public in the UK. When the teacher Mr Dadier, played by Glenn Ford, is having trouble with the class bad boy, he wants to take him to the principal's office but is faced with the taunt of "You gonna make me, daddio?". In this instance the use of the term 'daddio' was merely a mocking variation on the teacher's surname but the word itself had been around a long time. As part of the 'jive' vocabulary that accompanied the jazz and swing music of the era, it surfaced on a popular recording back in 1946 when it was used in Ella Mae Morse's "The House of Blue Lights". It had been just a short bop, skip and a jump before the word was used in a pejorative sense as a reference to anyone who was either a figure of authority or just too old to be 'cool' or 'hip', two amongst many other terms that would eventually form a lexicon for the rock n' roll generation. It was therefore no surprise when, a little later, a record with the title 'Don't You Rock Me Daddio' became a hit too.

The man who would one day be voted the 'greatest Briton' of all time, Winston Churchill, had been called many things during his many years in the public eye, 'imperialist' and 'warmonger' to name just two, but probably never 'daddio'. No one at the time had much cause to question his authority anyway but just a few days after 'Blackboard Jungle' opened the great man himself, now eighty, stood down as Prime Minister and Anthony Eden took over the leadership. Once in power he wasted little time in calling a General Election and at the end of May the Conservatives were returned to government with an increased majority.

The new Prime Minister had felt secure enough to go the country straightaway as the Conservatives, under Churchill, had enjoyed a relatively untroubled four years during which rationing had come to an end, house building numbers had exceeded expectations, and taxes had been scheduled to be cut. Events such as the Queen's coronation and the stellar achievements of Roger Bannister and Edmund Hillary had also imbued the country with an element of self-confidence to go with the general background of peace and relative prosperity. The improvement in living standards was evident in the rapid increase in car and television ownership. There were almost four million private vehicles on the road whilst forty percent of homes now had the small screen. Four and half million tv licences had been issued compared with under three hundred and fifty thousand just five years earlier, and as a consequence this election was the first to be given extensive television coverage. Party political broadcasts were transmitted and on election night itself the BBC ran a results programme along lines still used today, with different constituencies falling over themselves in the race to be the first to declare. Also making its very first appearance was the 'swingometer', a pendulum attached to a chart indicating the projected outcome of the election as each result came in. It finally settled at slightly over one and a half percent in favour of the Tories who thus became the first party in power since the nineteenth century to actually increase its majority.

Making changes often comes when events leave little alternative but the Conservatives had managed the more difficult trick of doing it when things were going well. In their own field, Rovers and Marys were in a similar position, dominant at the level they were playing but knowing there was a need to move on. The Spartan League had served them well and they it but it was now time for a parting of the ways. It was really just a question of 'where to next?' The Notts Alliance had shown no obvious indication that the two Arnold sides, despite their continued success, were now deemed any more worthy of admittance than before and there were no other Nottingham based leagues that could offer any advancement from the Spartan League. Fortunately, an opportunity arose from an unusual source. The Central Alliance had been in existence since 1947 and was effectively an East Midlands regional league, drawing its clubs from Nottinghamshire, Derbyshire, Leicestershire and Lincolnshire. Its players could be paid and it was second only in status to the Midland League, the premier competition for part-time professional clubs in the area. Apart from a single season back in 1949-50, the Central Alliance had always run just one division. The experiment with a second tier had proven unsuccessful and a lack of teams had caused the division to be disbanded part way through the following campaign. Five years later the situation had changed and now, with eighteen teams having lodged successful applications, there was sufficient interest for the project to be revived. Despite the obvious reservations regarding the playing and changing facilities of both clubs, Rovers and Marys were two of the new intake.

It was a big step forward, one that not only confirmed that they'd outgrown the Spartan League but also showed that they were keen to progress and better themselves. However, success on the field had to be backed up by good organisation off it and to this end both clubs had made moves to strengthen themselves in that area. Rovers, in addition to its committee members, now had more than thirty vice-presidents, a title given to those supporters who contributed financially but had no say in the everyday running of the club. Marys, though, could call upon even more support. Not only was its committee twice the size of that of Rovers, its list of vice-presidents numbered over fifty. Finance was to assume a far greater importance in the running of both clubs, not least because of the additional travelling costs involved. Then there was the matter of player remuneration.

In the Realm and Spartan League days players in both camps were expected to pay for the privilege of playing. These payments were colloquially known as 'subs', no doubt derived from the word subscription, and were used towards basic club costs like hire of the pitch, cost of equipment and match officials' fees. Travel to most destinations for away games up until now could usually be arranged using public transport and players in general had been expected to make their own way there. Not that there hadn't been the odd rumour of financial assistance. Eric Woollacott, whose brother Len had just stepped aside as Marys' secretary in favour of Syd Gray, had this to say.

EW : Nobody was paid back then but although I can't be absolutely sure I seem to remember that Marys were quite generous with expenses for away games.

Whether this was the case or not, from now on both clubs would be going by coach when on their travels and Marys would even start running special buses to all their away games for their supporters too; two shillings and sixpence for adults and a tanner for the kids. Even Rovers' second team were ferried around together but there was a distinct element of second-class status about their arrangements in comparison to the first eleven.

FG : Rovers' bus was paid for from money set aside from the receipts of games against Marys...

AC : ...and the Reserves travelled to games in the back of supporter George Simms' furniture removals van.

The Saints also started to produce a monthly newsletter to let their supporters know 'what we are doing for your entertainment'. It wasn't of the quality of Marys' earlier attempt at producing the equivalent of a matchday programme but it covered the basics like fixtures and goalscorers and went on to say: 'Well folks we are doing our best to improve your football fare by entering into much better competition. Now all we ask is your continued support, both by financial and vocal means.' The publication, lovingly knocked out on an old gestetner machine was full of typing errors but all the more appealing for it. It certainly gave an indication that Marys were on the move, an impression borne out quite forcibly when they made a close season raid on their crosstown rivals and signed four of their best players.

The most surprising signature of them all was that of Rovers' left-half Bill Whitt who, apart from a short spell with Notts Regent, had been with the club right from its inception nine years earlier. I was intrigued as to the reasons behind his move and he kindly explained the logic behind his thinking.

BW : Marys were better organised than Rovers. They were always arranging friendlies and.....I got a pound a game playing for them as well.

Now a quid might not sound that much but at the time of writing its equivalent is around twenty pounds; better than a poke in the eye with a sharp pencil. I'd had an inkling that Bill's move, and maybe those also of centre-forward Les Peel and winger Roy Carter, might just have had an element of financial inducement about it. Why else would players suddenly decamp from a side that was, by recent results alone, superior to its neighbour. Even fifty years after the event Bill was still rather coy about the subject when I spoke to him and one must assume that it wasn't quite common practice at the club. Even Geoff Parr was in receipt of no remuneration at the time and he was the Chairman's son.

The fourth member of the *émigrés* was goalkeeper Sam Archer, but the circumstances of his change of allegiance, caused by an accident at work soon after the previous season had ended, were far from financially motivated.

SA : I was a joiner working at Clowers in Daybrook Square and was putting a moulding on a piece of oak using one of the large machines, a spindle moulder. It was a single piece of timber and I wanted to get the job done quickly so I didn't put the protective guard over the cutter. I was trying to be too bloody quick and my hand slipped. The cutter was slightly above the level of the wood and the next thing two fingers on my left hand had the ends hanging off and a third was badly chewed up. If it had been a bit lower it wouldn't have happened.

My foreman came over and said "What've you done now you silly bugger", wrapped my hand in a bandage and took me down to the old General Hospital. It was ten o'clock at night when I was on the operating table because I could hear the Council House clock chime. The surgeon stitched two of the finger ends back on but the third one had to be cut down to the first joint. It didn't really hurt then but it did two weeks later when the bandages were being taken off. It must have taken two or three hours of sweat just trying to get them off. It was murder.

I'd missed a couple of games before when I dislocated a finger on my right hand. The trainer came on and tried to pull it back into place but at that time all they really knew what to do was throw water at you with a sponge. It eventually seized up and I had to have a metal wire put in it.

I was off work for ten weeks and at that time I wasn't married and lived in digs up Calverton Road, near where the Longbow is now. It was just field after field and I spent hours walking up and down them killing time. The one thing that I did get was three hundred and sixty pounds compensation as it was an industrial injury and believe it or not that money helped me buy my very first scooter. I'd have got even more money if I'd damaged my thumb and first finger instead. Funnily enough I'd already had one go at one of the fingers when I shaved a bit off on another machine, a surfacer.

It happened during the close season so the cricket got kicked into touch straightaway. Bowling right handed didn't matter but when later on when I started playing again I had to stuff cotton wool in my glove when I was batting in case I got hit on it. Of course the football was affected as well. There was no chance of me keeping goal and I wasn't good enough to play in Rovers first team as an outfield player. Then somebody suggested that I could go and play with Marys' reserves so I did.

Sam's place in Rovers' goal was filled ironically by a guy going in the opposite direction, Dougie Hodgson, but it was obvious that Marys had come out on top in the player swap. Rovers' situation then went from bad to worse when all three Cunningham brothers, John, Ken and Brian, signed professional forms for Newark outfit Ransome and Marles.

ARNOLD'S LOSS AND RANSOME'S GAIN

The Cunningham Brothers, (l to r); John, Brian, and Ken

(Brian Cunningham Collection)

BC : My brother John's best friend was Ransome's centre-forward Ernie 'Plank' Williamson. He lived in Arnold and recommended John and Ken to the club. John had been for a trial with Forest and Ken with Coventry. They were invited to play in a practice match and I went along to watch. Ernie told me to bring my boots with me and I ended up playing as well. Everything went all right and all three of us ended up signing. The travel was difficult because you had to catch one bus into town and then another at Huntingdon Street bus station to take you to Newark so then my dad bought a car specially to take us all over there together. We still had to use the bus when he wasn't available.

It was hardly a surprise then that the eleven who played in Rovers' opening game of the season contained just three players who'd figured in the last fixture of the previous one. In the circumstances the three-one win they picked up in sweltering heat over at Awsworth against a Villa side just up from the Notts Amateur League looked pretty impressive. Two goals from John Pike, newly returned from Coventry, and one from Jack Brace appeared to have got Rovers off to the best of starts, but unfortunately it was a bit of a false dawn. The Awsworth side were destined to finish rock bottom at the end of the season and Rovers' only other win in the first eight weeks of the new campaign would be the return game with Villa in late September. The other six games were all lost, the last two by big margins too; six-nil away to Kimberley YMCA and an even worse mauling, eight-one, over at Creswell against the colliery's reserve string. By the middle of October, Rovers were just two points off the bottom.

Their poor start was bad enough but it was made doubly so by the fact that the side lording it over everyone else at the top end of the table was none other than Marys themselves. In stark contrast to Rovers' difficulties the Saints had hit the ground running and dropped just two points in their own opening eight games. With Geoff Parr back in goal they'd conceded only four goals whilst rattling in thirty two at the other end and had started with an impressive scoring sequence of five, three sixes, and a four. The new boys, including Keith Moore, back at the club after a brief spell away, had all settled in well with ex-Rovers Les Peel and Bill Whitt conspicuous amongst the goalscorers. Keith's brother Charlie, well into the veteran stage of his career, also weighed in with a hat-trick in his only game in that spell. Central Alliance football obviously held no fears for the maroon and golds.

MARYS 1955-56 : Back Row (l to r); E Thompson (Committee), E Mellors (Groundsman), D Parr, R Hinson, G Parr, H Wharton, W Whitt, C Lawson, W Parr (Chairman), S Gray (Secretary). Front Row; W Archer (Trainer), C Moore, E Stones, L Peel, A Webb, R Carter.

(Courtesy Football Post)

Over at Nottingham Road, though, the changes were being rung in an urgent fashion to try and come up with a winning combination. By their ninth game no fewer than twenty three players had been tried. Some of them, like Alec Casterton, had featured in more than one position as well. In the next game, home against bottom markers British Ropes Reserves, Alec, who'd already worn the number five and number six shirts in the opening weeks, was asked to play centre-forward. The ploy worked well because he opened the scoring after twenty five minutes and Rovers went on to gain a valuable two points, edging out their Retford opponents by the odd goal in seven. Alec wouldn't keep the number nine shirt for long as he would be needed to plug gaps elsewhere but, when injury didn't keep him out, his versatility would see him go on to add right-back and inside-left to the list of positions he turned his hand to during the campaign. Rovers' close victory didn't stop the juggling of players but it did lead to two wins from the next three league matches and an improvement of four places in their position in the league.

Marys' form over the same period remained impressive. They dropped just one point in four league games against the strong reserve eleven of Ilkeston Town and dismantled Cinderhill Colliery by ten goals to one in the first round of the county cup. Even though the miners' side were no great shakes, sitting as they were at the bottom of the first division of the Notts Alliance with no points from nine outings, this was still a notable victory as the competition was now the Notts Senior Cup and this was the Saints' debut at that higher level. Rovers had received a bye and so both sides were looking forward excitedly to a successful run in the Notts FA's premier competition for its non-league clubs. Unfortunately, but intriguingly for both sets of supporters, only one of them would progress beyond the next round; they'd been pulled out of the hat together and would be meeting at Church Lane in the first week of December.

Whilst Rovers and Marys had been experiencing quite contrasting fortunes in their own new venture, there was an innovation taking place in the wider world that would influence the lives of probably everyone in the country. On September 22 ITV launched its very first broadcast and television advertising became a way of life. I can vividly remember my dad twiddling the knobs on the little box he'd bought and positioned on top of our television set and waiting with baited breath while he tried to tune in the picture. It seemed to take for ages but eventually he managed it and we sat around eager to see the very first 'commercial'. It turned out to be for Gibbs SR toothpaste and although the voice-over went on about SR standing for Sodium Ricinoleate all I can really remember was the picture of a tube of toothpaste stuck in a large cube of ice.

As, in theory, the only difference between ITV and BBC was that one was funded by its advertisers and the other by licence fees, the chances are that they would both have broadcast a news story around a week later about an up and coming young American actor tragically killed in a car crash less than a month before his second film was due to be released. The movie was 'Rebel Without a Cause' and the actor James Dean. His portrayal of a troubled teenager having a difficult relationship with his parents, together with the look that he brought to the screen, struck a chord with the under twenties, but it was his tragically early death that made him the iconic cult figure that he is today.

Social historians often bracket 'Blackboard Jungle' and 'Rebel Without a Cause' together as the point at which rock n' roll and changing attitudes amongst the younger generation collided to give voice to that section of the population that had until then always been taught to know its place. In fact the very first mention of the word 'teenager' that I've ever seen only seemed to reinforce that old world order. The Nottingham Evening News carried a headline inside an edition back in April 1950 that read 'TEEN-AGERS SHOULDN'T WEAR BLACK'. The hyphen would later be dropped of course but on the basis that kids are genetically programmed to do the opposite of what they are told it was no surprise when black later became the colour of choice for all manner of adolescent groups, rockers, punks and goths to name just three.

With James Dean already gone but destined never to be forgotten there was a chance that one or two of Arnold's young footballers might attempt to adopt his look, if not necessarily his attitude, but just a fortnight after the release of 'Rebel' they'd be in need of virtues of a far more fundamental nature; attitude of a different kind. With three weeks still to go to the mouth watering prospect of Rovers and Marys meeting in the Senior Cup, there was to be a dress rehearsal when the two teams met down on the Bottom Rec for league points. Whilst Rovers' list of players, now at twenty six for the season, was ten more than Marys', and the two teams were separated by ten places and eleven points in the table, the fact that this was a local derby meant that nothing of any great significance should be read into what had happened so far this season. Another large crowd and scores to settle were just two of the ingredients that meant it should turn out to be another close encounter of the local kind.

And it did; the ninth local derby ended just as the very first two had in a three-all draw. Rovers' old goalscoring partnership of Jack Tulley and Les Peel were prominent again, only this time of course they were on opposite sides. Jack opened the scoring for the red and whites after just eight minutes and repeated the feat before half-time after Les had grabbed an equaliser for the Saints. Rovers' usual number two Franny Greensmith had been picked at left-back to help counter the threat of Charlie Moore on Marys' right wing, whilst the number six shirt of each team was worn by a Whitt brother, Bill for the Saints and younger sibling Ron for Rovers. It all made for a tight contest and there was very little to choose between the two sides as the game progressed, although the home side did come close to claiming the winner. Ron Whitt, who'd only been in the side a few weeks, was playing against Marys for the very first time.

RW : I remember the game well, it ended three-three, and I hit the bar with a header. Then I got injured and ended up hobbling out on the left wing. There were no substitutes allowed so they just stuck you out there and told you that when the ball came to you to just take it into the corner. When they tried to get the ball off you they kicked seven bells out of you even though you were already injured.

Luckily for Ron his knock had a fortnight to clear up as Rovers were without a match the following week and he'd recovered sufficiently to be able to take his place in the side for the three-two win over Linby Colliery Reserves as the red and whites maintained their recent improvement in form. Marys had mixed fortunes in their own couple of games before the Senior Cup clash with Rovers, beating Awsworth Villa but dropping a couple of points away to Belper Town Reserves. This setback didn't affect their position at the top of the table so both sides headed for the Top Rec with much the same thought; it would be them going through into the next round.

ACTION FROM THE SENIOR CUP : DOUG HODGSON SAVES FROM LES PEEL'S DIVING HEADER, 3 DEC 1955

(Courtesy Football Post)

Of course in cup ties there can only be one winner and whilst the Saints kept the same line-up from the first game Rovers tinkered with their side slightly in trying to gain an edge; Franny Greensmith reverted to right-back and Ken Renshaw took the number four shirt. In blustery conditions before another large crowd Marys, despite home field advantage, got off to the worst possible start as the visitors' centre-forward Jack Brace collected a pass and shot on the run past Geoff Parr. From then on and despite having the wind in their faces the Saints laid siege to Rovers' goal. Les Peel and Charlie Moore both hit the crossbar and Rovers' centre-half Ken Dove had to clear off his own goal line on no fewer than three occasions. As is often the case when a team is taking a pounding the red and whites rode their luck and held out until the break. Probably realising that they had taken Marys' best shots and were still standing, they had much the better of the second period and ran out three-one winners. Not only did they end the Saints' interest in the Senior Cup for another year, Rovers also emphasised their dominance in the series of head-to-head matches between the two clubs. In the ten clashes so far, the Nottingham Road side had won five to Marys' two, with the trio of three-all draws completing the picture. At least the maroon and golds wouldn't have long to wait to try and extract their revenge; the return league game on the Top Rec was just three short weeks away, scheduled for the traditional crowd-pulling ten thirty start on Boxing Day morning.

The Saints had maintained the comfort of top spot in the league but they were taken apart seven-one at the Manor Ground the following week by the second string of Ilkeston Town, their third defeat in a row. It didn't help that on the same day an unchanged Rovers' side despatched Belper Town Reserves, the team who'd started Marys' poor run of results, by three goals to one. It seemed that there could be a crisis of sorts brewing, especially when

Les Peel made the surprising decision, viewed from the outside at least, to return to the Rovers. Maybe he'd been unsettled by the recent downturn in the Saints' form or maybe he hadn't settled in as well as his consistency in front of goal had indicated. Whatever the real reasons for him jumping ship he knew that he'd be unable to take part in any further rounds of the Senior Cup for Rovers as having just played against them he'd become 'cup-tied', ineligible to take any further part in the competition. He would also be aware that the least of Rovers' problems this particular season had been the centre-forward spot where Jack Brace was already closing in on twenty goals just halfway through the campaign. The red and whites overcame the problem of fitting their new signing in by leaving out left-winger Jimmy Raven, an early season acquisition from South Normanton, moving Jack Tulley over from the right flank to take his place, and handing Jack's number seven shirt to Les. The forward line now was Peel, Maddocks, Brace, Pike, Tulley; every one of them a natural goalscorer and a combination liable to fill opposing defences with a sense of foreboding.

Ironville Amateurs were the first to feel the force of this new attacking formation as Rovers smashed in seven goals past them and then followed that up with another four the following Saturday, Christmas Eve, against Shirebrook Miners' Welfare Reserves. With just one defeat in their last ten matches Rovers had moved steadily up the table to fifth place whilst Marys were still league leaders thanks to a four-nil victory the same day against Heanor Town's second eleven. The set up for the Boxing Day clash couldn't have been better and again there was little to choose between the sides. Each side was looking for that little edge to give them an advantage and what followed made this one of the most memorable derbies the two teams would ever contest. Eric Thompson was on the Saints' committee at the time.

ET : If you were with a team in a Nottinghamshire league the rules allowed you to play for another club in the Central Alliance because that was a Derbyshire league. 'Kegga' Parr and the committee wanted to get their own back on Rovers so they turned out a couple of Gedling Colliery players, Walter Kirk and Johnny Goodson, to strengthen the team. I think they'd tried it the Saturday before against Heanor when they won four-nil.

RW : There was a rumour about Marys using guest players and I think that 'Nark' Anthony, Rovers' chairman, tried to do the same.

In actual fact Rovers fielded almost the same side that had played less than forty eight hours earlier, except that Alec Casterton took over at left-half from Ron Whitt and Franny Greensmith returned at right-back.

RW : I turned up on the morning of the game expecting to play but there was no shirt for me. I was really annoyed to be left out.

Ron had been filling in for Alec whilst he was either out due to an injury he'd picked up early in November against Sutton Town Reserves or popping up in another position to cover anybody else who was unavailable.

AC : You had to be versatile. By the time I'd finished I'd played in every position for Rovers except goalkeeper and when I got injured against Sutton I was playing left-back. There were ridges in the pitch on the Bottom Rec and I fell awkwardly and injured my wrist. 'Tazza' Dove was the bucket and sponge man but his knowledge of being a trainer as regards football was more or less zero. My hand looked like it was hanging off and 'Tazza' tried to set it. He shouldn't really have touched it, he should have just put it into a splint and got me off to hospital. It was a Colles' fracture but the hospital wouldn't reset it because I'd still got all my movement. I was off work for four or five weeks until they took the cast off.

The derby was Alec's second game back after his lay-off and his memories of the day are pretty vivid.

AC : We all went out to celebrate Christmas the night before and on Boxing Day morning I walked from Basford and joined up with John Pike on Oxclose Lane where we'd arranged to meet. You could see people walking towards Arnold from all over the place, everyone heading for the ground. We joined up with Jack Tulley and Jack Brace up at Roy Carter's house, that was our meeting place, and then went down to Calverton Road School to get changed.

In front of what Alec reckons was the biggest crowd ever to attend an Arnold derby, the wisdom of Marys' inclusion of a couple of 'foreigners' in their side was severely questioned.

AC : Marys had got it into their heads that they were going to walk all over us with their star studded team but it backfired on them.

ET : Trouble was Marys got sucked in using these players. They forgot that by now Marys and Rovers were already better teams than Gedling.

Unfortunately for 'Kegga' and company, the Saints had no answer to Rovers' incessant probing and a day that started out with high expectations pretty soon started to rapidly deteriorate.

AC : I went up for a header with Marys' Ernie Stones and he did his neck stretching for it. It could have been shoulder to shoulder but I heard the crack as we went up and hit one another. I think they took him off straight away and when I saw him in town later on in the evening he'd got a collar round him. There was no serious injury but it was bad enough to stop him carrying on. We all went in hard, we all played hard.

Ernie's altercation with Alec would see him sidelined for the best part of three months, but that wasn't the only skirmish involving Rovers' left-half that morning.
AC : Somebody went into Bill Whitt, it could have been Franny [Greensmith]. Bill was down injured and I went to pick him up saying "Get up you silly old so-and-so". Fran just turned to me and said "Leave him!" I'll not tell you what he actually said because I don't swear but he wasn't happy because he thought of Bill as a traitor, a turncoat for leaving us for Marys.

Walter Kirk's fearsome reputation as one of the toughest players around at the time had been well earned and even though it was meant to be the season of peace and goodwill to all men he soon let Rovers' players know that festivities had been put on hold when he tried to remove John Pike from his clothing.

JP : Walter Kirk was a hard player and my shorts were all ripped by one of his tackles. The Rovers' crowd were all booing him but I was laughing like hell. He was alright, Walter, he was there to nail you, but he just couldn't catch me.

So, with the Saints down to ten men and struggling to accommodate their guest players and Rovers quite obviously up for it, the match turned into a nightmare for the home side.

RW : I seem to remember that John Pike scored three or four. He had a blinding game.

Whatever John's tally was would probably have been enough to win the game for Rovers on its own but there was much worse to come.

GP : I'm sure that Les Peel got five.

Charlie Moore's younger brother Albert, who was scoring regularly for Marys' reserves, was amongst the large crowd who could hardly believe what they were seeing.

AM : John Pike had a blinder. I think he got three. Rovers gave a marvellous exhibition of football and completely controlled the game. They thoroughly deserved to win and Marys never had a chance. And I'm saying that as a Marys' man through and through.

AC : Jack Tulley played brilliantly against Walter Kirk. I think Les Peel scored four.

Now whether John Pike scored three or four or Les Peel contributed four or five remains open to question but what is not in doubt is that the final scoreline unbelievably finished eight-nil in Rovers' favour and Marys had been well and truly routed in their own back yard.

Interestingly, at least by today's standards and considering that he'd spent a large part of the morning retrieving the ball from the back of his net, the Saints' last line of defence, Geoff Parr, accepted the humiliating defeat in good grace.

GP : I know we got beat eight-nil but I have to say that I enjoyed the game. You wouldn't think it but I actually played ok, but Rovers were just much too good for us on the day. Some days you get beat, and we definitely got beat that day. We had no complaints. There were no hard feelings. Both sides still went to the top room of the Seven Stars after the match for sandwiches and a drink.

No matter how good the fare on offer, it must have taken some swallowing by the home contingent. The Football Post reported the result as a 'sensation' and it was certainly that. It's not often that a team at the top of any self-respecting league loses at home by eight clear goals, especially to their nearest rivals and in front of one of the biggest crowds ever to gather in the town for a football match. The fact that it was Marys' heaviest post-war home defeat seemed almost an irrelevance and there was no doubt that it would take quite a while to live down the embarrassment.

Five days later Rovers fine form continued as they finished the year by extending their unbeaten run to nine games with a four-two home victory over Stanton Ironworks but Marys week, already memorable for the wrong reasons, took yet another turn for the worse. This time it was an individual player who suffered, rather than the team as a whole. It was a perfect day for football as the Saints made their first trip to the humble surroundings that passed for the home of Long Eaton Zingari. It was Marys' first ever visit to the Derbyshire club but one that would be remembered by Charlie Moore in particular for a very long time.

ET : Geoff Parr took a corner and Charlie went up for the ball with the goalie. The keeper caught Charlie in the back with his knee but there was no malice about it. Charlie left the field and then came back on again a bit later.

AM : I wasn't at the game because I was playing for the reserves but later that night Charlie took bad and he was shipped into hospital and ended up losing a kidney. I'll always remember it was New Year's Eve because Charlie went in for his operation one year and came out the next. He was off work for ages and even when he went back he could only manage part-time to start with because he got tired very quickly. Of course it finished his football career and he never played again. Apart from that he was fine and after all he did live to be eighty four.

It might have been the end for Charlie as a player but it didn't stop him from devoting many years of his post-playing career into helping run the Saints, along with brother Albert, until well into the nineteen seventies.

Of course injury never comes with a welcome sign and nor does the hangman's noose, but just five months earlier Ruth Ellis became the last woman to be executed in Britain after she was found guilty of shooting her lover, racing driver David Blakeley. If that unfortunate lady warrants an entry in the annals of 1955 then another female deserves a place for the most commendable of reasons.

Two days before Rovers despatched Marys from the Senior Cup Rosa Parks, a black American seamstress, boarded a bus in Montgomery, Alabama and sat with three other blacks in the fifth row. Under the segregation laws then in existence the first four rows were reserved for whites only. A few stops later, the white rows were filled but one white man was left standing. According to the law, blacks and whites couldn't sit on the same row so the driver asked all four of the blacks seated in the fifth row to move. Three complied, but the seamstress refused and was arrested. Her action led to a boycott of the city's buses by its black population, a situation that took nearly a year and much civil unrest to resolve. It wasn't until November the following year that the US Supreme Court declared segregation on buses unconstitutional that the Montgomery Bus Boycott was officially over. Whilst the gains achieved by the boycott were small in comparison to what would be achieved later it was an important start to what became known as the Civil Rights Movement, a campaign that would reach its zenith in 1965 when basic civil rights were finally guaranteed for all Americans, regardless of race.

Thankfully, this country never operated an official state-supported policy of *apartheid* but even on the buses that served Arnold back in the nineteen fifties there was segregation of a different sort and an element of prohibition too. Standing was forbidden on the upper deck but back in the days when smoking wasn't considered to be the anti-social pastime it is today you could light up to your heart's content. Smoke, being smoke, still funnelled its way down the staircase and with these being foggier and smoggier times anyway passengers downstairs continually ran the risk of an occasional bout of coughing and spluttering. Just in case anyone might have thought of clearing their throat, there was a sign at the front of the bus to remind them to reach for their hankie; it read "NO SPITTING".

Fortunately 1956 would see the government take a giant step forward in eradicating air pollution as the Clean Air Act would finally get passed later in the year. If it didn't exactly herald the end of 'pea-soupers' it certainly limited their frequency, although ironically the year itself started with just the kind of weather that the legislation was introduced to combat. Heavy fog had hung around Nottingham all morning of the first Saturday in January, putting many matches in doubt right up until the kick-off. The gates at Meadow Lane were only opened to the public on the referee's say so just twenty five minutes before County's cup tie against Fulham was due to begin and both Marys and Rovers ended up without a fixture.

Seven days later it was the turn of snow, ice, and torrential rain to wreak havoc with the football programme but this time the two Arnold sides escaped the worst of the elements. A much changed Saints' side travelled to the Gatehouse Ground to play Linby Colliery Reserves. Sam Archer, who of course had been Rovers' first team goalie until his accident at work, had done so well on the right wing for the second eleven that he was one of the players called into the first team. He fully justified his promotion by scoring Marys' first goal in a four-three victory and summed up his elevation thus:

SA : I don't suppose I was that rubbish, then.

AC : Sam wasn't a bad winger at all. He used to whip the ball over really well.

Now whilst Sam was getting his name on the scoresheet for the Saints, his old club were engaged in the next round of the Notts Senior Cup where their opponents were Raleigh Athletic from the Notts Alliance. With quite a few of the Rovers' side being employees of the cycle manufacturers there was a tremendous level of interest in the tie and a crowd of just over two thousand packed the Bottom Rec. There had been heavy rain throughout the night and again during the morning of the match, leaving the surface extremely slippery. This was no deterrent to Rovers' nippy forward line and not longer after the kick-off the red and whites had seen two efforts, one from Jack Brace and the other from John Pike, come back off the crossbar with the goalie beaten. Unfortunately the visitors took the lead against the run of play after ten minutes but a quarter of an hour later John Pike equalised from a Jimmy Raven cross. The scores stayed level until half-time but two goals before the hour mark from Jack Brace gave Rovers a two-goal lead that ultimately proved too difficult for Raleigh to claw back. The game ended four-two to Rovers, a victory that was all the more admirable as the cyclists had themselves knocked out Eastwood Town the round before by three goals to one.

Marys, with just the league left to concentrate on, were still not having the greatest of times and yet the loss of points by sides nearest to them meant that they were hanging on to top spot at the end of January. Rovers had just one game for points in the month and drew three-all with Ilkeston Town Reserves to keep in touch with the Saints, six points behind with two games in hand. Alec Casterton reckons it was one of the most memorable games of his career.

AC : The game was played in hail, rain and sleet. Even then it was a cracking game and Johnny Pike in particular scored two goals and played a blinder. It was so bitter that Ken Dove, who was cold even on hot days, couldn't undo his boot laces because he was that frozen. We chucked him in the big bath to thaw him out.

The Nottingham Road side though were preoccupied at this time with the Senior Cup and just a fortnight after seeing off Raleigh they were rewarded with another home tie, this time against Central Alliance Division One side British Ropes. Rovers made just one change to the eleven who had been successful in the previous round. John Pike had decided to have a second stab at making it as a full-time professional and had signed a two year contract with Derby County for a basic three pounds per match. Alec Casterton took over at inside-left but Ron Whitt was unlucky once again. Just as he might have thought that he would be back in favour the number six shirt was handed to Ken Atherley.

Another large crowd was anticipated down on the Bottom Rec as Forest had a blank afternoon, Notts were playing away at Brentford, and the only other game of any consequence in the locality was Gedling Colliery's FA Amateur Cup first round replay against Northern Nomads up at Plains Road. However, conditions on the morning of the two games were particularly grim and up at Mapperley fog was drifting across the pitch to such an extent that it was impossible to see from one goal to the other. Visibility was that bit better down in Arnold as Rovers laid siege to their visitors' goal. The home side did everything but score and were caught out on the break, conceding a soft goal that gave the Retford side the lead at half-time. Not to be deterred, the red and whites fought back to equalise after the break and that was the way the tie stayed until the ninety minute mark. Thankfully the light was good enough for extra time to be played and with Rovers now in the ascendancy they notched a second in the final half-hour to secure an impressive victory.

In a winter already notable for its poor weather snow came back in February to make playing conditions difficult at best. The elements restricted Marys to just two home games during the month, both of which they successfully negotiated; seven-four against Ironville Amateurs and four-three against Kimberley YMCA. Rovers, though, came undone either side of their next county cup tie and lost both their league games to slip back to tenth place. The Saints, whilst nowhere near as fluent as in the opening half of the season, remained top of the pile with only the second elevens of Creswell Colliery and Ilkeston Town having dropped fewer points.

However, the big attraction in the town during the month was Rovers' Senior Cup game against old Spartan League rivals Aspley Old Boys. This was the Quarter Final stage of the competition, the last eight, and the red and whites had again had the luck of the draw, being first name out of the hat for the third consecutive round. The Old Boys weren't to be taken lightly because, unlike the two Arnold clubs, they'd already had experience of the Senior Cup before this season and had achieved a good deal of success in the competition too. Even though Roy Carter had recently followed Les Peel's lead in swapping the Top Rec for the Bottom one both players were cup-tied and with no John Pike either, Rovers would have their work cut out if they were to make it to the semis.

Snow had been mostly cleared from the pitch but at kick-off the surface was still very slippery and it was the visitors who acclimatised themselves better to the conditions in the early stages, going ahead through a header from right-winger Fidler after just a quarter of an hour. Things got worse for the home side as goalie Doug Hodgson was beaten by a second header before the break, this time scored by centre-forward Grimshaw. Both goals had come from crosses from left-winger Stan Balchin. Alec Casterton, back at left-half, remembers the occasion ruefully.

AC : Aspley had a good side; Fidler, Stainwright, Hornbuckle, Balchin. It seemed that every time they went down they scored. Every chance, every half chance. It was just one of those games.

Indeed it was, because Aspley added another three in the second half with Rovers powerless to do anything about it. Drawing a complete blank themselves they ended up on the wrong end of a five-nil hammering and whilst it wasn't quite the ending that had been envisaged beforehand there could be no complaints. And whilst Rovers' players and fans might have been severely down in the dumps as a result, over on the other side of the Atlantic a young man was professing to be a bit heartbroken too but in reality was far from it as he was just about to embark on a career that would see him become immortalised as the 'King of Rock n' Roll'.

Elvis Presley had been signed by the massive Radio Corporation of America (RCA) just before the turn of the year and in January had made his first appearance on national TV. The same month he'd recorded the seminal 'Heartbreak Hotel' and whilst footballers were sloshing their way through snow over here, the record was working its way up the American charts until it finally hit top spot, giving the young singer his first but definitely not his last number one record. The world of popular music would never be the same again as hit followed hit during the rest of the year, with 'I Want You, I Need You, I Love You', 'Hound Dog', 'Don't Be Cruel', and 'Love Me Tender' all reaching the top of the charts. The impact of this latest icon of the younger generation wasn't limited to the music either. Just as James Dean helped inspire a look and a certain style, so Elvis reinforced it. His appeal became even more enduring to those of a certain age when his gyrating movements from the waist down, later to land him with the nickname 'Elvis the Pelvis', led to uproar in the media and resulted in the absurd spectacle of TV showing him only from the waist up despite hardly moving when he was singing the religious song 'Peace In The Valley'. Even though he was just a good ol' country boy at heart, the young Mississippian found himself unwittingly at the vanguard of an invisible movement that was challenging the old conservatism in his country and which would eventually repeat itself across the Atlantic.

There were a number of riots at his earlier concerts leading to the National Guard being called out to prevent any repeat and a court in Jacksonville, Florida called him a savage, saying that his music was undermining the youth of America. He was regarded as a threat to the moral well-being of American women and even the mother of his future wife Priscilla allegedly said that he 'arouses things in teenage girls that shouldn't be aroused'. His music was called wicked, heathen, and obscene by those of a nervous disposition as well as being seen as a danger to American culture. Considering that this was the very same culture that had seen the instrumental 'The Poor People Of Paris' by Les Baxter's Chorus and Orchestra hold the top spot in the charts for six weeks prior to Elvis' arrival there were many who probably thought that this 'danger' was worth the risk. When fellow singer Roy Orbison first saw him perform he was moved to say that 'there was no reference point in the culture to compare it' whilst some time later Beatle John Lennon would be quoted as saying 'before Elvis there was nothing'.

Whilst Elvis' star had risen rapidly, Rovers' had fallen almost as quickly when losing all three of their games in February. Now, with just a couple of months left in the season, they had a dozen games left in which to try and improve on the tenth place that their recent dip in form had seen them slip to. The forward line took on a familiar look too; from seven to eleven it read : Jack Tulley, Ron Maddocks, Les Peel, Jack Brace, and Roy Carter. Even though Roy, Jack Brace, and Alec Casterton were the only three players who had started the season in the side back in August, a season in which the red and whites had used no fewer than thirty three different players, three whole teams' worth, Rovers still managed to keep a fairly settled formation in the run-in. It showed in the results too with just one match being lost, two drawn, and nine won, including seven in a row to close out the campaign. One of the wins was against Shirebrook and the after match socialising showed that the spirit in the camp was pretty good too.

Not only was Jack Tulley one of the most prolific goalscoring wingers in local football, he was also the team's practical joker, as a number of his teammates were only too willing to testify. He was on particularly good form after the Shirebrook match.

FG : Jack was a real joker. We went to Shirebrook and after the game we went in the pub and played dominoes. After we'd finished Jack put the dominoes in Ken Dove's pocket but Ken never knew they were there. Next morning when Ken woke up the police were at his door!

Sometimes you'd have your case there and when you picked it up Jack had put a couple of house bricks in it. He was a real comic was Jack.

JP : Not only was he one of the best footballers I've ever seen for a little bloke but what a comedian he was. I can remember him putting two bricks in somebody's overcoat pockets. He was a practical joker, always smiling. I liked him very much.

AC : Oh Jack was a case, he would do anything. He used to turn the cold water hose on me after the game because I was the young one in the side. He had fantastic balance, either way. I've seen him jump up on a table and hop around the pint glasses on it on one foot, never spilling a drop.

Joking aside, other notable playing achievements in the run-in were the scoring of double figures against Heanor Town Reserves and a victory by the odd goal in three against the second eleven of Creswell Colliery who were fighting Marys for top spot in the race for the championship. When the final table was drawn up Rovers finished in sixth place, just three points behind the runners-up; a tremendous achievement considering their awful start to their new Central Alliance venture.

The Saints' chances of picking up the league trophy had been much the stronger of the two Arnold sides, despite the in and out form they'd shown following their blistering start to the season. A glance at the fixture list for March showed that it would be a make or break month for the maroon and golds as they had to face strong opposition from the coalfields. A tough match against Ollerton Colliery was sandwiched between home and away games against their nearest challengers Creswell Colliery Reserves.

Marys had continued to hit the net consistently but they'd been letting them in rather too frequently at the other end too. Geoff Parr had reverted to outside left and his place in goal had been taken by Bob Kinton, but the new keeper had had a baptism of fire and had suffered the misfortune of having to pick the ball out of his net twelve times in his first three matches. When that became sixteen after just twenty five minutes of the home game with Creswell the writing was on the wall both for his tenure in the Saints' goal and for the team's chances of retaining top spot for much longer. To be fair Marys put up a spirited resistance during the remaining sixty five minutes and scored four times themselves but with the miners adding another couple they went down fighting by six goals to four. The defeat brought Creswell to within a single point of the Saints despite having played three games fewer and when, four weeks later, the miners completed the double with a four-nil victory Marys' chances of honours in their first season at this level had evaporated.

With Bob Kinton's tally now standing at an unfortunate eighteen goals conceded in just four games it was inevitable that a change would be made and the week following the crucial six-four setback to Creswell the committee turned to Len Rockley, who had originally made his debut in a friendly back on Christmas Day 1952. Len had featured for both the first and second elevens since that time but had been away for two years on National Service until late 1955. Now he'd been given the chance to establish himself as the first team keeper for the foreseeable future and he grabbed it with both hands. The first goal that he conceded on his return to the side took four hours and thirty eight minutes to arrive. He'd been the last line of a defence that hadn't been breached for three straight games and it was only when Creswell opened the scoring not long after the kick-off in the return game that he experienced the disappointment of letting a goal in. He also kept three more clean sheets in the last five games of the season as Marys did their utmost to cling on to second place in the table. Ultimately they fell that little bit short, finishing in fourth spot just a single point behind Ilkeston Town Reserves and Wilmorton and six behind the champions Creswell.

Ironically, if a hybrid of Marys' first fourteen games and Rovers' last twenty could be spliced together, then the combined effort of the Arnold sides would have been enough to win the league by three clear points. It was a pity that neither of the sides could sustain their performances for a whole season but, even so, it had been a very successful start to their sojourn in the Central Alliance. Both sides had had to cast about for players who could make the big step up to the higher level and there had been a significant degree of wastage along the way. Marys eventually ended up giving try-outs to even more guys than their neighbours, at least thirty four and counting.

It was strange in a way too to see no silverware heading Arnold's way after four uninterrupted years of success but there was no doubt that it was going to be harder for the two clubs to add to their trophy cabinet now they'd moved up a level. It still hadn't stopped the local rivalry from giving the local fans three games to remember and one in particular that will be hard to forget by anyone who was there that fateful Boxing Day morning. As to who was the better side, well it is hard to say as there was hardly a Rizla paper between them. Both teams had their purple patches and Marys did, after all, finish two places higher and two points better off than Rovers. However, on the basis of the latter's great dominance in their head to head clashes, it would be hard to argue against the claims, yet again, of the Nottingham Road outfit.

ROVERS : FIVE CHAMPIONSHIPS, SIX CUPS (INCL ONE SHARED)

MARYS : ONE CHAMPIONSHIP, THREE CUPS (INCL ONE SHARED)

REGENT : THREE CUPS

CHAPTER TWELVE 1956-57

As the phenomenon that was Elvis gradually became less threatening he was inevitably embraced by America's major contribution to popular culture, Hollywood. When 20th Century Fox released his acting debut 'Love Me Tender' later in 1956 it had a far greater impact than the movie critics of the time could have imagined, especially to kids outside the USA who'd not had much chance to catch a glimpse of him, or the top half of him at least, other than from still photographs or the occasional clip on television. Whatever it was that had swathes of American females swooning at his concerts and television performances, it would soon be magnified up there on the silver screen, and young British ladies of an impressionable age, together with almost as many curious male associates, would be able to see what all the fuss had been about.

In the middle years of the fifties it was possible, if you lived in Arnold and were an Elvis fan as well, to catch him down at the local cinema because, amazing as it may seem in these days of Multiplexes, the town had its own picture house, the Bonington. In fact if Daybrook is included there were two as the Roxy, situated on Ribblesdale Road adjacent to its junction with Mansfield Road and Thackerays Lane, was no more than three or four bus stops or a good brisk walk away from the doors of the 'Bonno' itself.

The Bonington was sited diagonally opposite the building that is now home to The Ernehale pub but back then was a branch of the Co-op on the crossroads formed by St Albans Road, Arnot Hill Road, and Nottingham Road. My mother used to take me there quite regularly, especially on a Friday night, and whilst I can't remember seeing 'Love Me Tender' there I can recall acting as her escort when she wanted to view the latest in a line of musicals that were amongst her particular favourites. I'd probably been with her to see 'Oklahoma' the previous year but the one that sticks in my memory the most is Rodgers and Hammerstein's 'Carousel'. Released earlier in the year it introduced 'You'll Never Walk Alone' to those not already familiar with it from the stage play that had debuted on Broadway just over ten years prior to it being adapted for the big screen. Some time later Gerry and the Pacemakers, despite taking it to number one in the UK charts, would murder the song whilst at the same time paving the way for it to become the terrace anthem of their hometown football club Liverpool and then sometime thereafter of Glasgow Celtic too.

The reason that I accompanied my mother to the flicks was quite simple. Back in the mid nineteen fifties it was still considered inappropriate behaviour for a woman on her own to frequent any public place of entertainment, lest it should give the wrong impression as to her character. Pubs especially were no-go areas for a sole female whilst cinemas weren't far behind in expecting her to attend with a companion in tow. My younger brother was just a toddler and as my father's love of musicals wasn't quite as enthusiastic as his wife's he was more than happy to do the baby sitting. Of course my chaperoning skills came at a price, not least of which was a visit to the sweet shop next door to the Bonington the very moment we alighted from the number fifty two bus that stopped right outside.

It was called the 'Arcadia Confectionery & Tobacco Stores' and was effectively the kiosk for the cinema, which wasn't quite as strange as it may sound because both operations were owned by the same family, the Wardles. I can remember the shop more clearly in the sixties and seventies but it was one of those places that always gave you the impression that it had hardly changed at all down the years. The gentleman who ran the shop always wore a kind of dark house jacket and was very dapper with a thin pencil moustache. I know from experience that he was very strict and at a time when the return of empty pop bottles was rewarded with a penny or two refund he would never part with his money if there was even a shadow of a doubt in his mind that it was one that he had originally sold. Of course as this was many years before the mass-packaged supermarket system that actively encourages the purchase of more than you really want or more importantly actually need – a six-pack of this or 'twelve for the price of ten, twenty percent extra free' of that – a youngster like me could make a few pence go a long way. With most items that took my fancy being available loose it was two ounces of these and two ounces of those and if I really played my cards right then I might be able to increase my goody bag with a selection of those 'four for a penny' sweets that were teasingly placed at the front of the glass counter at just the right height for a seven year old.

Now whilst I might have been familiar with the wares on sale at the 'Arcadia Stores' it was a different matter altogether when it came to the next building along. This was home to two separate businesses, a butcher's shop and Mrs Spouge's fancy goods and hardware emporium. I am assured by members of both Rovers' and Marys' camps that there was an illicit bookies 'at the back' of the butchers which they may or may not have made personal use of, but there was a secondary element to the business next door too, one which many of the town's players had definitely availed themselves of. It was Bill Spouge's physiotherapy practice, one that he ran out of the back room of his wife's shop. Alec Casterton, who was more often in the wars than not, recalls the gentleman's prowess.

AC : Bill was an ex-boxer, which probably explains his broken nose, but he was a good cricketer as well. He used to look after players from Forest and Notts as well as the City Police. I think he also had a diploma in herbalism, something like that. You usually ended up with your leg in a bucket full of herbs to get the swelling down because he knew what concoctions to mix so that he could get at the problem to feel what was there. He put bones back in place and he was one of the first people to get hold of an infra-red lamp. I sometimes spent the whole day round there when I was coming back from an injury. He was very good.

Of course injuries were an occupational hazard of every footballer, full-time or part-time, professional or amateur, and whilst there is a generally accepted view that the lower the standard the greater the degree of 'clogging' that goes on, an exaggerated emphasis on the physical side of the game rather than its technical and skilful aspects, there is no doubt that even as Rovers and Marys took steps to improve their status in life the rigours of football in the fifties would inevitably take their toll.

The Central Alliance, just like its more senior neighbour the Midland League, was no place for the faint-hearted, no stage for the fancy-dan, but it was serious in its attempts to increase its own credibility in the non-league scheme of things and to this end it had decided to extend its boundaries to include teams from outside its current heartland. Although it wouldn't affect the playing schedules of the two Arnold clubs in the coming season, the impact of spreading the league's wings would certainly be felt in the near future but for now it only affected the top division which had needed to be extended into two roughly geographic sections, north and south. It was the latter of these two sections which had a newer, more exotic look about them. It still contained teams from Derbyshire, Leicestershire and Lincolnshire but its cosmopolitan look came from the arrival of sides from Norfolk, Cambridgeshire, Northamptonshire and Bedfordshire. With the increase in private car ownership and the attendant embracing of travel as the norm rather than the exception, expectations within football were being stretched too. Where once upon a time football outside the full-time professional ranks was invariably a local pursuit, now it was becoming a regional one, and the boundaries of the region were pretty elastic too.

There was just one slight anomaly in the reorganisation of the league and that was that two teams, Wilmorton & Alvaston and Ollerton Colliery were both elevated to the top division even though they'd finished just 3rd amd 5th in the second division the previous season compared with Marys' and Rovers' 4th and 6th positions respectively. Just what it was that the other two clubs had that enabled them to clinch their promotion ahead of Arnold's finest was privy only to the league itself. There had been talk the previous season when the expansionist plan was being mooted that the Saints might be included in the Northern Section of Division One, leaving Rovers marooned where they were. The Football Post even posed the question "Would Arnold St Marys ...be willing to forego their local rivalry with Arnold Rovers?" Personally, I think the answer was obvious. Given the fact of Rovers' dominance in recent years and the desire by 'Kegga' Parr, Syd Gray and the rest of Marys' committee to advance the cause of their own club, any chance to leave their town rivals behind for any reason would have been one they'd have grasped wholeheartedly. It didn't come to that though and the football fans of Arnold would have to content themselves with another season of the Central Alliance at second division level. There would however be a major change in proceedings for both clubs, courtesy of a bit of wheeling and dealing in the world of commerce.

In actual fact it was a little more parochial than that. The Daybrook-based Home Brewery had for some time wanted to build a new public house at the bottom of Gedling Road at its junction with Brookfield Road and Derby Street. When eventually completed in 1958 it would be known as the Friar Tuck and would operate under the licence previously held at the Butcher's Arms on Front Street. As part of the *quid pro quo* that saw them given the go-ahead to develop the site the Brewery had generously given some six acres of adjacent land to the Arnold Urban District Council back in 1950 to be used in perpetuity by the people of Arnold. This was designated as a King George V (KGV) playing field and was intended to enable the local population to enjoy 'outdoor games, sports and pastimes' as laid down by the original King George's Fields Foundation some twenty years earlier on the death of the King in 1936.

As a result of this gift a variety of facilities were provided, not all of which have survived into the twenty-first century. As it happened the project had taken some time to come to fruition because tenders weren't sought for the initial laying out of the football pitch until February 1954 but at least it remains, along with the cricket pitch and children's playground. Unfortunately the original putting green and tennis courts are no more than a pleasant memory. Even as I write it seems that there are those in the district who would like to see the playing of the nation's two most popular sports disappear from Gedling Road too. These anti-sport killjoys appear to have no appreciation of tradition in the town either because, in the case of the winter game in particular, football has been played on that particular piece of land since at least the early nineteen hundreds.

A football pitch on the site of the current one is clearly shown and named as such on a 1904 Ordnance Survey map of the area currently held in the Arnold Library, and just a couple of years later the ground was actually shared by two local sides; the matter-of-factly named Arnold and the more exotically titled Daybrook Olympic. In an echo of Marys' and Rovers' own more recent changing facilities at the Seven Stars and Greyhound pubs respectively, the young players of a hundred years ago were expected to 'dress' at the Horse and Jockey before making their way down Front Street, fully kitted out amidst the Saturday afternoon shoppers, on their way to the pitch. The ground was also used down the years for other events, most notably the annual Flower Show, but now in the mid fifties it would once again be home to two local football clubs as Marys and Rovers readily accepted the Council's invitation to leave the Top and Bottom Recs behind and share the facilities of the new and, as the Football Post reported it, 'well appointed enclosure'.

Quite what they meant by 'well appointed' is not clear, especially as the re-development of the site was in its embryonic stage and there were as yet no changing facilities for the players and officials. A solution was sought, and found, that would make playing away against the two Arnold sides a pleasure for visiting teams; off the pitch at least. For the immediate future players would have the use of what the locals called the Arnold Baths but which might more correctly be referred to as the Arnold Public Baths and Swimming Pool. Located just a couple of hundred yards away from the pitch, it sat opposite the side of the Bonington Cinema on Arnot Hill Road and adjacent to the back of the Library which fronted on to Nottingham Road. Much as before there was the necessity of a bit of a walk to the ground itself, this time along Hallam's Lane, but back then this was a relatively sleepy little backwater quite unrecognisable from the busy thoroughfare it is today. These arrangements worked well, at least apart from one particular occasion involving an unfortunate Bill Whitt; an incident recalled with some relish by team-mate Sam Archer.

SA : Normally we got back to the baths around a quarter to five and by the time we'd taken off our muddy football gear and had a shower the Baths Superintendent had cleared the public out of the swimming pool. On this particular day Bill had finished showering and decided to take a dip straight afterwards. He'd got nothing on as he left the changing room but unfortunately for some reason there were still people using the pool. It was very embarrassing for Bill but it made me chuckle.

The Council wanted the two teams to put showers into the pavilion that was planned to serve the various facilities but the cost was beyond the budget of the clubs at the time. Running costs for all clubs at Rovers' and Marys' level were not inconsiderable and the move to Gedling Road led to an increase of over five hundred per cent for the hire of the pitch alone. Rovers had been paying around five pounds a year for the privilege of playing on the Bottom Rec and now they would have to find a sum of twenty seven pounds and ten shillings at their new venue. Transport costs were obviously greater in the Central Alliance than in the Spartan League and there was always the thorny issue of having to find extra money to induce better quality players to the clubs to enable them to compete at the higher level. Neither club had been able to charge admission when using the Recs and this practice continued at KGV with the main source of income, apart from the players' own subs, being the half-time collection. All this was about to alter at just the right time, courtesy of a change in the law of the land.

There had been moves in Parliament the previous year for a Private Member's Bill to legalise small sweepstakes, a change in legislation that would provide a financial lifeline for clubs like Rovers and Marys who would be in need of additional sources of revenue if they were to pursue their dreams of advancement. When the Small Lotteries and Gaming Act hit the statute books in August it introduced so-called 'societies' lotteries', which were small public lotteries conducted by societies established for charitable or sporting purposes but not for commercial gain. In essence this enabled clubs like the two Arnold ones to run what was effectively a glorified weekly raffle, known as a 'Tote' but which paid out cash prizes rather than the usual bottle of whisky or a box of chocolates. The amount that could be won was usually a fixed percentage, normally fifty, of the value of the tickets sold less agents' commissions. Obviously the more tickets that were sold, the greater the prize money, and the greater the prize money, the more tickets were sold. Not only was it incumbent in these changing times to attract better players on the field, it was becoming just as important to attract successful agents off it, and there was no disguising that the two were inextricably linked.

This change in the law would eventually have far-reaching effects for any number of clubs of the status of Rovers and Marys but at the start of the new season it was, with the exception of the ground move, very much a case of business as usual for both sides, just as it had been a couple of weeks earlier when England beat Australia at Old Trafford to retain the Ashes, courtesy of a spectacular performance by Jim Laker. The Surrey off-spinner took all but one of the twenty Australian wickets to finish with nineteen for the loss of only ninety runs, the best ever bowling analysis in the long history of Test Cricket. However, if the magnitude of his tremendous achievement still resonates strongly down the years, the response to his record breaking efforts at the time were greeted in a far more muted fashion.

This was of course a time when most everything was done, certainly in this country, at a more sedate pace and in a quieter and a noticeably far more understated manner, even on the sports field at the very highest levels. When Jim Laker took his last and nineteenth wicket to clinch the series and write himself into the record books for all time, he casually took his jumper from the umpire, slung it over his shoulder, and led his side back to the pavilion to a round of polite applause. It was in sharp contrast to the antics of today; there were no high-fives, no group hugs, no running around the field with a stump in hand. Off the field the reaction was pretty much the same. There were no central contracts for test players so the hero of the hour was due back at the Oval in London to play for his county the next day and as he drove back down from Manchester he called in at a pub to stretch his legs. Even though the news of his nineteen wicket haul had been on the radio and television news bulletins he wasn't recognised by any of the patrons as he sat in silence drinking his pint and tucking into a sandwich.

He wasn't recognised by his country, either, destined never to be invited to Buckingham Palace to receive a gong from the Queen. That he'd been unfortunate to be around at a time when England actually had the upper hand over its fierce rivals from Down Under was one reason for this lack of recognition but had he been of this era, with its circus of vacuous celebrity and dearth of national sporting success, there is every chance that he would have been honoured. After all Paul Collingwood, bit part member of the England cricket squad that regained the Ashes in 2005, unbelievably received the MBE having achieved scores of just ten and seven in his only two innings in the series. For those who would like to see an end to the honours system, the perversity of elevating a guy who scored just seventeen runs over that of a player who achieved sporting greatness only helps to reinforce their argument for its dismantling. It was a pity really that the OBE ranks above the MBE otherwise Mr Collingwood could have been awarded that instead, given that it's initials are often mischievously said to stand for 'Other Bugger's Efforts'.

This was a phrase that could never be applied to the players of Rovers and Marys, and it was entirely by their own labours that they'd adapted so well to life in the Central Alliance. However, whilst the red and whites stuck with the same eleven or twelve players who'd had such a marvellous second half to the previous season, the Saints had cast around for new blood and by the time their opening game came around Norman Burton had taken over at left back and the attack had a completely new look about it with left-winger Geoff Parr the only recognisable name amongst the forwards.

A new combination always needs time to settle in and that certainly looked the case as Marys went down six-two over at the Manor Ground against Ilkeston Town Reserves. The Derbyshire side had finished second the previous season and had hammered the maroon and golds by seven goals to one in the corresponding fixture so it was too soon to draw conclusions from the result. Unfortunately, they then went over to Newark to meet new boys Ransome and Marles Reserves and suffered a six-three reverse and in their first game at Gedling Road lost to Belper Town's second string by the odd goal in five.

ROVERS SIDE WHO PLAYED IN THE VERY FIRST MATCH AT KGV 1 SEP 1956
Back Row (l to r); J Barnes (Secretary), F Greensmith, G Wileman, D Hodgson, P Holmes, K Dove, A Casterton. Front Row; J Tulley, R Maddocks, L Peel, J Raven, R Carter (Alec Casterton Collection)

This latter game wasn't the inaugural match at KGV. That honour fell to Rovers who, having fared better than Marys and beaten Belper's reserves on their own ground five-four in their opening fixture, entertained British Ropes Reserves on the first day of September and brought competitive football back to the location after many years' absence. They did it in style too and the Retford side must have felt like unwanted guests at a private party as the red and whites thrashed them by nine goals to nil. Ron Maddocks wrote his name into the history books with the first goal at the 'new' Gedling Road after just three minutes and eventually finished with a hat-trick. Evergreen Jack Tulley, who would be in his fortieth year during this campaign, scored three of his own whilst a couple from Les Peel and one from Jimmy Raven completed the rout.

THE VERY FIRST GOAL AT KGV 1 SEP 1956 ROVERS v BRITISH ROPES RESERVES, SCORED BY RON MADDOCKS AND WATCHED BY JACK TULLEY (Courtesy Football Post)

Whilst the Saints' worst start to a season in the post-war era saw them lying next to bottom of the division, a marked contrast to the tremendous run they'd opened with just twelve months earlier, Rovers' own great form had carried over into the new term. They were given a bit of a reality check the next Saturday though when they came back from another visit to Derbyshire having been on the wrong end of a seven-one scoreline. Heanor Town's reserves were the side giving out the thrashing this time and there was little doubt that they and their close rivals Ilkeston would be amongst the title contenders in the months to come. Thankfully the red and whites seemed to have suffered no lasting damage as, seven days later, they played their second match at KGV and despite facing the previous season's champions, Creswell Colliery Reserves, they exceeded all expectations as well as improbably bettering the nine-nil score of a couple of weeks ago; this time they fired eleven goals past the hapless visiting keeper to make it a mighty twenty goals in just two games at their new home. The following week Rovers completed the double over the colliery side, this time being restricted to just a couple of goals, but much harder tasks were facing them as the next two fixtures, both at Gedling Road, had the league's two leading teams as visitors.

First up were Sutton Town Reserves, currently in second place and still unbeaten with eleven points out of a possible twelve. Almost from the kick-off right-back Franny Greensmith had to make a spectacular clearance off his own goal-line to prevent the visitors from gaining an early advantage and then Rovers countered themselves with Les Peel putting them ahead after ten minutes. Sutton bounced back to equalise but Jack Brace, making what would prove to be a rare appearance this season, restored the home side's lead a few minutes before the break. Unfortunately, it wasn't quite enough as with another equaliser, this time on the stroke of half-time, and a third in the second period, the visitors ran out close winners by the odd goal in five.

It had been a very close contest, one that could have gone either way, and there was every chance that this would be the case seven days later when league leaders Ilkeston Town Reserves visited KGV. It also promised to be a high scoring game too considering that both teams were averaging five a match so far this season but the most intriguing aspect to the fixture, at least for the first half-hour, was that Rovers played with a man short. Happily the visitors didn't make the best of their superiority in numbers and in a ten minute spell straight after the sides were evened up the home team hit the woodwork three times. Pete Holmes, Les Peel, and Jack Tulley were the unfortunate players but the latter made amends by opening the scoring on the forty minute mark. Unlike the previous week it was a lead that they didn't surrender and this time the game finished three-two in their favour to leave them lying handily in sixth place in the league and very much in touch with the leading pack.

During this same period Marys' faltering fortunes had taken a turn for the better but it couldn't be put down to luck. Syd Gray had been on the lookout for new players to bolster the squad and he managed to get the signature of three guys whose presence in the side just happened to coincide with the Saints' revival. Left-half Barry Brace, who was also comfortable in the number three shirt, returned after a year with Gedling Colliery, whilst forwards Geoff Lawton and Ron Hart made their first appearances for the maroon and golds in the number seven and number ten shirts respectively. His debut was the only game in which Geoff figured on the right-wing, eventually settling in at inside-right after a spell at centre-forward, but Ron played solely as an inside-left, forming a strong partnership with Geoff Parr over on Marys' left flank. Unlike Barry Brace and Geoff Lawton, Ron wasn't a local guy. He was currently serving with the Military Police at Chilwell but he originally hailed from Rotherham. The Yorkshireman had spent some time on the books of Halifax Town a couple of seasons earlier and his experience and ability would result in him proving to be an extremely useful acquisition for the club. With the help of these new and returning additions the Saints won four of their next five matches, including a thrilling five-four Notts Senior Cup First Qualifying Round victory over previously unbeaten North Notts League side Warsop Main. They also became the first team to take a point off Sutton Town Reserves in the league, holding them to a three-all draw a week before their opponents returned to Gedling Road to narrowly overcome Rovers.

By now it was the middle of October and the next couple of weeks were dominated by a couple of bizarre encounters with Thoresby Colliery. Maybe that should be 'planned encounters' because the first one never actually took place and the second one lasted just seventy five minutes. The first of the two entries on the fixture list was the visit of the miners' side to play Rovers at KGV. Well they would have been visitors had it not been for the home side deciding to make a last minute trip of their own; to Blackpool, for the town's Illuminations.

Now, there is nothing wrong in popping off to see the East Midland's favourite west coast resort light itself up every year between the beginning of September and early November, hundreds of thousands of people do it, but a snippet in the Football Post hinted at a modicum of displeasure from the Central Alliance itself that its fixture schedule could be disrupted for something as trivial as a week-end shindig. It probably did smack a little of amateurishness for the club to postpone a match for such a reason, but then again they were still to all intents and purposes an amateur club and none of its players were tied to the obligations of a legally binding contract unlike some in the league. As to the actual timing of the visit, the fact that the local side were hosts to Preston North End that weekend might have had some bearing on the matter. This it needs to be remembered was a time when Blackpool were a force to be reckoned with, sitting in third place in Division One, the forerunner of today's Premiership, with a certain Stanley Matthews on the right wing whilst Preston, no slouches themselves, had a fairly decent winger of their own, Tom Finney. For the record books the game ended in a comprehensive four-nil victory for the home side, and as has been mentioned in an earlier chapter, the team's two stars were eventually knighted; for their own efforts, naturally.

The second incident with the North Notts colliery side was, by contrast, something that actually happened rather than didn't, and on the field of play as opposed to off it. Seven days after they were originally due at Gedling Road the miners arrived for their game with Marys. The teams were well matched with the scores level at one all when, with around fifteen minutes left to play, Thoresby's inside-right raced in to put his side ahead. In doing so he ended up following the ball into the goal and grabbed the net to steady himself. Unfortunately, he brought the crossbar down as a result and as no replacement was available the match had to be abandoned. Whether the guy injured himself in the process was not reported but when the two teams met the following week up at Thoresby he wasn't in the side. Not that the miners missed him because they ran up three goals without reply before the break. Thankfully Marys staged a tremendous second half comeback to snatch a point as the game ended four apiece. Whilst the Saints were engaged with Thoresby, Rovers racked up a couple of high scoring victories, eight-one and six-four, to edge up to fifth place in the table on this last Saturday in October; more pertinently, only two teams had dropped less points than them too.

Now as interesting as Marys' and Rovers' efforts on the football field were locally, there had been a couple of situations going on in the wider world that were far more intriguing, and which were about to escalate into something far more serious. The first of these was what became popularly known as the Suez Crisis, one of the most important and controversial events in the country's post-war history. Three months earlier and ironically on the first day of 'Laker's Test' at Old Trafford, the Egyptian President, Colonel Nasser, announced the nationalisation of the Suez Canal. Of course the Canal, which had been partly owned by British interests, was of great strategic importance, linking, as it did, the Mediterranean and Red Seas and the oilfields of the Middle East with its western consumers without the need to make the long trip around the southern tip of Africa. Probably the only humorous incident to come out of the crisis precipitated by the President's actions was a comment by the Old Trafford groundsman Bert Flack. He'd come in for heavy criticism for his preparation of the playing surface for the Fourth Test and when interviewed by the press about this he protested his innocence whilst saying "Thank God Nasser has taken over the Suez Canal. Otherwise I'd have been plastered over every front page like Marilyn Monroe."

Three months after Nasser's move, and following much discussion at diplomatic level and in the corridors of power, Israeli forces invaded Egypt. This was the first act in a plan, or rather a plot, cooked up by Britain and France that would then see them have no option but to send in their own forces and seize back the Canal as an act of intervention between 'warring' nations. Unfortunately, especially for the Prime Minister Anthony Eden, the military action was condemned by the country's biggest ally the United States, had no backing from the United Nations, and was used as a cover by the USSR for their own invasion of Hungary that took place even as the British and French troops were about to re-take control of the Canal. British public opinion too was deeply divided over the use of force.

When the Americans showed their displeasure by putting financial pressure on the British Government, the Cabinet had little alternative but to order a cease-fire, effective at midnight on November 6, just seven days after the Israeli invasion. The Crisis, regarded by many as signalling the end of Britain's role as a world power, had impacted badly upon the Prime Minister's physical well-being as well and just two months after the ending of hostilities ill health led to his resignation in favour of Harold Macmillan.

The world's two leading players were now indisputably the USA and the USSR, as evidenced by the latter's unopposed crushing of the Hungarian uprising, another conflict that was over almost as soon as it had begun. The bitter fighting and resultant bloodshed did have an impact on the world of football though. The Hungarian Champions, Honved, were playing a European Cup tie in Spain when the revolution took place and three of their most famous players, internationals Ferenc Puskas, Zoltan Czibor, and Sandor Kocsis, all decided to defect to the West. Puskas in particular found even more fame and fortune when he subsequently joined Spanish giants Real Madrid, culminating in probably the most memorable European Cup Final of them all in 1960 when he scored four goals in a seven-three victory over Eintracht Frankfurt at Hampden Park, Glasgow.

Puskas was a nominal inside-left, the number ten, but he was allowed the freedom to work his magic all along the forward-line. It had been said that he was fat, overweight, and past it when he'd signed for Real, but if that was the case then every team in the world would have liked someone so out of condition as him. Marys were happy enough with their own inside-left, Ron Hart, but Rovers had been struggling to find someone to hang onto the number ten shirt and by the end of the season would have used no less than eight players in that position. The fourth to try was none other than Bill Whitt, who'd just re-signed for the red and whites after his fifteen month spell with the Saints. With brother Ron playing at left-half it proved to be a happy homecoming for Bill as he helped Rovers to an eight-nil win against Sutton-in-Ashfield outfit Metal Box, but a fortnight later, whilst the high scoring continued, they were beaten six-five by Ransome and Marles Reserves in a thriller over at Newark.

That same day, the last Saturday of November, fans at Marys' home game against Shirebrook Miners' Welfare Reserves had seen double figures too, with nine of the ten strikes happily counting in the Saints' favour. The match had marked the first appearance of new centre-half Dennis Wheat, recently signed from Gedling Colliery and whose addition it was hoped would be the answer to the club's own problem position. No fewer than five number fives had been tried prior to his debut and although the team hadn't been having too much difficulty in front of goal their defensive record of conceding forty goals in their last dozen outings certainly showed there was plenty of scope for improvement. All in all it had been a bit of an in and out month for the maroon and golds. They'd been knocked out of the Notts Senior Cup at the Second Qualifying Round stage by Bestwood Colliery, with the Notts Alliance outfit coming from behind to win a closely fought contest two-one, and they'd finished on the wrong end of a five-three scoreline over at Heanor Town Reserves. However they had managed to beat another of Derbyshire's contenders for the title when they entertained the second eleven of Ilkeston Town; the final score was five-two, a result that gave Marys their first ever win at KGV.

Marys' teamsheet at this time had taken on a bit of a confusing appearance. Not only did the side contain two Parrs and a couple of Disneys, it also had three Dennises, two Geoffs, and a pair of Rons, as well as a Ken and a Len; there'd also been two Burtons and two Jacksons playing together in earlier games. Maybe it was 'Kegga' Parr and Syd Gray's master plan to confound the opposition and it certainly seemed to work on the first Saturday of December when, against all the odds, the Saints visited Priestsic Road to meet the unbeaten leaders Sutton Town Reserves and ended up taking them to the cleaners. The maroon and golds had been just one of two teams to take points off the home side so far this campaign, and when the scores were level, two-all, at the break it looked as though the game might end in another draw. One of the Disneys, Ken, and one of the Parrs, Geoff, had scored Marys' two goals, but they were only a taste of what was to come as the visitors added five more goals in the second period with Sutton too shell shocked to reply.

The following week the Saints' tremendous run of form continued when they played host to the struggling reserves of Linby Colliery. The miners' side were in a poor way and started the game with just nine men. Marys took no pity and quite rightly punished them severely, with Ron Hart in particular relishing the chance to impose both his and the team's superiority over their unfortunate visitors by scoring all of the first four goals in just over a quarter of an hour including a hat-trick in four minutes. Ken Disney added a first half hat-trick of his own as the maroon and golds ended up not only hammering their opponents by fourteen goals to nil but also bringing about their demise. For the second time in just three seasons, Linby Colliery Reserves withdrew prematurely from the competition in which they were playing, only this time their record wasn't expunged. Wilmorton and Alvaston, members of the Central Alliance Division One North, agreed to set up a second eleven to fulfil the miners' outstanding fixtures.

This annihilation of Linby had made it an amazing thirty goals in just three games for the Saints but the only negative aspect had been a problem with the new playing surface at Gedling Road, one that had caused this latest match to have to be relocated to the Top Rec. The fans had certainly taken to the fare being served up by both Arnold sides in their new environment and the attendances at KGV were averaging over the five hundred mark, but this situation was in danger of being threatened as the state of the pitch itself was beginning to give cause for concern. It had been laid down by a firm called En-Tout-Cas who had been in business since 1909 and who specialised in providing playing surfaces for various sports uses. They were a nationally known, reputable organisation so there was no accusation of cost cutting, especially as they had won the contract by open tender back in 1954. The underlying problem with the ground, which I experienced personally as a player there some twenty years later, was that it drained very poorly. Any amount of heavy rain on the morning of a match would invariably see the game having to be called off. Thus was the case now, and it would only get worse. Good fortune saw Rovers' two December home games avoid postponement but Marys weren't so lucky. They managed to move their match against Linby back up to Church Lane but they weren't able to repeat the process; their games scheduled for the last two Saturdays in 1956 both fell victim to the elements. Rovers' Alec Casterton recalls the teething problems at KGV.

AC : There was a problem with the drainage at King George's right from the start. I think they must have laid the pitch on cinders or ashes because after a while they started working their way up to the surface. It was quite dangerous too because I was watching Marys in a night match and my good mate Dennis Wheat picked up a nasty injury as a result. Someone made a back for him and he ended up falling head first along the ground and taking the skin off one side of his face.

Whilst the Saints were sitting out three fifths of the month Rovers' good form continued right up until the last Saturday of the year. They picked up seven points out of a possible eight as well as notching up consecutive scores of seven, six, and six. The usual suspects were on the scoresheet but were joined at this time by Pete Holmes, a utility player who was enjoying a particularly productive purple patch with seven goals in two straight games. The red and whites' nine game unbeaten run had seen them climb to third in the table and with only a visit to Shirebrook to come there seemed no reason to believe that they wouldn't extend it into double figures. They were due to play the reserve eleven of the Miners Welfare club and with their opponents occupying a position below half way in the division there was every expectation that Rovers might come away with both points. There was one slight problem, as left-half Ron Whitt explains.

RW : We went up to Shirebrook and we were sitting in the dressing room getting changed when one of our committee men came in and said "Lads, I've got some bad news. Their first team game's been postponed and they're going to play them instead of the reserves." There wasn't much we could do, but I know that we put up a good fight. I think they only just beat us in the end.

Ron's recollection was pretty spot on. Rovers went down five-three despite being level at two apiece at half-time. The rumour that Shirebrook were going to play the whole of the first eleven wasn't far off the mark either but in the end the home side settled for the inclusion of just five first team regulars. It was a ploy that was commonplace as Alec Casterton recalls.

AC : The most difficult thing about playing in the Central Alliance was the fact that reserve teams often used first team players. We'd play against Creswell when they had Messenger and Dennison in their side, guys who'd played for Burnley and Notts.

Of course this situation wouldn't change unless Rovers and Marys graduated to the top division of the Central Alliance so for now it was a matter of putting up with the iniquity of the division's make-up. At least the red and whites would know in advance that they'd definitely be playing the first eleven of their next opponents. This was because the fixture was the Notts Senior Cup tie against Retford Town, winners of the trophy three times since the war and most recently in 1954-55. They'd just dropped down into the second division of the Yorkshire League but were expected to provide strong opposition for Rovers, exempt until this stage of the competition thanks to their fine run the previous season. On a very heavy surface that wasn't really to the visitors liking, Retford went ahead in just the third minute. It was an uphill battle all the way for the red and whites as they conceded twice more before the break and despite having had their fair share of the play in the second period they eventually went down by four goals to one. It was no disgrace to go out to the North Notts side because even though they didn't go on to win the Senior Cup they did end up winning the league championship to reclaim their place in the top flight.

With both Arnold sides now knocked out of the season's only cup competition all attention was now focused on how well they could do in the second half of the league campaign. At the turn of the year Rovers were still hanging onto fourth spot but despite Marys' recent explosion of goals, their poor start and lack of games as a result of the recent postponements meant that they remained stuck in mid-table.

Quite a few motorists shared those same feelings of inertia, thanks to the imposition of petrol rationing just before Christmas. If the British people had thought that shortages were a thing of the past then this sanction, a direct legacy of the Suez Crisis, was a reminder that they weren't, that the potential for them was ever present. The fact that they are often beyond the control of government was summed up in an answer Prime Minister Harold Macmillan once gave to a reporter who'd asked him what worried him most. He famously replied "Events dear boy, events".

Whilst President Nasser's actions had their negative aftermath on the country as a whole they had the opposite effect on my own family. My dad worked as a panel beater, repairing cars, at A K Austen, a garage in Carrington. Just across the busy Mansfield Road was Mapperley Park, home to the well-off middle classes, many of whom had their vehicles fixed by my father. One day he was engaged in conversation with one of the garage's clients, a doctor, who ran two cars. As he was a member of the medical profession his main vehicle was exempt from rationing but the second one, used by his wife as a run about, was not. The car stood idle more often than not and the fuel restrictions, despite not being expected to last more than four months, also hit the motor car industry, causing the value of used cars to drop. The doctor decided to cut his losses and sell and my father became the proud owner of a very nice Ford Ten. A few months later rationing ended, car prices returned to their earlier levels, and my dad sold his recent acquisition at a profit. He'd always hoped that one day he would be able to start his own business and the funds generated from the sale of the car helped him get some capital together to fulfil his dream. Most of the money went on tools and equipment but there was just a little left over to buy a van to replace our lovely family car. Unfortunately, for the foreseeable future our family outings were less luxurious than they had been. The van was an ancient, small, bright red, wooden-framed ex-Post Office vehicle which my brother and I had to gain access to through the double doors at the rear. There were no seats in the back, it was dark and extremely basic, and we all breathed a sigh of relief a couple of years later when the business was starting to pick up and my father could afford to buy a second-hand Land Rover. It was hardly a Rolls Royce, but by comparison with the old mail van it certainly felt like one.

Despite the lack of movement on the roads, Marys managed to make a bit of progress of their own in January, edging up the table by winning two of their four matches and drawing the other two with Rovers holding onto fourth place courtesy of back to back victories over Kimberley Town. Unfortunately, they'd slipped up two-nil at home to Heanor Town Reserves, although even that was a big improvement on the seven-one thrashing they'd suffered at their hands back in September. A quick glance at the table showed that it was dominated by the three reserve teams of Ilkeston, Heanor and Sutton, hardly surprising given that their first teams were also leading their sections of the top division. Of course, these were exactly the kind of clubs whose operating level Arnold's two representatives were trying to reach and only time would tell just how successful Rovers and Marys would be. In the meantime, though, neither club was looking much beyond the next game; the first Saturday of February just happened to be the date of the first Arnold derby of the campaign.

It was in the fixture list as Rovers' home game but there was no particular advantage to be gained by either side under the current ground-sharing arrangement, that is until the Gedling Road pitch was declared unplayable yet again and the match was moved at short notice down to Rovers' old stomping ground on the Bottom Rec. The last time that Marys had beaten the red and whites was almost two and a half years previously, back in October 1954, and they'd never once succeeded in lowering their local rivals' colours at Nottingham Road.

This hold that Rovers seemed to have over the Saints was the subject of quite a bit of banter between the two sets of players, as Alec Casterton recalls.

AC : There were quite a few Marys' players who didn't like to play us because of the jinx we seemed to have over them. One or two of them were quite nervous, especially as we played in front of those big crowds. Harry Wharton was one of them. He was a bit older than me and I saw him on the evening before the game and he had a worried look on his face. It wasn't that late and I said to him "Harry, you should be at home, wrapped up in bed. You've got a lot on tomorrow." I don't know what it was but they couldn't do anything against us at that time.

The worried look on Harry's face was probably caused by the fact that he hadn't played for the first team for three months. Now, called up in place of Barry Brace who'd gone down with laryngitis, he'd been pitched right back in at the deep end, Marys' only change to a settled side that had been unbeaten since Dennis Wheat's arrival. The impact of the new centre-half hadn't gone unnoticed either because, along with full back Norman Burton, he had attracted the attention of scouts from no less a club than Arsenal. Rovers too had been keeping a largely unchanged side but would give a debut to George O'Dowd, recently signed from Gedling Colliery, whilst hoping that newcomer John Barkes from Grantham would make the troublesome number ten shirt his own.

Before kick-off excitement naturally ran high amongst both sets of supporters but had they had eyes on anything other than the players, they would have noticed that the referee was accompanied by two more men in black; independently appointed linesmen. Normally for most matches at local level it was difficult enough to get hold of a referee, let alone someone to run the line but the Central Alliance did at least have a pool of officials upon which they could call. However, this didn't usually run to providing linesmen. That was left to the two clubs involved who were both expected to have someone in their ranks capable of assisting the referee with throw-in and offside decisions. The requirements were that they were passably fit and able to keep up with play, had half decent eyesight and displayed a fair degree of impartiality. Now a lack of partisanship would have been a rare quality at a time like this, a local derby in front of over a thousand people or more, so the authorities, quite rightly, decided to take no chances and called in three officials from different parts of Derbyshire.

To be fair, the clashes between the town's finest were always keen but clean and the latest meeting was no exception. Rovers took an early lead through Roy Carter but Marys came back with two goals of their own through Geoff Parr and a Norman Burton penalty, both just before the break. It looked as though the Saints might be in with a chance of their first win on the enclosure but two goals before the hour mark, from Les Peel and Ron Maddocks, swung the balance of the game back in the home side's favour. There was no way back for the visitors and Rovers, having further extended their lead a little later, ended up worthy winners by four goals to two. It was a fine recovery by the red and whites but it probably left Marys wondering just what they had to do to overcome their bogey side; it had been the twelfth game in the series and the Saints had won just twice. Four had been drawn whilst Rovers' continuing dominance of these head-to-head meetings was reflected in their seven victories.

Whilst the defeat was obviously a blow for Marys, they didn't let it affect them too much and bounced straight back with a string of fine performances, winning six and drawing one of their next seven matches. The only point dropped was at home to Heanor Town Reserves who were by then clear leaders of the division, and even then the Saints gave them a run for their money. Paying scant attention to the visitors' reputation, Marys tore into them from the start and thanks to scoring efforts from Geoff Lawton, Dennis Parr, and Ron Hart went in at half-time three-nil up. Dennis had been moved from his normal position at right-back to centre-forward, where he would stay for the rest of the season, but that wasn't the only switching around going on during that spell. Poor weather had again rendered KGV unplayable so the Saints ended up playing three consecutive home games at different places. The Heanor fixture was sandwiched between a five-one win against Stanton Ironworks on the Top Rec and a six-one victory over Metal Box on the Bottom Rec, ironically giving the maroon and golds their long awaited first ever win at that venue. On their travels they hit seven against two Miners Welfare sides, Loscoe and Shirebrook Reserves, despite the latter game being played with three inches of snow on the ground.

During this decent spell of Marys, Rovers own good form continued. They won four of their five games whilst losing only to second placed Ilkeston Town Reserves, albeit by seven goals to two. Just like the Saints the red and whites had to transfer a home game due to the state of Gedling Road, in their case back to the Bottom Rec, as well as succeeding in emulating their rivals' high scoring feats with tallies of six, seven, and nine of their own. By the last Saturday in March Rovers had inched up to third place with Marys just two points behind them on level games in sixth spot. It appeared that, barring a miracle, the title would go to one of the two reserve elevens of fierce rivals and neighbours Heanor and Ilkeston, but there was every chance that an honourable third place finish was quite within the grasp of either of the Arnold sides. Unfortunately, both teams proceeded to make life difficult for themselves when they went and lost their last game of the month.

MARYS v ROVERS 20 APR 1957 (EASTER SATURDAY) : Back Row (l to r); R Hinson, H Wharton, L Rockley, C Lawson, N Burton, B Brace, W Archer. Front Row; A Branston, G Lawton, D Parr, R Hart, G Parr.

(Arnold Library Collection)

There were just eight matches left to play and five weeks in which to fit them. The toughest fixture for both Marys and Rovers was the one that saw them meet each other on Easter Saturday. Prior to the derby they rattled off three straight wins apiece, scoring thirty-two goals between them in the process and setting things up nicely for their thirteenth meeting. There were a couple of changes in the line-ups compared with the first game but the most significant one was the return of Sam Archer in Rovers' goal. Sam had been back at the club a few weeks and had also figured for the first eleven on the right-wing, just as he had for Marys the previous season, but now he was back, despite his hand injury, in his favoured position between the sticks.

SA : When the nurse was treating my injury when I first went to the General I said to her "Well that's my life buggered up then" but she said that it wouldn't be and she was right. It took a while but I soon got used to it and eventually I ended up back in goal. It's surprising how well you can adapt.

Marys, whose home game it was, could catch Rovers up or even overtake them if they were to win and in front of another large crowd at KGV, its numbers boosted by the sunny weather conditions, they set off far more quickly than the red and whites and were two up inside the first twelve minutes thanks to goals from both of their wingers. Outside-right Alan Branston scored the first and the second was netted by left-winger Geoff Parr after his brother Dennis had beaten four players and laid on a perfect pass for him. Ten minutes later Bill Whitt reduced the arrears but soon after the Saints regained their two goal advantage with a second from Alan Branston, his shot taking a deflection off Alec Casterton on its way in. Rovers stepped up their own attacks but their pressure came to nothing and it was Marys who struck again right on the half hour through Ron Hart. There was no further scoring in the first half and it was a very chastened Rovers' who went in at the break trailing four-one.

With a three goal lead the Saints could have been forgiven for thinking that the game was there for the taking but anyone with any experience of a number of the sides' previous encounters would know that it was never over until it was over. Whatever was said amongst the Rovers' players at half-time had the desired effect because first Les Peel clawed one back and then Ron Maddocks added two more in quick succession to bring the scores level. With both sides taking it in turns to attack, the two defences needed to put up a solid resistance. They did, and with the last ten minutes of the match generally accepted as the most thrilling seen at Gedling Road all season, no quarter was asked and none given as the two sides slugged it out to the finish. The game ended four apiece with both sides having given their all and it was a shame that the epic contest only earned the two protagonists a single point each.

MARYS 1956-57 : Back Row (l to r); S Gray, C Moore, N Burton, R Hinson, H Wharton, L Rockley, D Wheat, B Brace, L Wildgust. Front Row; G Lawton, J Whalley, D Parr, R Hart, G Parr

(Barry Wildgust Collection)

With the spoils being shared Marys hadn't succeeded in narrowing the gap on Rovers so the red and whites could afford to drop a point in their last four matches and still stay ahead of their rivals. As it turned out they made things difficult for themselves by winning three of the games but going down surprisingly by the odd goal in three away to Thoresby Colliery. Marys, never giving up the slim hope of catching them in the home straight did everything they could in their run of four games, all played at home in the space of just over a week.

Finding a rich vein of goalscoring form, not only did they win them all fairly convincingly, they also rattled in thirty goals to give their fans a rousing finale to the campaign in its last week, hitting eleven past British Ropes Reserves and ten against Loscoe Miners Welfare a couple of nights later.

It had looked an improbable task but in the final analysis, Marys' goal blitz enabled them to overtake Rovers on goal average right at the death. The Saints had lost just once in their last sixteen games and only twice in the twenty four outings since Dennis Wheat made his debut; their poor start, in which they lost their opening three fixtures, had left them with a big gap to make up, but in the end they just did it. The red and whites, despite their occasional losses, had recorded a steady stream of victories all the way through the season to claim fourth place just ahead of Sutton Town Reserves. Whilst the Ashfield side finished with the same number of points as both Arnold clubs, they had the worse goal average of all three sides. Pretty much as had been expected, Heanor ended as champions with Ilkeston taking the runners-up spot.

All in all it had been an excellent first year at Gedling Road. Despite the problems with the pitch, home fans had been rewarded with high scoring by both sides no matter what the venue. In their thirty four home fixtures the two teams had hit close on a hundred and seventy goals between them, 'near as dammit' to five a match, as the locals might say. As to who had been the better team taking the season as a whole, well that was almost too close to call, but if pressed a case could just about be made in favour of Rovers. Even though they had a marginally inferior goal average to Marys, they did after all finish level on points with them after a thirty-four match campaign whilst maintaining their dominance in their head-to-head battles. Whatever the argument, the success of the two teams certainly augured well for the future, even if the honours board did remain unchanged for the second year in a row.

ROVERS : FIVE CHAMPIONSHIPS, SIX CUPS (INCL ONE SHARED)

MARYS : ONE CHAMPIONSHIP, THREE CUPS (INCL ONE SHARED)

REGENT : THREE CUPS

CHAPTER THIRTEEN 1957-58

Whilst the two Arnold clubs had consolidated their places in the Central Alliance, the end of the previous campaign had brought about some noticeable change elsewhere in the football world. Stanley Matthews, now forty two years of age, played his last game for England in a four-one victory over Denmark, although remarkably he would continue playing league football until he was fifty. Notts County had skirted with relegation from the Second Division all season but just managed to hold on their status whilst Forest left the section for all the right reasons by gaining promotion to the top flight. They finished runners-up to neighbours Leicester City and, in a sign of the times, one point ahead of third placed Liverpool. Forest's elevation meant that Division One football returned to Nottingham after an absence of more than thirty years whilst at the same time coinciding with its sixtieth anniversary as a city.

With the last bout of petrol rationing finally ending the day before Matthews' swansong, things could be said to be looking up for most people, unless you happened to be one of the few inhabitants of the largely deserted Christmas Island who were specifically advised by the Government that it was better if they didn't; eight thousand feet above them Britain was exploding its first hydrogen bomb. This particular device had an explosive force of 'only' three hundred kilotons and even though it was twenty times as destructive as the one dropped on Hiroshima in 1945 it was still not as powerful as those being developed by the USA and the USSR. The Pacific islanders had been advised to stay indoors and avoid the temptation to gaze at the flash that accompanied the bomb's detonation so as to minimise damage to their eyes. Whilst the 'Wizard of Dribble' was saying his farewell to the international footballing world in Copenhagen, those living on Christmas Island were spectators too, unwitting ones to an experiment that would see nuclear proliferation lead just five years later to the Cuban Missile Crisis. Then, just about everyone with an interest in living would be contemplating saying farewell, and not just to the footballing world either.

Conspiracy theories abound whenever there is talk of weapons of mass destruction. Countries have even gone to war on the basis of what was thought rather than what was actually known with regard to such capabilities and recent times have also shown us how government departments like to time the announcement of difficult stories so that they coincide with more uplifting ones. An earlier chapter referred to the ending of tea rationing being announced on the same day that Britain's first atomic bomb was being tested and now, five years later, history was more or less repeating itself. There were loud cheers in the House of Commons when the lifting of petrol restrictions was announced. Not only that, the Commercial Travellers' Association announced that their members would be 'overjoyed' at the news. Quite what they felt about the UK's entry into the arms race as they filled up their tanks and resumed hawking their samples up and down the country the next day was not recorded.

Despite the fact that the world's major powers were quickly escalating their capability for mutual annihilation, the summer of 1957 wasn't without its more uplifting moments. Harold Macmillan, addressing a rally at Bedford football ground, was clearly of the mind that the country's economic standards were not only rising but were at a level never seen before, not only just in his lifetime but in the history of the country. "Let us be frank about it", he said, "most of our people have never had it so good". His words became one of the best known political quotations of modern times.

Being only eight at the time politics didn't figure high on my personal agenda but, looking back, it was obvious that the growing consumer culture that was gradually replacing post-war austerity had impacted on me too. Most young boys of a certain age are interested in toy cars, die-cast scale models of the real things, but until 1953 the choice was limited to one make; Dinkys. Then along came a smaller range called Matchbox toys, to be followed three years later by my favourite brand; Corgi. Now there was a greater choice and the competition between the manufacturers led to improvements and innovations in the vehicles themselves.

One day of course I would put them all to one side and move onto my next interest which, the constancy of my love of football apart, was music. Exactly two weeks before the Prime Minister's speech a certain meeting had taken place elsewhere in the country that would have a profound effect not only on my own musical preferences but on those of many millions around the globe as well. At the Woolton Church fete in Liverpool, a fifteen year old Paul McCartney was introduced to a sixteen year old John Lennon and the seeds were sown for a song-writing partnership that would blossom and grow, underpin the music of the Beatles, and send twentieth century culture off on a different trajectory.

The year would also see major developments in other branches of the arts that would result in works that expressed a definite anti-establishment sentiment. American author Jack Kerouac's novel "On The Road" was published, based mainly on his own life and the trips he'd made with friends across America over the previous few years. Kerouac was part of a loose group of writers known as the 'Beat Generation' whose stream of consciousness style was inspired by both jazz and drugs, especially drugs. Their influences extended into choice of lifestyle too and when later in 1957 the Russians launched Sputnik I, the first artificial satellite to successfully orbit the Earth, the San Francisco Chronicle columnist Herb Caen coined the term 'Beatnik', mischievously implying that the 'Beats' might be found wanting when it came to rallying around the flag. His new word came to be associated with any member of the younger generation who showed signs of exhibiting such unwanted traits as a general lack of cleanliness and tidiness, or a propensity towards idleness; "They're only Beat you know when it comes to work" he wrote. The suffix '-nik' also suggested the worst slight of them all, that the 'Beats' and their followers might just be communist sympathisers at a time when American paranoia over everything Russian was at its zenith and it was 'better to be dead than red'.

In reality they were just another group of people whose behaviour, style of dress, and point of view were decidedly unconventional and in many ways their ideas if not their look were mirrored on this side of the Atlantic by a group of writers who were given the soubriquet 'Angry Young Men'. Although not an organised artistic movement as such, their work was characterised by an outspoken dissatisfaction with the status quo and championed the working classes in their struggle against the class distinctions of the day, a divide seen to be encouraged by the Establishment. Nottingham author Alan Sillitoe was numbered amongst them when he wrote 'Saturday Night and Sunday Morning', a novel about a young man working at Raleigh. He himself had worked at the cycle factory some years earlier but had escaped the drudgery and monotony of the hard working, hard drinking, hard loving and hard living routine of his book's anti-hero, Arthur Seaton.

Quite a few of Arnold's footballing finest had been or were Raleigh employees; Harry Redgate, Ken Pritchard, Brian Cunningham, Ken Dove, Pete Holmes, to name just a few, as well as Alec Casterton whose time there lasted just three weeks. None of them fitted the stereotype of angry young men but they could all at one time or another have been called hungry young men, especially where matters of football were concerned; hungry for action and hungry for success. For those still playing, together with their non-Raleigh team mates, there was the prospect of an increase in both as the new season approached; the Central Alliance had decided to introduce a cup competition exclusively for second division sides. If the form that Rovers and Marys had demonstrated in achieving their high finishes in the previous campaign could be maintained during the coming months, there was every chance that one of them might lift the new trophy.

For the Saints in particular, there was also the potential for a good run in another cup competition as they became the very first Arnold side ever to make an appearance in the FA

Amateur Cup. There were no expectations at Gedling Road that Marys could realistically challenge the traditional big hitters like the Northern League's Bishop Auckland, current holders of the trophy and winners for the past three years in a row, or their southern counterparts from the Isthmian League such as Wycombe Wanderers or Wimbledon, but they had a decent chance of making a bit of progress in the early stages of the competition. The best performance by a local side in recent years had been that of Gedling Colliery, who had on a number of occasions worked their way through the qualifying rounds only to come up against that season's eventual winners no less than three times; the Bishops twice and Pegasus once. This latter club were the success story of the early nineteen fifties in top quality amateur football. They drew their players from England's elite universities, Oxford and Cambridge, and for a while their exploits captured the public's imagination to such an extent that the 'sold out' signs were posted wherever they played, including Gedling's own Plains Road ground in January 1954. Temporary accommodation was erected around the perimeter of the pitch and six thousand spectators, an all-time record crowd for a match played in what is now the Borough of Gedling, braved the icy conditions to see what all the fuss was about. The miners' side included two players who would later join Rovers, George Wileman and George O'Dowd, and although they held the opposition to just a single goal lead until around the hour mark, the visitors' superior skill told in the end and they eased to a six-one victory.

Nor was it just the taking part that was of interest to Marys, there was also the not insignificant matter of the financial rewards that could be gained from participation in the competition. Such was the draw of football at the time that the Amateur Cup finals of the nineteen fifties had been played in front of capacity crowds at Wembley, whilst the semi-finals also attracted large crowds to neutral league grounds such as Arsenal's Highbury Stadium and Newcastle's St James' Park. At the end of each season the FA made a re-distribution from the proceeds of the tournament to each competing team, the amount received being dependent upon the progress made, so a good run would obviously provide the Saints with a welcome infusion of funds.

In terms of new blood amongst the players, the side that opened the new season showed little change from that which had finished third in the previous one, the only notable addition being that of Harry Burton at right-back. Harry had made a couple of appearances during the last campaign but it would be this one in which he became a regular in the side. Rovers too had adopted a similar approach, sticking with the guys who'd got them their fourth place finish the last time around.

Now both clubs knew that it was imperative to get off to a good start, not only by winning games but also by making use of the light nights to fit in one or two midweek matches whilst they could. As it happened, neither of them got off to much of a flyer, with Rovers' season in particular struggling to even make it off the ground. The red and whites were fixtureless on three of the first seven Saturdays of the new campaign, including the opening day, completed no midweek games and didn't make an appearance at Gedling Road until the third week in October, by which time they'd played just four league games compared with the nine achieved by a number of other sides in the division. It didn't help that the club had organised another weekend at the Blackpool Illuminations but at least this time, unlike the previous year, they had kept a clear space in the fixture list. For those players who went to Bloomfield Road to see Blackpool play there was at least a game for them to remember. The home side thrashed Sunderland seven-nil whilst giving the run around to the visitors' new centre-half, Charlie Hurley. He probably wondered just what he'd let himself in for following his big money transfer from Millwall as his new team found themselves a goal behind after just forty five seconds and three down by the ninth minute. On those occasions that Rovers actually played rather than watched, their form on the field matched the stop start nature of their season off it; they picked up a solitary win, drew twice, and went down heavily by five goals to two at Long Eaton Zingari. The one highlight of the period was a victory by the same margin over Notts Alliance Division One side Lenton Gregory in the first qualifying round of the Notts Senior Cup.

By contrast, whilst Rovers were absentee tenants at KGV as well as just occasional participants away from it, Marys had had a full fixture list, playing five times at home and ten in total, courtesy of two midweek games and their participation in the Amateur Cup.

Unfortunately, this had lasted just two rounds, both of which had seen the Saints drawn out of the hat against a team from the Central Alliance Division One. The maroon and golds had home advantage on both occasions and whilst they saw off Linby Colliery fairly comfortably three-one in the Extra Preliminary round, a fortnight later they fell to another pit team, Clay Cross and Danesmoor Miners Welfare. It was a tight contest with Len Rockley in good form in Marys' goal but despite having taken an early lead through inside-left Ron Hart, the Saints were finally edged out by the odd goal in five. The game turned out to be Ron's last for the club and would precipitate a search for a successor that would see no fewer than ten number tens wear the shirt before the season was out. Marys had better luck with their Senior Cup campaign though, despatching Midland Amateur Alliance side Nottinghamshire by five goals to one, a game which saw the return of Keith Moore after a year's absence and the goalscoring debut of the maroon and golds' fifth outside-right of the season so far, Mick Cripwell. Unfortunately, the Saints' league form had been as indifferent as Rovers' and they'd picked up just six points from their first six outings, winning three and losing three. To make matters worse, two of their defeats had come at the hands of old rivals Aspley Old Boys who'd at last taken the plunge to leave the Spartan League, two years after the Arnold clubs had made the move.

Marys' monopoly of Gedling Road finally came to an end some two weeks after Goose Fair had packed up and left the Forest and with Bonfire Night just around the corner. Rovers' visitors were Sutton Town Reserves and the two sides put on their own display of fireworks in the form of a ten goal thriller which ended in a six-four victory for the home side. However, having belatedly whetted the appetite of their fans with their sparkling display, the red and whites found themselves back on the road again for the next three weeks, the first two of which brought unwelcome defeats. Goals were again in plentiful supply as Rovers visited Heanor Town Reserves. The two teams provided another exciting spectacle for those watching but the Derbyshire side just got their noses in front to finish winners by the odd goal in nine. The following week it was the turn of Rufford Colliery to act as hosts, this time in the second qualifying round of the Senior Cup. The miners' side, like Rovers' opponents Lenton Gregory in the previous round, were members of the top division of the Notts Alliance, so another tough contest was anticipated. The visitors actually got off to the better start with a goal from newcomer John Exton after just ten minutes and there was very little to choose between the two teams. Although Rufford fought back with a couple of goals of their own, a Les Peel equaliser brought the sides level. The score remained locked at two apiece but with extra time looking almost certain, the home side broke away to snatch the winner with just three minutes left on the clock. Rovers' hopes of a long run in the competition had been dashed but they put their disappointment behind them seven days later by thrashing bottom markers Stanton Ironworks eight-two. The visit to the works' side also marked the end of the red and whites' nomadic spell that had seen them play no fewer than eight of their opening nine matches away from home. It can not have been good for the club's funds that it would be the middle of November, and almost three months into the season, before the half-time collecting bucket was sent round a second time.

Whilst Rovers were counting the cost of their unusual fixture list, Marys on the other hand had had plenty of opportunity to boost their own coffers. Aided by three home ties in cup competitions, the Saints had had the use of Gedling Road no less than eight times in comparison to their rivals' solitary appearance. When Rovers had been making their first appearance at Gedling Road Marys had travelled to Shirebrook and blitzed the Miners Welfare reserve outfit eleven-two but back at KGV they failed to capitalise on home ground advantage and took just a single point from the visits of Ilkeston Town Reserves and their counterparts from Heanor. Goals were in plentiful supply at the time with everyone in Marys' forward line scoring regularly but the Derbyshire sides were capable of causing defences trouble themselves. The games ended six-four to Ilkeston and four apiece against Heanor. When two more points were dropped the following week at leaders Kimberley Town, the Saints were stuck in mid-table with just eleven points from eleven matches. Apart from their double figure victory over Shirebrook the other highlight had been the pasting given to Bilsthorpe Colliery in the Senior Cup. Whilst one North Notts pit side was putting Rovers out of the competition at the same stage, Marys showed scant respect for the status of their mining visitors from the top tier of the Notts Alliance and saw them off by six goals to nil with Dennis Parr, still operating at centre-forward, leading the way with a hat-trick.

The amount of goals hitting the net at this time probably led to one or two restrained gestures of congratulation between the players, a handshake here and a pat on the back there, but to listen to the Chairman of the Football Association one might have imagined that the game was gripped by an epidemic of unmanly behaviour. Speaking at a referee's dinner in Wales, Sir Stanley Rous expressed his indignation at the practice of players hugging and kissing each other after a goal had been scored. "It is a dreadful habit" he said, one "which has crept in since the war. No-one runs along to kiss the goalkeeper when he has made a magnificent save." Well they do now Sir Stanley, and it's probably a good job that he's not here to see it, let alone having to watch the unedifying spectacle of a bunch of young, fit athletes writhing around on top of each other in a scene straight out of a Roman orgy just because one of them has scored a tap-in from a couple of yards out.

Now whichever way the upright young men of Arnold's two sides went about their own celebrations, they'd have plenty of chance to practice them over the next couple of months because despite the stop-go, in-and-out nature of their seasons so far, both teams were about to embark on an excellent spell of form to the end of the year.

Following their defeat against Kimberley, Marys set about the opposition in some style and racked up five straight wins at an average of five goals a game. Individual highlights included Geoff Lawton's hat-trick against British Ropes Reserves in the League Cup and a back-heeled goal by Dennis Parr against Nottingham Forest B but by far the most impressive team performance came in the third round of the Senior Cup. Ironically, Kimberley provided the opposition just two weeks after their previous meeting only this time Marys had ground advantage, the fourth time out of five that they'd been drawn at home in knock-out competitions this season. The Saints' near neighbours were clear leaders of the division at the time but it is often said that league form means nothing in a cup-tie and Marys set off at a cracking pace to prove the old adage correct. In fact Dennis Parr almost scored directly from the kick-off. Having won the ball with the game just seconds old he caught the opposition defence napping, swerved past the centre-half and only the keeper's save stopped his shot from entering the record books as one of the quickest ever recorded. The Saints' pressure following this dramatic start brought an early goal only for the visitors to equalise after twenty minutes. However, Kimberley's hopes of making a game of it were short lived as the maroon and golds ripped through their defence to add three more goals in a nine minute spell before half-time, and three more for good measure after the break. As equally satisfying as the result was the fact that every one of the home team's forwards ended up on the score sheet.

Marys' good run had seen them through to the semi-finals of the League Cup and the fourth qualifying round of the Senior Cup. In addition their league position had improved to seventh, just four points behind new leaders Heanor Town Reserves in what was shaping up to be the most open title race the division had seen since its reintroduction. The Saints might have been even higher had they not had the disappointment of the postponement of a home fixture the Saturday before Christmas. Scheduled to meet Shirebrook Miners Welfare Reserves, the home side were all changed and raring to go but only six of the opposition had bothered to put in an appearance. Marys were by now charging admission to their matches and whilst quite a number of spectators had already parted with their money and had chosen their favourite spot around the perimeter of the pitch, even more were waiting on the approach to the ground to see whether the missing visitors would be showing up. They didn't, and the disappointed fans either dispersed immediately or queued up to get a refund. Amazingly the situation almost repeated itself the following week when British Ropes Reserves were due to make the trip down from Retford. This time though all eleven visiting players did eventually turn up but only after the kick-off had been delayed for the second week in a row. Even then the last of them didn't take the field until the game was twenty minutes old and it was hardly a surprise that the Saints saw off their challenge by five goals to two.

Whilst Marys were enjoying their resurgence in form Rovers were having an even better run of their own. Following their victory at Stanton, they notched up a further seven straight wins, six of which were in the league, to move themselves rapidly up the table from fourth bottom to next to top. With most of the leaders dropping points to each other the red and whites now had, improbable as it may seem, the best record in the division, and were just a point off the lead with two games in hand. This amazing change had been achieved in just eight weeks; not quite with the spectacular goalscoring of their town rivals but with impressive performances nonetheless. Standouts were victories over Kimberley and Aspley Old Boys in the league and the elimination of Sutton Town Reserves at Priestsic Road in the first round of the League Cup. The side had taken on a settled look now that Ken Crump had joined his ex-Raleigh team mate John Exton to form a strong half back line either side of number five Alec Casterton. John Pike had rejoined the club and Ron Maddocks was prominent on the scoresheet, claiming a notable hat-trick in Rovers' three-two victory over Creswell Colliery Reserves, a game which also saw the debut of right winger John Douglas.

Both Marys' and Rovers' excellent spells of form had been played in better than average conditions given the time of the year, but as 1957 drew to its close the weather took a seasonal turn for the worse. Rovers' last fixture of the old year, an away trip to Belper Town Reserves in the second round of the League Cup, fell victim to the bad weather and seven days later the red and whites' home game against Ransome and Marles Reserves had to be postponed too, though on this occasion due to lack of availability of a ground rather than the state of it. The first Saturday of the New Year was set aside for the fourth qualifying round of the Notts Senior Cup and with the Saints having been drawn at home yet again, this time to another Notts Alliance top division side Bestwood Colliery, the staging of the tie, as was the tradition, took priority over league fixtures. Having already handsomely despatched their three previous opponents in this season's competition Marys went into the match strong favourites. The colliery side were having a poor season and despite treacherous conditions underfoot, the pitch being both frozen and muddy by turns, the Saints assumed command early on and never let up the pressure, running out easy winners by five goals to nil. It could have been even more but the visitors twice kicked off the line with the keeper beaten.

The following week Marys were involved in an unusual set of circumstances that saw them just scrape a victory over Long Eaton Zingari but incur a fine in the process. At the eleventh hour the Saints had to make five changes from the side that had been unchanged for the previous five matches. First team regulars Len Rockley, Ron Hinson, Dennis Wheat, Geoff Lawton, and Dennis Parr were all unavailable and there was no option other than replace them with guys from the second team. It was this last minute decimation of the reserve team that caused the problem. Unable now to field a side, the reserves didn't show up for their game against Sherwood Rangers in the Notts Amateur League. Unfortunately the home side did, along with the match referee, and the league's management committee took a dim view of the proceedings. They fined Marys ten shillings and sixpence for the non-fulfilment of the fixture and ordered them to pay the ground expenses together with the referee's fee and expenses. With the hybrid first eleven just edging a win by the odd goal in seven to pick up two valuable league points, the Saints' own committee probably thought that it was a sum worth paying.

Whilst this little scenario was being played out Rovers' game at Belper in the League Cup finally got under way. The luck of the draw had gone against them yet again, this being their fourth away tie in a row, but as befits a team with eight straight wins behind them they didn't let a two week break affect their form. Attacking from the start they were two up after a quarter of an hour thanks to goals from Jimmy Raven and Ron Maddocks, and even though the home side pulled one back, Ron restored the lead on thirty-five minutes. From there on Rovers' command of the game was never really threatened and they ran out winners by six goals to three. Jimmy Raven continued his goalscoring form with a hat-trick in the following week's six-two victory over Nottingham Forest B and seven days later Rovers were back at Belper to repeat their earlier cup win, this time by four goals to one. Unusually, given that bad weather across the country had played havoc with the fixture list, Marys' game at Gedling Road included, the Derbyshire club's Christchurch Meadow ground had been playable when two weeks earlier it had succumbed to the elements.

Now if the weather was a little iffy at this time thousands of miles to the south it was many times worse. Just a few days before Rovers' latest game at Belper, Dr Vivian Fuchs had met Sir Edmund Hillary at the South Pole. They were members of a joint Commonwealth Trans-Antarctic expedition which had set off from opposite ends of the continent the previous November, Fuchs and his British team from Shackleton Camp near the Weddell Sea and

Hillary's New Zealand team from Scott Camp near the Ross Sea. The plan had then been to retrace the latter's route back to Scott Camp together and in doing so enable Fuchs and his party to complete the 2158 mile crossing. However, poor weather had meant that the British party, who'd arrived at the Pole two weeks after Hillary had reached it, was almost three weeks behind schedule with climatic conditions rapidly worsening. Undeterred, the joint party set off and after a journey of ninety nine days finally reached their destination at the beginning of March. It was the first surface crossing of the Antarctic and, on his return, Dr Fuchs was rewarded with an immediate knighthood for his feat of successfully finishing what had come to be known as 'the last great journey in the world'.

Whilst the intrepid explorers were completing the second leg of their historic journey, Rovers continued to battle the elements too although on the first day of February there was a temporary respite from the worst of the weather. The red and whites had at last been given a home draw, their first of the season, and their reward was the visit of Aspley Old Boys in the semi-final of the League Cup. They'd already beaten their old rivals at KGV back on Boxing Day and they got off to the perfect start in trying to emulate that result when, despite some early pressure from the Old Boys, Les Peel scored with a speculative effort from all of forty-five yards. Although Aspley recovered from this setback to gain an equaliser, two more goals from Ron Maddocks and another from John Douglas saw Rovers repeat the four-one scoreline of the holiday game. Having secured their place in the final, where they would await the winners of Marys' tie with Heanor, the red and whites were at home again the following week and extended their fantastic winning run to thirteen games with an odd goal in five victory against Ilkeston Town Reserves. The weather had taken another turn for the worse and it was a surprise that the condition of the Gedling Road pitch proved playable. Over thirty English and Scottish League fixtures were postponed, including Notts' and Mansfield's home games as snow, frost, and a rapid thaw upset the football programme once more. Some grounds had been covered by more than six inches of snow and at local level play was impossible at three of the area's major public recreation fields: Victoria Embankment, Bulwell Hall Park, and Highfields.

All this was just a minor inconvenience because just two days earlier a real tragedy had taken place involving appalling weather conditions and a football team that also played in red and white. With all due respect to Rovers, this team was one of the most famous in the land; Manchester United. At the time they were the English champions and had qualified to play in the current season's European Cup. The side was young with an average age of just twenty-four and contained a number of internationals including Roger Byrne, Tommy Taylor and the peerless Duncan Edwards, as well as future England legend Bobby Charlton. Managed by Matt Busby, their tender years had earned them the nickname 'Busby's Babes' and in the days when football followers were far less tribal in their support of the game than they unfortunately seem to be now, the Reds' success in Europe was being eagerly followed across the country. They'd reached the quarter final stage of the competition and been drawn to play Yugoslavia's Red Star Belgrade. The tie was played over two legs and with the advantage of a win in the home game, a three-all draw in Belgrade had been sufficient to secure United a place in the last four.

A great future awaited the young side as they boarded their British European Airways flight at Belgrade Airport. Take off had been delayed because a United player had mislaid his passport but otherwise the journey was untroubled and the plane touched down in Munich for a scheduled refuelling stop. The weather in the Bavarian capital was appalling and two attempts to take off on the second leg of the flight had to be aborted, leading to the fateful decision to try a third time. The aircraft never got off the runway and ended up breaching a fence surrounding the airport and smashing into a nearby house. Of the forty-three passengers on board, twenty-three lost their lives, eight of them players, and two more of the team never played again as a direct result of their injuries.

The incident was timed as having taken place at four minutes past four in the afternoon, local time, but with a time zone difference of an hour the news started to filter through in the UK in the middle part of the afternoon. I'd arrived home from school as usual at around four o'clock and was looking forward to a pre-dinner treat, maybe a slice of bread and dripping or a packet of sweet cigarettes, the kind of things that a nine year old needs for a balanced diet, when I heard the news on the radio that there had been a plane crash involving Manchester United. I recollect that specific information as to casualties was pretty sketchy to start with but by the time my dad came home from work with a late edition of the evening paper the victims were already being named in the stop press column.

Now whilst I was a football fanatic even at that early age and had a natural interest in Marys' and Rovers' exploits, I was already bound by some invisible force towards the almost terminally underachieving Magpies of Notts County. Indeed, even this very season they were again skirting with relegation, and unfortunately it would turn out to be a case of one struggle too many. To be fair, they had looked like avoiding the drop once again until Lincoln City performed a feat of escapology that Harry Houdini himself would have been proud of. At the beginning of April the Imps were rooted to the bottom of the Second Division table with just five wins from their thirty six matches. They'd also just lost their last eight games too and were odds-on favourites to be playing third division football the following season. That was until they contrived, improbably, to win every one of their last six matches and push my beloved County through the trapdoor by just a single point. There was a sense of inevitability about Lincoln's whole comeback through the closing weeks of the campaign and my heart sunk each time the news of their latest victory came through. When the last and decisive result came through, a three-one home win over Cardiff City four days after the Magpies had finished their fixtures, I was inconsolable.

It wasn't that I was a mardy child but County were the sporting love of my life and I'd so much wanted them to stay up. I wasn't normally in the habit of losing control of my emotions but this was now the third occasion that I'd shed a tear over something to do with football. The first had been Notts' ejection from the Cup a few years earlier against York, referred to previously, but the second time was nothing at all to do with the Magpies. It was in fact that very moment when I began to look down the newspaper at the list of names of those who'd died at Munich. I'm not sure why it touched me so much but it did and, judging not only by contemporary reports but historical retrospectives too, it seemed that I wasn't alone. In the aftermath of the crash public sympathy was widespread and it's hard not to draw the conclusion that the tragic circumstances in which so many young men were cut down in their prime was a significant factor in the club's subsequent popularity. Indeed, in their first league match following the accident, ironically at home against Forest, a new post-war record crowd of over sixty-six thousand were in attendance.

Just forty eight hours after the crash, every game that had managed to survive the weather was preceded by the traditional mark of respect of a minutes' silence. Despite the widespread postponements, Marys' match joined Rovers' in being just about playable, although given the eventual outcome of the game everyone connected with the club might have wished that it had joined the other fixtures and been called off. Away at Sutton Town Reserves the Saints gave a debut to full-back Norman Gough but went down to their heaviest defeat of the season, four-nil, leaving them below halfway in the table with just nineteen points from seventeen games. Even without the awful events in Munich, the last four weeks had been the worst of Marys' season.

It had started with a four-two defeat away at Heanor Town Reserves in the league, had been followed by the postponement of a home League Cup tie against the same team the following week, and had continued with a gallant but ultimately disappointing clash with Eastwood Town in the Notts Senior Cup. The tie was the First Round Proper and with just eight teams left in the competition was in reality a quarter final. Marys' luck with home draws had finally run out and they had to travel to Coronation Park to meet the current leaders of the Notts Alliance. Eastwood, as befitted their position, were no mugs and had hammered Aspley Old Boys in the previous round by seven goals to two. They'd also go on to win their next league fixture by twelve goals to one so no-one in the Saints' camp were under any delusions as to the severity of the task ahead. In the event the game turned out to be a thriller from the very first kick and Marys were awarded the accolade of being the best visiting side seen at Eastwood this season. Scoring first through Geoff Lawton the Saints outpaced the home side in the early stages but were behind at the break thanks to two goals late in the half. After the interval the maroon and golds soon equalised and whilst their opponents were temporarily down to ten men through injury they took a grip of the game, adding two more goals for a four-two lead. Once Eastwood had been restored to a full complement though the game swung back in the hosts' favour and it was Marys' turn to come under pressure. Unfortunately, their defence was breached twice more to force the game into extra time and with the excitement mounting it was the Badgers who secured victory with the ninth and last goal of an enthralling tie. It was a disheartening way to end the game but their performance had showed that the Saints were quite capable of doing even better in the competition in the near future.

Following Marys' poor showing at Sutton, their form improved even if the weather didn't. In a five game spell to the middle of March the Saints won four of them and drew the other whilst getting back on the goalscoring trail with a vengeance. The first of the sequence was a tight two-one victory over Kimberley played in treacherous conditions at KGV, followed by a share of the spoils in a four-all draw against Ransome and Marles Reserves. For the next match, the two Dennises, Parr and Wheat, were involved in a shirt swap. The younger of the Parr brothers had been playing at centre forward for just over a year although before that he had spent most of his time with the club as a defender. Dennis Wheat had been the first choice centre-half, earning glowing reports, since his signing the previous season and the change certainly looked an intriguing one at the time. Any doubts as to the wisdom of the move were soon dispelled when the new number nine hit two goals in the first forty five minutes against Creswell Colliery Reserves. Four-one up at the break Marys added another five in the second period to give themselves a major boost in advance of the following week's League Cup Semi-Final against Heanor Town Reserves.

The Saints' luck was in once more as they'd been drawn first out of the hat yet again but as the game kicked off home advantage meant very little. For the first half hour a snow storm obliterated play and it wasn't surprising that the game remained goalless. Once the conditions began to improve play became more expansive and goals from Keith Moore and Dennis Wheat helped the home side settle down. Leading two-one at the break Marys rammed home their superiority in the second period and finished comfortable winners by six goals to two. Even more importantly their win had given the town's football followers yet another all-Arnold cup final to look forward to and with the two sides yet to meet in the league the run-in to the end of the season promised to rank with any seen before.

The first of the local derbies was just a fortnight away but before that the maroon and golds travelled to Stanton to meet the division's bottom markers. The result was never in doubt as an all-out offensive from the off brought the Saints their first goal after just three minutes, two more before half-time and another four by the final whistle. The only black mark was the sending off of Keith Moore and an opponent after an exchange of blows. It must have been a pretty serious altercation because at that time referees appeared so reluctant to apply the ultimate sanction that a player needed to commit GBH to even get a talking to.

Whilst Marys' good run had brought them seven league points they remained stuck halfway up the table. Rovers too hadn't moved from their spot in second place, but that was as a result of a dearth of games rather than a lack of success. The red and whites, thanks to poor weather and ground unavailability, had managed to play just three matches to the Saints' five but despite heavy conditions they'd extended their fantastic run to sixteen straight wins with three more victories that were steady rather than spectacular, with Ron Maddocks again prominent amongst the goalscorers. Rovers' league position was misleading though because the leaders Ilkeston Town Reserves were just two points ahead but had played five games more and third placed Ransomes, who were on level points with the Arnold side had played six matches more. The teams with the next best record for least points lost were Heanor with eleven and Kimberley and Sutton with twelve each, so considering that the red and whites had dropped just six the prospects of them taking the title were pretty good. The only downside was that with just six Saturdays of the season left they still had thirteen league matches to play.

So, after seven months of avoiding each other, the two Arnold sides were finally set to meet three times in just six weeks and as luck would have it the two league games would be played back to back on the last two weekends of March. The first was Marys' home game and a big crowd turned up for the long awaited meeting. They were well wrapped up too because although it was a bright day it was accompanied by a chilling wind.

GEDLING ROAD PACKED FOR THE 22 MARCH 1958 DERBY (Courtesy Football Post)

Rovers drew first blood with an early goal from Les Peel and as was the norm when the two sides met play was fast with both teams forcing the other onto the back foot. The Saints gradually came more into the play and on the half-hour Dennis Wheat equalised from a Mick Cripwell cross. The score remained at one apiece at the break but only thanks to a fingertip save by Rovers' keeper Sam Archer from Keith Moore's terrific shot just before the half-time whistle.

RAY BENNETT THWARTED BY FRANNY GREENSMITH AND KEN CRUMP 22 MAR 1958 (FP)

The two teams, much as might be expected, had been evenly matched, but it was the visitors who had the better of the opening period of the second half. With the biting wind at their backs Rovers pinned Marys back and it was inevitable that their pressure would tell. Ron Maddocks fired in a goal bound shot which had Len Rockley well beaten but Dennis Parr came to the rescue and blocked the effort on the goal line. Unfortunately, in doing so, he'd used his hands and a penalty was awarded to Rovers. Nowadays Dennis would have been automatically sent off for committing what is known as a 'professional' foul, a slight misnomer considering that it applies to all players whether paid or not, but back then he stayed on the field without even a ticking off from the referee. To make matters worse, the red and whites' left-back George Wileman proceeded to fire the ball wide from the penalty spot and the visitors had missed a golden opportunity to take command of the game. It turned out to be a costly miss. Encouraged by this let off Marys came back strongly and just after he'd hit the bar with one effort, Mick Cripwell made no mistake the second time to put the Saints ahead. It was a lead that they didn't relinquish and a third goal later in the game sealed a decisive victory. It was a pity that as Marys were effectively out of the title race the game brought them little more than the two points and bragging rights for a week but they had succeeded where sixteen other teams had failed and brought to an end Rovers' great run lasting almost five months.

Seven days later the red and whites had the perfect opportunity to make amends, especially considering that the outcome of the first game had effectively turned on the missed penalty and that on another day the result could just as easily gone their way. Conditions were heavy underfoot and impeded both sides' style of play but both goalmouths soon saw plenty of action nevertheless. Sam Archer in Rovers' goal saved a fierce shot from Mick Cripwell and at the other end the ball was kicked off Marys' goal line three times in as many seconds with the keeper beaten. With the match finely balanced Keith Moore eventually broke the deadlock with a header to give the Saints the lead, one that they maintained until half-time. Immediately after the break Len Rockley made a great save from Les Peel at point-blank range and the score remained at one-nil until well into the second half when Rovers, seeking to maintain their hundred percent home record, fought back and grabbed the equaliser. Neither side could add to their score in the final stages and the game ended one apiece. Whilst it was the first point dropped by the red and whites at home all season, they remained the only team in the league unbeaten at on their own ground. Despite slipping back to fourth in the table they had lost the fewest points of any side in the league and if the fighting spirit they'd shown in the two clashes with Marys was anything to go by then they were still in with a great chance of taking the title.

The Saints' successes over Rovers had taken their own unbeaten run to seven matches, a sequence that they then extended to ten with three convincing away victories in which they scored no less than sixteen times. However, Marys' ultra slim chances of finishing top would have required results to go very badly wrong for the teams above them in the table but when they picked up just a point from their next two outings they were left only with the prospects of a top five or six finish at best. Even with little to play for other than pride the Saints finished off the league campaign with a flourish by winning their last four matches. Once again they'd had a tremendous second half to the season, losing just once in their last sixteen games, but had seen their efforts stymied by a poor start. At least they had the consolation of knowing that the all-Arnold League Cup Final gave them one last chance to pick up some silverware.

The team who stood in their way in that competition though had had more important things on their mind. Having dropped those three points to Marys, Rovers had bounced straight back with maximum points from an Easter double, a three-one victory over Ironville Amateurs on the Saturday and an excellent three-nil win against fellow title contenders Kimberley Town on Easter Monday. Their title chase was back on track and when they completed another, rather more unusual, double the following week they strengthened their position as favourites to land the championship.

With nine matches remaining and the season rapidly running out of time in which to play them, Rovers and their next opponents British Ropes Reserves hadn't yet met so they agreed to play each other twice on the same day. The Retford side were scheduled to make the trip to Gedling Road and so the clubs decided that to ease fixture congestion they would play a double header. The ground advantage clearly lay with Rovers but they gave a disappointing display in the first half of the opening game and even went behind just after half-time. The visitors were sitting next to bottom of the league at kick-off and this wasn't quite what the home fans had been expecting. Thankfully the red and whites were stung into action and a wave of constant attacking finally brought its reward with the equaliser from John Pike and the winner from Jimmy Raven. It had been a close run thing, a bit too close for comfort in fact, but two points were in the bag with the prospect of more after the tea break. Both clubs had taken the precaution of having spare players on call and were able to make changes for the evening match but happily, this one proved far less problematical for Rovers as they eased to a four-one victory. Les Peel with a couple and John Pike with his second of the day were the scorers, along with John Douglas who was one of the players introduced for the second game. When the red and whites beat Shirebrook Miners Welfare Reserves at home two evenings later they were back at the top of the table. With just six games left they'd opened up a two point gap over their nearest challengers Sutton Town Reserves; just as importantly they also had a game in hand of them too.

Rovers, unbeaten now in six matches and with five wins on the trot, had recovered well after the disappointment of the two local derbies. If they could steer clear of injuries and keep their nerve then the title looked like being theirs for the taking. Then, just when it was least expected and certainly when it was most unwanted, a communication arrived to put a dampener on proceedings. It concerned the previous Saturday's games with British Ropes. Despite the agreement reached between the two sides, it transpired that the Central Alliance hadn't given their permission for the second game to take place and that the result would not be allowed to stand. Rovers would have to travel to Retford at a date to be arranged to fulfil the fixture, not an easy task considering that the calendar was already choc-a-block. They were already committed to playing their final six league games in an exhausting ten day spell and, when the two clubs found one of the few slots available to them both, this became an even more gruelling seven games in eleven days.

The attitude of the league certainly seemed harsh. They themselves had given permission for a match between the two colliery sides of Creswell and Linby in Division One North to be played for four points but that was because neither side were in contention for honours. Whether Rovers and their Retford opponents had approached the Central Alliance for permission to play a four pointer isn't known but it would probably have been turned down on the grounds that it might have given an unfair advantage to the red and whites in the title chase. The compromise reached by the two clubs had seemed sensible in the circumstances, and after all it was a *bona fide* contest refereed by a neutral, accredited official.

Even with seven games now to go though, it was still Rovers' title to lose and when they took three points from their next two matches the situation hadn't changed, except in the league table where the chalking off of the disallowed win had dropped them back to second place, wedged between the only other two teams who could win the championship.

	P	W	D	L	F	A	P
Sutton Town Res	29	21	3	5	112	57	45
Arnold Rovers	27	20	4	3	85	46	44
Kimberley Town	28	20	2	6	106	53	42

In actual fact the above table never appeared in any newspapers because for some illogical reason the official Central Alliance version that was published right through to the end of the season confusingly and incorrectly continued to include the result of Rovers' second game against British Ropes.

Despite this, Rovers' destiny remained in their own hands as they travelled the short distance to Melbourne Road to meet old rivals Aspley Old Boys for their third game in four days. Ominously, injuries were already beginning to bite. With everyone available Rovers had already beaten the Old Boys twice this season, four-one on both occasions, but centre-half Alec Casterton had been ruled out of the run-in and an even bigger blow had been the loss of inside-right Ron Maddocks. The number eight had been in excellent form all season and had racked up a tremendous tally of thirty-nine goals so it was a major setback for both the player and the team when he suffered an ankle fracture against Shirebrook. Despite Rovers putting up as good a performance as might be expected in the circumstances, the home side prevailed by two goals to nil. All of a sudden the red and whites were under a bit of pressure, probably not quite as great as the Football Post would have it when referring to the defeat at Aspley as a 'severe setback', but pressure nonetheless, especially as their next game less than forty-eight hours later was away against leaders Sutton Town Reserves.

The FP gave the clash the title of 'Division II championship decider' but that was not exactly correct. Obviously, a loss by either side would be damaging but it wouldn't necessarily be fatal. Of course a win for Rovers would be the perfect outcome and even a draw would be a good result and, with the regular half-back line missing completely and Jack Brace being called up for a very rare appearance in the forward line, it seemed, with just five minutes left to play, that a precious point was about to be gained. Rovers had had much the better of the first half and had taken the lead with a header from Mick Holmes just before the break and although Sutton had equalised around the hour mark the game stayed deadlocked at one apiece. Unfortunately, with the players enquiring just how much time was left, the home side's centre-forward slipped through the red and white's makeshift defence to snatch a dramatic winner. It was a bitter pill to swallow because not only had the advantage in the title race switched dramatically to the Ashfield side, Rovers' were now in the position of having to rely on Sutton and Kimberley dropping points to give themselves renewed hope of claiming the trophy.

With little or no time to recover from the ever increasing number of knocks they were picking up, Rovers somehow managed to produce two great wins on the Monday and Wednesday night, seeing off the reserve sides of Belper Town four-one and Heanor Town by the odd goal in three. It had been a great effort from the red and whites and had kept their outside chances of the title very much alive. Then came tremendous but unexpected news; Kimberley Town had dropped a crucial point against Aspley and Sutton had been beaten in their penultimate game of the season. Rovers could hardly have dared hope for both their nearest rivals to falter and now they just had. All of a sudden in this hectic, draining, but very exciting climax to the season, the momentum had switched back yet again and the Arnold side were just two games from a fantastic League and Cup double.

The final league game of the season, the rearranged fixture against British Ropes Reserves, had been shoehorned into the schedule in about the only place it could have been; just twenty-four hours after the Heanor game and only two days before the League Cup Final against Marys. The league table, had it appeared in print, should have looked like this:

	P	W	D	L	F	A	P
Sutton Town Res	32	23	3	6	123	60	49
Kimberley Town	32	23	3	6	122	60	49
Arnold Rovers	31	22	4	5	92	52	48

Sutton had won their last game of the season by eight goals to nil to edge above Kimberley by the narrowest of margins and with Rovers' goal average being significantly inferior only a win would enable the red and whites to clinch the title right at the death.

Whatever state of mind and health Rovers' party of players, committee men, and fans were in as they made their way up the A614 to Retford on the evening of the first Thursday in May, there was no escaping the fact that it was a very patched up eleven who eventually took the field for the club's most important game yet in the three years that they'd been in the Central Alliance. The opposition, next to bottom in the table, would normally have held no fears for the red and whites but there was always a sneaking suspicion that a midweek fixture against a reserve outfit late in the season might just see them bolstered by the inclusion of one or two first teamers.

Now whether this was the case is a matter of conjecture because no report of the match exists and present-day memories of the game amongst everyone that I've spoken to are, at best, vague and rather more usually completely non-existent. The local weekly newspaper, the Retford Times, didn't even include the result of the match in its next edition despite being crammed full of scores from minor games in the district. Thankfully, the Nottingham Evening Post came to the rescue in its Friday editions. There, tucked in amongst the scores from the previous day's fixtures was 'British Ropes Reserves 1 Arnold Rovers 2'; the red and whites had taken the title. A couple of days later the newspaper followed this up with a small item that confirmed that Rovers, despite being hampered by injuries, had taken the championship with fifty points.

Considering what had been at stake the last league game of the red and whites' campaign had attracted a minimum of attention but that would certainly not be the case with the climax to the season as a whole, the eagerly awaited clash with their greatest rivals Marys on the Saturday evening in the final of the Central Alliance Division Two Cup Final.

Such was the interest in the game that a match day programme was produced by local printers W H & H Parr. It cost sixpence and featured the team line-ups, pen pictures of both sides, and over two dozen adverts from local businesses. It was the first publication of its kind for eight years and it would be half as long again before another was produced in Arnold on a regular basis. Both sides posed for the traditional pre-match photographs before the action began with the one featuring Marys clearly showing the Friar Tuck pub still being built. With over two thousand fans in attendance the Home Brewery might have wished to have finished its construction a bit earlier. The Rovers' shot was as interesting for the players who were missing as it was for the eleven actually snapped by the cameraman. The walking wounded were back for the big game but long term casualties Alec Casterton and Ron Maddocks were obviously missing. There was one other notable absentee from their ranks too; cup-tied John Pike would be taking no part in proceedings either.

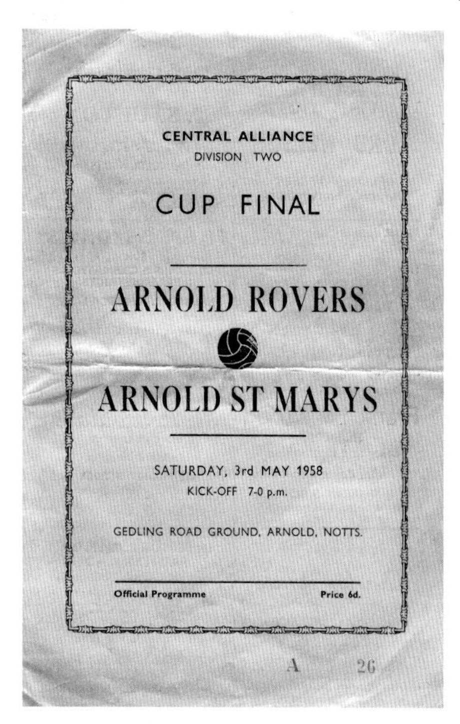
CENTRAL ALLIANCE
DIVISION TWO

CUP FINAL

ARNOLD ROVERS

ARNOLD ST MARYS

SATURDAY, 3rd MAY 1958
KICK-OFF 7-0 p.m.

GEDLING ROAD GROUND, ARNOLD, NOTTS.

Official Programme Price 6d.

M. J. THOMPSON
COAL & HAULAGE CO., LTD.
COAL - COKE - COALITE
AND ALL TYPES OF OTHER FUELS

M. J. THOMPSON
HIGH CLASS
PROVISIONS - COOKED MEATS
GREEN GROCERY Etc.

20 CALVERTON ROAD, ARNOLD, NOTTINGHAM
Telephone: Nottingham 26-7671

ARNOLD ST MARYS Football Club

L. Rockley
N. Gough H. Burton
R. Hinson D. Parr J. Whetton
M. Cripwell K. Moore D. Wheat P. Smith G. Parr

Referee: J. R. Hirst (Retford)
G. Walker (Aspley)
F. Nuttall (Warsop) Linesmen

R. Carter J. Raven L. Peel M. Holmes J. Douglas
K. Crump W. Whitt J. Exton
G. Wileman F. Greensmith
S. Archer

ARNOLD ROVERS Football Club

SEVEN STARS
After the Match
SEVEN STARS
for Prize Ales every night

RADIO - TELEVISION
FURNITURE
From the Good Service Store
SIMPSON'S
1 HIGH STREET, ARNOLD
Telephone Nottm. 262102

FRONT COVER AND CENTRE PAGE TEAM LINE-UPS CENTRAL ALLIANCE DIVISION 2 CUP FINAL PROGRAMME 3 MAY 1958

(Ron Hinson Collection)

In fact Alec and John had spent the afternoon together at the latter's house watching the FA Cup Final on television. Another patched up side, Manchester United, had taken on Bolton Wanderers in the traditional showpiece finale of the professional season. United, so cruelly ripped apart at Munich just three months earlier, had somehow managed to get to Wembley with a mixture of survivors and new signings but in the final analysis had come up just short against their Lancashire rivals led by centre forward Nat Lofthouse, nicknamed the 'Lion of

Vienna' thanks to his exploits in the England shirt a few years earlier in a famous victory over the then powerful Austrian national side. Bolton's talisman had scored both their goals in the two-nil defeat of United but it was his second that lives in the memory. Back in the days when goalkeepers had nowhere near the kind of protection they are afforded these days, Lofthouse bundled United's keeper Harry Gregg, ball and all, over the line and was accredited with the goal.

This maltreatment of the man in goal would eventually be outlawed, but a few hours after the Bolton centre-forward had clinched a cup-winners medal for himself and his team, his actions, if not necessarily the same outcome, were repeated down at Gedling Road.

AC : I can remember Keith Moore coming through like Lofthouse and trying to knock Sam [Archer] over the goal line. Sam just set himself and Keith bounced off him. He had no chance.

MARYS 3 MAY 1958 CENTRAL ALLIANCE DIVISION 2 CUP FINAL : Back Row (l to r); S Gray, R Hinson, D Parr, W Parr, J Whetton, L Rockley, N Gough, H Burton, L Peck. Front Row; W Archer, M Cripwell, K Moore, D Wheat, P Smith, G Parr, - -.

(Arnold Library Collection)

The one thing that Marys did manage to repeat successfully was the scoreline. They too were without a couple of players who had played a part in the successes of the season but to be fair the eleven who ended up playing in the final had been picking themselves for weeks in the run-in. Only Phil 'Piddy' Smith was a relative newcomer in attack, the rest had been banging goals in for fun all year. If the respective goal tallies of the two centre-forwards fielded by the Saints during the season, the Dennises Wheat and Parr, were combined, the total would have been thirty-two. Geoff Parr had hit an impressive twenty-three goals from the left wing whilst the pairing on the opposite flank had been pretty prolific too. Number seven Mick Cripwell and his inside-right partner Keith Moore had hit the target twenty-five and twenty times respectively. Little wonder that they were thought by many judges to be the best right wing partnership in the division.

With this kind of firepower and with many of the Rovers' side running on empty, there was very little chance that having manoeuvred themselves into a two goal lead the Saints would relinquish it. They didn't, and another fantastic season had been brought to its climactic conclusion with the two Arnold sides sharing the spoils; to Marys the Cup and to Rovers the League.

Three years earlier both clubs had made the tentative step up from the Spartan League and now their success had shown that they were obviously ready for the next stage in their fascinating rivalry. It would have been pointless trying to split the two sides over the whole season because although the Saints had had the better of Rovers in their head to head matches, including the League Cup Final, Rovers had clinched that all-important league title. The honours board needed amending though and now read:

ROVERS : SIX CHAMPIONSHIPS, SIX CUPS (INCL ONE SHARED)

MARYS : ONE CHAMPIONSHIP, FOUR CUPS (INCL ONE SHARED)

REGENT : THREE CUPS

CHAPTER FOURTEEN 1958-59

The summer of 1958 was one of the most pleasant in living memory; well in mine at least. It was great to be alive and nine years old living in Arnold, Nottingham, even though my beloved Magpies had just been relegated. After all, my young mind figured that we'd soon be back whence we'd come; how could I know that I'd be twenty-five with two young children of my own before County regained their position in the second division?

Hula hoops, the plastic kind, were whizzing round various parts of the anatomy of kids all over our estate, and apparently the world too considering that over one hundred million would eventually end up being sold. Christine, who lived next door to us, could keep two going at the same time, one around her neck and the other somewhere between her waist and hips. She made it look so easy that all the adults around our way made themselves look positively stupid as they tried to emulate her world-class technique. An inevitable part of growing up is that unfortunate moment when one's parents and their friends embarrass you with their 'trying-to-act-cool' antics; this was one of those occasions, unfortunately repeated three or four years later when they all discovered the latest dance craze 'The Twist'.

That was later though and this particular close season marked the beginning of a great chapter in the history of world football as a young seventeen year old, Edson Arantes do Nascimento, better known as Pele, burst onto the scene in the 1958 World Cup held in Sweden. This tournament had seen the four home nations qualify for the world's premier competition for the first and only time but none had progressed beyond the quarter finals. Television viewers back in the UK were amply compensated by the exploits of the precocious Brazilian youngster and his audacious ability, and one of his two goals in the final, where he flicked the ball over a covering defender and volleyed it past the despairing dive of the Swedish goalkeeper, will live forever in the memory of those privileged to see it; that and the whole Brazilian side carrying a massive flag of the host country around the ground at the end of the game.

It was that time of year too when a little pocketbook publication, the Post Football Guide, made its annual appearance at local newsagents. Produced by the Nottingham Football Post, It had first seen the light of day way back in 1905 and, apart from the war years, had been issued every close season since. Distinctive in appearance with its yellow edged cover and spine, it contained comprehensive details of the season just finished, together with fixtures for the forthcoming campaign, for all of the region's League clubs. It also featured final tables for the Football League, Scottish League, Midland League, and Central Alliance, as well as having a section of photographs showing not just League clubs but also local sides too. There, on page one hundred and eighteen, was a team picture of Rovers under the caption 'CENTRAL ALLIANCE (DIVISION II) CHAMPIONS', the first time a photo of an Arnold side had ever featured in the Guide, whilst page two hundred and twelve clearly showed the red and whites sitting proudly at the top of the table, a point ahead of Sutton Town Reserves.

If only it were true.

The unfortunate fact of the matter was that Rovers weren't champions at all. The first Football Post of the 1958-59 season tried to explain why in its Central Alliance round-up:

"At this late hour it has transpired that after all, Arnold Rovers, although they have been presented with the trophy, and may still be in charge of it, were not second division champions. The final table, it appears, when officially issued in May last, credited the Rovers, in error, with a win in the replayed game against British Ropes Reserves at Retford, whereas the verdict went against them. Instead of having 50 points as shown in the official table of results, they had obtained only 48, and as an outcome, the Arnold club finished third to Sutton Town Reserves, the correct champions, and Kimberley Town, who finished level, on the 49 points mark. Sutton have a very slight advantage indeed on goals average. The correct final records were:"

	P	W	D	L	F	A	P
Sutton Town Res	32	23	3	6	123	60	49
Kimberley Town	32	23	3	6	122	60	49
Arnold Rovers	32	22	4	6	93	54	48

The FP summed up the bad news thus:

"These facts will create deep disappointment in the Arnold district."

Well, as understatements go, it was pretty much spot on, and the 'facts' certainly didn't go down too well amongst certain of the players.

AC : They all said we'd won the championship and then it turned out we hadn't. We were all choked about it, well me and Johnny Pike were anyway because we'd lived for it. They told us officially that we'd won it and then they reversed it. They took it off us.

CENTRAL ALLIANCE (DIVISION II) CHAMPIONS

118

Arnold Rovers—Back row (left to right) : K. Crump, W. Whitt, J. Exton, S. Archer, F. Greensmith, G. Wileman. Front : J. Douglas, M. Holmes, L. Peel, J. Raven, R. Carter.

IF ONLY – THE INCORRECTLY CAPTIONED PHOTO TAKEN PRIOR TO THE CENTRAL ALLIANCE DIVISION 2 CUP FINAL v MARYS 3 MAY 1958 (Courtesy Football Post)

Just how the situation was allowed to arise will remain shrouded in the mists of time. The Central Alliance tables published in the Football Post each week were all over the place right from the start of each season. You didn't have to be a statistical anorak to know that in every league table the total number of wins must equal the total number of defeats, the total number of goals scored by all the teams must equal those conceded, draws must add up to an equal number and so on. Unfortunately, all this seemed to be beyond the management of one of the supposedly superior leagues in the region. Even the Central Alliance league table in the last edition of the previous season's Football Post was littered with errors and it was no surprise that confusion abounded.

Indeed, given both the lack of information and the contradictory nature of that which was known, Rovers might have actually travelled to Retford for that fateful last league game not knowing whether they needed a win or a draw to clinch the championship, or even whether they'd already won it. With it being their seventh game in eleven days it was no wonder the league didn't know whether it was coming or going. It was a pity they hadn't let the result of the original game between Rovers and British Ropes Reserves stand; at least that way no one would have been in any doubt that the red and whites had won the championship fair and square.

In the final analysis though Rovers had come up short; the league table above shows just how short. There were of course those who thought that the bigger clubs in the Central Alliance, who could attract crowds of four and six thousand to games between themselves, had an agenda that precluded 'amateur' clubs like Rovers from doing well. Clubs that had a first team in the top divisions and their reserve elevens in the second tier were viewed with a particular suspicion, and there was little doubt that pressure to annul the second victory over British Ropes Reserves had been brought to bear on the league by at least one of those clubs.

AC : I don't think that the top teams in that league liked the idea of an amateur side winning it. They were professional clubs, the players were getting paid and they had permit players even in their second teams. It wouldn't have looked very good.

Unfortunately, Rovers' troubles that particular summer, relatively speaking at least, didn't end there either. Despite finishing higher than their ground-sharing neighbours and rivals Marys, they found themselves stuck in Division Two whilst the Saints miraculously ascended to the top tier. Even Kimberley Town, who'd finished runners-up by the narrowest of margins and three places above the Saints, would be staying where they were for the time being.

Whilst there was no question of impropriety, just how had Marys managed this trick of levitation? Well, the clues had been there for quite a while.

With the change in the law in 1956 that had seen football clubs begin to recognise the possibilities of organising their own lotteries, usually in the form of 'tote' tickets, Marys had been one of the first off the mark, certainly quicker than Rovers.

LR : My father, Len Rockley Senior, worked at Saxbys, the bleachers and dyers at Basford. One day he saw someone selling tote tickets and he introduced it at Marys.

AC : It soon became a case of who was selling the most tote tickets, who was getting the most commission. Marys were one of the first. Eventually Rovers had one too, they had to. Marys though were better on the financial side, on how to make money and exploit situations.

Confirmation of their savvy came when the Saints had also been rather quick off the mark and had started charging at the gate, maybe even contravening the very spirit of what was intended when Gedling Road was designated a King George the Fifth playing field.

AC : I'm not sure that Marys should have been charging at the gate. They did things and thought about [the consequences] later. They didn't care about anything like that.

LR : The committee, Syd Gray, 'Kegga' Parr and the rest couldn't care less about anybody else, they just lived for Marys.

AC & FG : I don't think Rovers ever charged at the gate.

Marys aggression with the tote and at the gate weren't the only manifestations of their ambition.

SA : Rovers didn't train as a team but when I worked at Clowers there was a wall at the side belonging to the Baptist Church in Daybrook Square. There was a large area of grass on the other side and I used to nip over it with one of the lads at break time or after work and have them banging the ball to each side of me so that I could practice diving and improve my reflexes.

AC : Rovers didn't have any regular training until later on when we went to the Drill Hall.

LR : Even when Marys were in the second division of the Central Alliance we trained twice a week. The sessions took place on a Tuesday and Thursday evening in the gym at Robert Mellors' school. They were taken by the PE teacher, Mr Shapland, a rugby player, and they included a fifteen minute spell of circuit training. It was hard but very interesting.

Not of course that a lack of organised training had found Rovers wanting when it came to the actual playing of matches, far from it.

AC : Marys were always more professionally minded than Rovers but that's why we always rose to the challenge. We had the ability where it counted; on the pitch.

Ability, it seems, that the Saints never tired of trying to poach from their closest rivals. Bill Whitt, Les Peel, Roy Carter and a few more besides had been enticed away from Rovers and it might have been even more.

AC : Marys would do anything to get one up on Rovers no matter how they did it. They were always trying to poach players from us, including me. Buying you boots and things like that. Syd Gray said to me "If I could get Jack Tulley and Ron Maddocks out of your team we'd have them playing tomorrow no matter who we've already got." They were ruthless as regards replacing players and it didn't bother them.

Trying to weaken your nearest rivals whilst strengthening your own side wasn't a strategy exclusive to Marys, but Rovers weren't the only club they tried to raid and by 1958 they had begun to set their sights even higher. Colin Collindridge had played over three hundred league games for Sheffield United, Forest and Coventry City, scoring over a hundred goals, and had been a teammate down at the City Ground of Sid Thompson, a skilful wing half cum inside forward who'd had a couple of dozen games in the first team. The Saints had identified them as being just the type of players needed to take them to the next level.

AC : Marys wanted to venture into the permit side of football, sign more professionals. Well, they were paying some of their players anyway. They were more forward thinking on that side of things.

LR : Syd Gray was the man responsible. He was a bricklayer and worked at Calverton Colliery in the Maintenance Department. He got Sid and Colin nice steady jobs at the pit as well as signing them for Marys.

This hard evidence of the Saints' ambitions as a club had probably convinced the Central Alliance management that the unusual promotion of a team finishing just fifth in the table was a risk worth taking. Maybe Rovers had been invited too, but there was little chance that the offer would have been taken up in any case.

AC : Rovers didn't think their finances would run to that sort of thing. It was as if we knew our place, that the club had reached its level. We'd not got the money or the financial clout behind us and the brains to put it into practice.

PW : As long as they'd got a match to look forward to Rovers' committee were happy. I don't think they wanted to go any higher. Marys took it much more seriously, they didn't just think of it as having a bit of fun on a Saturday.

And of course whilst there's absolutely no shame in such an admittance, the marked difference in the approach of Arnold's two clubs went beyond just their own philosophies. At a stroke, Rovers had conceded their position as footballing equals of their town rivals and brought an end to the glorious spell of the last twelve years when they'd not only severely questioned Marys' position as the pre-eminent team in town, but had actually assumed the mantle for themselves.

From now on there would be no more head to head clashes in front of four figure crowds and the only chance of meeting each other in competition would be in the Senior Cup. As it turned out they would never once be drawn out of the hat together, largely because Marys' continued success in the competition meant that by the time their name went in it, Rovers had invariably been eliminated in an earlier round.

For all of Arnold's footballing neutrals with a love of a rivalry, and especially for the fans of Rovers, the next five years were to be extremely painful. Not only did they have to watch Marys go from strength to strength, they had to witness the slow and painful sight of a once successful club in terminal decline.

Marys had fully vindicated their promotion to the Northern Section of the top division of the Central Alliance by almost winning the title at their very first attempt. More than holding their own against fully professional town teams such as Ilkeston, Heanor, and Matlock, they finished level with another Derbyshire side, Belper Town, on fifty four points from just thirty four matches, and only missed out on the championship on goal average. Rovers though, giving truth to the old sporting adage that if you stand still, you end up going backwards, could only manage an eleventh place finish in the second division. However, before long, even eleventh would begin to look like an achievement.

In 1959-60, and almost as if to remind the red and whites of their diminished status in the town, Marys' reserves made their debut in Rovers' division and proceeded to finish five places higher than them, seventh to their twelfth. In fact Rovers never once finished above the Saints' second string in four years of trying.

The following season, 1960-61, Marys won the Notts Senior Cup for the first time in their history and finished fifth in the league. This was the season that the Midland League had been suspended for a year and many of its sides had ended up in the Central Alliance. For the Saints to figure so high in a final table containing teams like Matlock Town, Goole Town, Worksop Town, Gainsborough Trinity, and many others was a fine accomplishment.

In fact fifth, their position again in 1961-62, was the lowest that the Saints ever finished in their stay in the top flight of the Central Alliance but in this, the fourth season since Marys and Rovers had gone their separate ways, the red and whites, in stark contrast, had hit absolute rock bottom. It could be said that finishing twenty second out of twenty two meant that the only way was up, but for the red and whites there was to be no up. Twelve months later they finished at the foot of the table once again whilst this time managing to accrue the meagre total of just three points. This performance, or lack of it, would have been bad enough in itself but was made many times worse by the tremendous success of both Marys' sides. The Saints' second eleven finished at the opposite end of the table to Rovers and took the title in style. The two teams' comparative records were:-

	P	W	D	L	F	A	P	Pos
Marys Reserves	22	19	2	1	112	30	40	Top
Rovers	22	1	1	20	31	93	3	Bottom

In the top division, Marys' final tally was just as impressive as their reserves'.

	P	W	D	L	F	A	P	Pos
Marys	28	24	3	1	149	24	51	Top

As it happened, the 1962-63 season would be the last in the Central Alliance for both Arnold clubs. Just eight years after they'd moved up together into the competition as rivals and equals, they were both about to take their exits at the same time too, unfortunately in diametrically opposite directions.

Rovers' exit was ignominious; down through the trapdoor to a twilight existence in the junior leagues until they existed no longer. Marys' route out of the Central Alliance was far more attractive; onwards and upwards to the Midland League, the region's premier competition outside the Football League, where they would become one of its strongest clubs. One that would be good enough in just a few years' time to qualify for the first round of the FA Cup and play hosts to Bristol Rovers, and then some time later meet Port Vale at the same stage of the venerable competition and even play well enough to take them to a replay.

Back in the summer of '58 though this was all still a long way off and the implications of the close season manoeuvrings of Marys were some distance from being appreciated. By the end of the year changes of an even more far reaching nature would be taking place throughout the country. On the weekend beginning Saturday 30 August, riots between blacks and whites took place in Notting Hill, London. Just over a month later the first passenger jet crossed the Atlantic and then just before Christmas, the first motorway in the UK was officially opened. Life certainly appeared to be speeding up.

The following year Forest won the Cup and Harold Macmillan's Conservative Party was returned to power in the October election, which was also notable in that it saw a certain 'Iron Lady', Margaret Thatcher, first enter Parliament as MP for Finchley.

But, lest I forget, the underlying desire behind this review of football in Arnold, starting in the immediate post WWII years and ending in 1958 for reasons explained above, was to find out which of the two protagonists, Ken Renshaw for Rovers and Len Rockley for Marys, was correct. Just who had been the better, the red and whites, or the maroon and golds?

Well, in terms of plain facts and statistics you'd be hard pressed to argue against Rovers. If, in modern day parlance you asked the players with the most appearances for the two clubs in that era, Franny Greensmith at Rovers and Ron Hinson of Marys, to 'show us your medals', then Franny's would easily outnumber Ron's. For purposes of illustration the revised honours board, now minus Rovers' 'yes they've won it, no they haven't' Central Alliance Division Two league title, looks like this.

ROVERS : FIVE CHAMPIONSHIPS, SIX CUPS (INCL ONE SHARED)

MARYS : ONE CHAMPIONSHIP, FOUR CUPS (INCL ONE SHARED)

REGENT : THREE CUPS

No-one would argue that Marys' Spartan League winning side of 1949-50 was the better team that season but often it was hard to choose between the two sides. In fact it may be pointless trying to come up with a tally on a season by season basis. However, considering that Notts Regent's trophy winning sides coincided with their team containing more than just a few absentees from Rovers, then the case for the red and whites being the most **successful team** over the period under review is indisputable. Their ten and a half trophies in twelve years compares more than favourably with the Saints' haul of four and a half. Then of course there is the more immediate yardstick of the results of the two teams' head to head clashes; sixteen in all, of which the Saints won just four, two of those in the last season the teams would ever meet, compared with Rovers' seven.

Of course it's a cruel world and despite Rovers' greater success on the field of play, there is more to a club than just the eleven players out on the pitch on any given Saturday. Marys' 'Kegga' Parr and Syd Gray would have been annoyed to see their club's position challenged by the upstarts from the Bottom Rec and it would have hardened their resolve to resume their place as the town's foremost club. If being a better club means being more organised, more dynamic, more ambitious, more ruthless, more professional, then the Saints off the field were all of these things and more besides. The years 1946 to 1958 might have seen their noses put out of joint slightly, but in the end they were just a springboard to bigger and better things for 'Kegga' and Syd and the rest of Marys' committee.

In the wider scheme of things those same years had been a springboard for the country's aspirations too. The dismal grey days of rationing, clothes coupons, and utility furniture were receding into the past. With eight million licences issued, up by five and a half million since the Coronation, television was in most people's homes and private car ownership was becoming the norm. The mile had been run in less than four minutes, Everest had been conquered, and the Antarctic crossed. Elvis Presley had just joined the US Army and although many said that his music was never as potent from there on in, it hardly mattered. Rock 'n Roll was here to stay and the youth of the western world had found its voice. It had been a struggle at times but the country had finally progressed from austerity to prosperity. Harold Macmillan might not have been speaking for all of the people with his 'never had it so good' remark, but it struck a chord with many.

For lovers of football in Arnold the fifties had indeed been a glorious time. Rovers and Marys had forged a rivalry that had not been seen in the town since the nineteen twenties when a previous incarnation of the Saints had been engaged in a number of sterling contests with Arnold Wesleyans. Unfortunately, this latest rivalry would prove to be the last. The days of two teams of local footballers facing each other in front of over one, two, and three thousand avid supporters would be no more.

And the fact that it has never been repeated makes the rivalry between the two clubs even more special. That the teams created such excitement, that the players showed so much pride in what they were doing, took so much pleasure from it, gave and received their hard knocks like real men but remained friends at all times, says a great deal about those remarkable days.

In the final analysis it could be said that Rovers won most of the battles with Marys but ended up losing the war but a military metaphor hardly seems appropriate in the context of their friendly rivalry. In these days of a politically correct, anti-competition, 'medals for everyone' agenda, it might sound like a bit of a cop-out to say that ultimately there were no losers in the story I've tried to tell but in truth I don't think there were. Alec Casterton sums it up perfectly:

AC : We would have played all day if they'd let us, we loved it so much. It didn't really matter who beat who because the real winners were the people of Arnold. Whenever we played the atmosphere was wonderful, it was unique.

And unique it was, a time never to be repeated, a time when life was slower and more civilised and probably all the better for it, a time when summers were hot and snow fell every winter, a time when a generation of young, fit men from around the district put on their football gear and were transformed into more than mere players. They became kings, and no ordinary ones at that. For one glorious spell back in the fifties they were Arnold's very own...

KINGS OF THE RECS!

STATISTICAL SECTION

In many ways this section has been the most difficult part of the book because back in the forties and fifties an exhaustive attention to detail or accuracy didn't seem to be a pre-requisite of local league secretaries, especially at the level that Rovers and Marys played at.

Despite the problems of accessing information I am pleased that nearly every result of the almost eight hundred that the two teams played in the period under review has been verified, together with well over ninety percent of the actual scorelines in those matches.

I have resisted the temptation to expand this section because I felt that to do so might detract from the main idea behind the book; that of trying to tell the story of Rovers' and Marys' battle for supremacy. The statistics are here to support that story, and are in no way meant to be a definitive record.

I am hoping to use the additional information that I have gathered in a future volume of the evolving history of football in Arnold, but for now I hope that those of you inclined towards an appreciation of facts and figures will find the following pages of interest.

HONOURS

ROVERS	1946-47	NOTTS REALM LEAGUE DIVISION 2
	1951-52	NOTTS REALM LEAGUE DIVISION 1
	1952-53	NOTTS REALM LEAGUE DIVISION 1
	1953-54	NOTTM SPARTAN LEAGUE DIVISION 1
	1954-55	NOTTM SPARTAN LEAGUE DIVISION 1
	1948-49	NOTTS JUNIOR CUP
	1951-52	ARNOLD & DISTRICT BENEVOLENT CUP
	1952-53	NOTTS REALM LEAGUE SENIOR CUP
	1952-53	NOTTS INTERMEDIATE CUP
	1952-53	ARNOLD & DISTRICT BENEVOLENT CUP [TROPHY SHARED]
	1953-54	NOTTM SPARTAN LEAGUE CUP
MARYS	1949-50	NOTTM SPARTAN LEAGUE DIVISION 1
	1952-53	ARNOLD & DISTRICT BENEVOLENT CUP [TROPHY SHARED]
	1953-54	NOTTS INTERMEDIATE CUP
	1954-55	NOTTM SPARTAN LEAGUE CUP
	1957-58	CENTRAL ALLIANCE DIVISION 2 CUP
REGENT	1949-50	NOTTS REALM LEAGUE SENIOR CUP
	1950-51	NOTTS REALM LEAGUE SENIOR CUP
	1950-51	NOTTS JUNIOR CUP

SEASON BY SEASON SUMMARY : ALL GAMES

	ROVERS							MARYS						
SEASON	P	W	D	L	F	A	%	P	W	D	L	F	A	%
1946-47	30	21	5	4	127	30	78.3	23	14	2	7	87	65	65.2
1947-48	29	19	5	5	96 +	49 +	74.1	22	8	2	12	56 +	88 +	40.9
1948-49	40	30	3	7	165 +	47 +	78.8	39	30	2	7	156 +	64 +	79.5
1949-50	31	16	5	10	69 +	59 +	59.7	37	31	3	3	171	56	87.8
1950-51	27	12	6	9	59 +	52 +	55.6	41	27	5	9	154 +	66 +	72.0
1951-52	31	25	3	3	116 +	45 +	85.5	29	17	4	8	141 +	79 +	65.5
1952-53	31	29	1	1	127 +	34 +	95.2	33	23	5	5	128 +	48 +	77.3
1953-54	34	30	2	2	168	50	91.2	34	30	1	3	121 +	32 +	89.7
1954-55	25	21	0	4	114	53	84.0	28	23	1	4	118 +	44 +	83.9
1955-56	38	23	4	11	118	92	65.8	36	22	4	10	113	78	66.7
1956-57	35	24	2	9	154	80	71.4	36	23	6	7	166	78	72.2
1957-58	38	26	4	8	114	67	73.7	43	29	4	10	166	79	72.1
TOTAL	**389**	**276**	**40**	**73**	**1427 +**	**658 +**	**76.1**	**401**	**277**	**39**	**85**	**1577 +**	**777 +**	**73.9**
LEAGUE	298	209	36	53	1151	523	76.2	299	206	32	61	1230	611	74.2
CUP	91	67	4	20	276 +	135 +	75.8	102	71	7	24	347 +	166 +	73.0
TOTAL	**389**	**276**	**40**	**73**	**1427 +**	**658 +**	**76.1**	**401**	**277**	**39**	**85**	**1577 +**	**777 +**	**73.9**
HOME	184	149	18	17			85.9	189	149	14	26			82.5
AWAY	170	103	21	46			66.8	181	110	21	50			66.6
NEUTRAL	21	14	1	6			69.0	19	9	3	7			55.3
tbc	14	10	0	4			71.4	12	9	1	2			79.2
TOTAL	**389**	**276**	**40**	**73**			**76.1**	**401**	**277**	**39**	**85**			**73.9**
SEASON AVERAGE	**32**	**23**	**3**	**6**	**119 +**	**55 +**	**76.1**	**33**	**23**	**3**	**7**	**131 +**	**65 +**	**73.9**

1946-47

NOTTS REALM LEAGUE DIVISION 2

	P	W	D	L	F	A	P	H	A
ARNOLD ROVERS	**26**	**19**	**5**	**2**	**119**	**23**	**43**		
COTGRAVE	26	18	6	2	102	28	42	2-2	1-1
LONG EATON SPB	26	18	3	5	121	54	39	3-1	2-2
CALVERTON UNITED	26	15	4	7	88	53	34	2-0	0-2
LONG EATON ZINGARI	26	15	3	8	104	46	33	2-0	3-1
SHELFORD UNITED	26	13	4	9	84	63	30	W	0-1
BASFORD HALL OB	25	13	2	10	76	58	28	4-1	4-1
RIGLEYS ATHLETIC	26	9	5	12	62	76	23	D	4-0
QUEENS DRIVE RANGERS	26	9	3	14	55	83	21	1-1	9-0
CARLTON STARS RESERVES	26	7	3	16	71	89	17	12-0	5-0
RADCLIFFE OLYMPIC RESERVES	25	7	3	15	39	96	17	9-1	4-0
RUTLAND UNITED	26	7	2	17	74	100	16	9-0	W
ROYAL NAVAL OCA	26	6	1	19	45	133	13	W	7-2
CASTLEDONIANS	26	2	2	22	30	139	6	10-0	W
	362	158	46	158	1070	1041	362		
ROVERS HOME	13	10	3	0	54+	6+	23		
ROVERS AWAY	13	9	2	2	39+	10+	20		

NOTTS REALM LEAGUE JUNIOR CUP

R1 : CALVERTON UNITED (-)	5-1
QF : CROSSLEY PREMIER (H)	1-0
SF : LONG EATON SPB (A)	1-2

NOTTS JUNIOR CUP

R1 : CITY TRANSPORT (H)	1-4

1946-47

NOTTM SPARTAN LEAGUE

	P	W	D	L	F	A	P	H	A
WORTHINGTON-SIMPSON	25	23	2	0	132	29	48	4-5	dnp
LINBY COLLIERY	21	19	1	1	152	17	39	1-2	0-6
ARNOLD ST MARYS	**21**	**14**	**2**	**5**	**82**	**55**	**30**		
RUDDINGTON	25	13	4	8	91	68	30	dnp	3-3
STAPLEFORD BROOKHILL	23	14	1	8	101	55	29	dnp	dnp
STAPLEFORD VILLA	25	14	1	10	82	62	29	4-2	dnp
ARMORDUCT CABLES	21	12	4	5	77	48	28	4-4	2-3
AVRO	21	12	1	8	60	44	25	W	2-3
EDWARDS LANE ESTATE	26	8	2	16	63	122	18	4-3	6-3
CARR FASTENER	25	8	2	15	50	100	18	3-0	4-2
BURTON JOYCE	26	6	5	15	52	100	17	W	W
DERBY & NOTTS ELECTRICITY PC	26	4	3	19	46	130	11	4-1	4-1
SOUTHWELL ST MARYS	25	3	1	21	40	116	7	5-2	6-3
BARLOCK TYPEWRITERS	26	3	1	22	38	145	7	8-4	6-1
	336	153	30	153	1066	1091	336		
MARYS HOME	11	8	1	2	37+	23+	17		
MARYS AWAY	10	6	1	3	33+	25+	13		

WORTHINGTON-SIMPSON FINISHED AS UNBEATEN CHAMPIONS

NOTTM SPARTAN LEAGUE CUP

R1 : BURTON JOYCE (H)	4-5

NOTTS INTERMEDIATE CUP

R1 :	bye or W
R2 : HUCKNALL COLLIERIES (A)	1-5

1947-48

NOTTS REALM LEAGUE DIVISION 1

	P	W	D	L	F	A	P	H	A
KEYWORTH UNITED	22	18	1	3	130	31	37	1-1	1-4
ARNOLD ROVERS	**22**	**15**	**4**	**3**	**74**	**37**	**34**		
RADCLIFFE OLYMPIC	22	17	1	4	88	23	33	3-2	1-6
BULWELL FOREST VILLA	22	10	3	9	63	60	23	4-1	2-2
COTGRAVE	22	10	3	9	61	61	23	6-1	0-3
WILFORD ROAD ATHLETIC	22	10	1	11	58	74	21	9-2	6-3
NOTTS CASUALS	22	7	4	11	52	63	18	4-1	2-2
CARLTON	22	6	5	11	43	52	17	1-0	5-1
NOTTS REGENT	22	7	3	12	37	56	17	4-1	1-1
ILKESTON MINERS WELFARE	22	7	2	13	43	69	16	4-1	3-2
HAZEL GROVE CELTIC	22	7	1	14	40	83	15	4-1	2-0
CASTLE IMPERIAL	22	3	2	17	24	96	8	3-1	8-1
	264	117	30	117	713	705	262		

	P	W	D	L	F	A	P
ROVERS HOME	11	10	1	0	43	12	21
ROVERS AWAY	11	5	3	3	31	25	13

RADCLIFFE OLYMPIC DEDUCTED TWO POINTS

NOTTS REALM LEAGUE SENIOR CUP

R1 : RADFORD CORINTHIANS (A)	2-2
R1R : RADFORD CORINTHIANS (H)	W
QF : HAZEL GROVE CELTIC (H)	4-1
SF : KEYWORTH UNITED (A)	3-5

NOTTS JUNIOR CUP

R1 : BEESTON OLD BOYS (A)	2-0
R2 : DUNKIRK (H)	W
R3 : NEWTHORPE UNITED (A)	1-4

1947-48

NOTTM SPARTAN LEAGUE DIVISION 1

	P	W	D	L	F	A	P	H	A
WORTHINGTON-SIMPSON	16	13	1	2	93	34	27	1-8	1-7
WILFORD VILLAGE	16	11	0	5	54	38	22	2-6	1-3
STAPLEFORD BROOKHILL	16	10	1	5	66	32	21	4-2	0-6
STAPLEFORD VILLA	16	10	0	6	57	40	20	1-8	1-9
BURTON JOYCE	15	8	2	5	42	29	18	dnp	L
RUDDINGTON	16	8	0	8	61	47	16	3-5	1-3
ARNOLD ST MARYS	**15**	**4**	**1**	**10**	**36**	**69**	**9**		
SOUTHWELL ST MARYS	16	3	2	11	32	67	8	5-5	2-1
BRAMCOTE & STAPLEFORD BL	16	0	1	15	13	98	1	5-1	W
	142	67	8	67	454	454	142		
MARYS HOME	7	2	1	4	21	35	5		
MARYS AWAY	8	2	0	6	15	34	4		

NOTTM SPARTAN LEAGUE CUP

R1 : WILFORD VILLAGE (H)	5-4
R2 : WORTHINGTON-SIMPSON (A)	1-4

NOTTS INTERMEDIATE CUP

R1 :	bye or W
R2 : RETFORD GROVE LANE (A)	2-1
R3 : BENTINCK COLLIERY COLTS (A)	2-2
R3R : BENTINCK COLLIERY COLTS (H)	W
QF : RALEIGH ATHLETIC RESERVES (H)	6-2 *
QF : RALEIGH ATHLETIC RESERVES (A)	4-6

* MATCH ORDERED TO BE REPLAYED FOR BREACH OF RULES

1948-49

NOTTS REALM LEAGUE DIVISION 1

	P	W	D	L	F	A	P	H	A
KEYWORTH UNITED	28	21	3	4	112	37	45	3-2	1-2
ARNOLD ROVERS	**28**	**21**	**1**	**6**	**130**	**38**	**43**		
NEWTHORPE UNITED	28	21	0	7	95	44	42	6-1	1-2
DAKEYNE STREET OLD BOYS	28	19	3	6	96	53	41	4-1	1-4
RADCLIFFE OLYMPIC	28	16	3	9	102	61	35	tbc	tbc
COTGRAVE	28	15	3	10	82	75	33	tbc	3-6
LONG EATON SILVER PLATE BAND	28	15	2	11	89	72	32	4-0	tbc
WILFORD ROAD ATHLETIC	28	13	5	10	82	58	31	6-0	2-0
BULWELL FOREST VILLA	28	12	4	12	88	78	28	4-2	4-3
NOTTS REGENT	28	13	2	13	68	66	28	7-0	tbc
HAZEL GROVE CELTIC	28	11	6	11	79	66	28	3-0	2-2
NOTTS CASUALS	28	7	3	18	63	99	17	4-0	7-1
CARLTON	28	4	1	23	42	105	9	tbc	8-0
GOTHAM UNITED	28	3	1	24	45	125	7	11-0	10-0
ST SAVIOURS	28	0	1	27	34	203	1	4-0	13-0
	420	191	38	191	1207	1180	420		
ROVERS HOME	14	11+	0+	0+	56+	6+	22+		
ROVERS AWAY	14	6+	1+	4+	52+	20+	13+		

NOTTS REALM LEAGUE SENIOR CUP

R1 : KEYWORTH UNITED (-)	1-3

NOTTS JUNIOR CUP

R1 : REMPSTONE & COSTOCK (H)	9-0
R2 : GAS SPORTS (A)	8-0
R3 : HUCKNALL BRITISH LEGION (H)	3-2
R4 : CITY TRANSPORT (H)	3-1
R5 : BROXTOWE (-)	3-0
QF : NEWTHORPE UNITED (H)	1-1
QFR : NEWTHORPE UNITED (A)	D
QF2R : NEWTHORPE UNITED (H)	3-2
SF : ST PATRICKS (Formans Ath Ground)	W
F : FERRY RANGERS (Meadow Lane)	**1-0**

ARNOLD & DISTRICT BENEVOLENT CUP

R1 : HENDON RISE (A)	3-0
QF : Withdrew	

1948-49

NOTTM SPARTAN LEAGUE DIVISION 1

	P	W	D	L	F	A	P	H	A
EAST KIRKBY WELFARE	24	19	2	3	110	43	40	4-2	3-6
ARNOLD ST MARYS	**24**	**19**	**1**	**4**	**107**	**46**	**39**		
BALDERTON OLD BOYS	23	14	4	5	81	44	32	3-2	1-3
STAPLEFORD VILLA	24	13	4	7	73	51	30	3-2	1-3
SUTTON COLLIERY	24	10	5	9	84	73	25	6-1	5-3
ANNESLEY WELFARE	24	11	3	10	70	73	25	6-1	1-1
WILFORD VILLAGE	23	11	2	10	74	83	24	10-2	2-3
NETHERFIELD ROVERS	24	9	3	12	68	75	21	5-1	5-2
BURTON JOYCE	24	9	3	12	53	63	21	7-0	7-2
STAPLEFORD BROOKHILL	22	9	2	11	65	63	20	3-1	4-3
RUDDINGTON	22	6	1	15	47	75	13	4-1	3-1
SOUTHWELL ST MARYS	23	2	5	16	48	93	9	6-2	5-0
MINISTRY OF SUPPLY ATHLETIC	24	2	3	19	42	135	7	9-4	4-0
	305	134	38	133	922	917	306		
MARYS HOME	12	12	0	0	66	19	24		
MARYS AWAY	12	7	1	4	41	27	15		

NOTTM SPARTAN LEAGUE CUP

R1 : ROBIN HOOD ATHLETIC (A)	4-1
R2 : BALDERTON OLD BOYS (H)	10-2
QF : WILFORD VILLAGE (H)	8-1
SF : SOUTHWELL ST MARYS (Gatehouse Ground, Linby)	6-1
F : EAST KIRKBY WELFARE (Gatehouse Ground, Linby)	D
FR : EAST KIRKBY WELFARE (Gatehouse Ground, Linby)	2-3

NOTTS INTERMEDIATE CUP

R1 : ERICSSON ATHLETIC (H)	3-0
R2 : MINISTRY OF SUPPLY ATHLETIC (H)	6-1
R3 : CHRIST CHURCH (A)	3-2
QF : NETHERFIELD ROVERS (A)	4-2
SF : EAST KIRKBY WELFARE (Gatehouse Ground, Linby)	1-0
F : MAPPERLEY (City Ground)	2-4

ARNOLD & DISTRICT BENEVOLENT CUP

R1 : LAMBLEY VILLA (A)	W
QF : tbc	W/O or W
SF : BESTWOOD COLLIERY (H)	L

1949-50

NOTTS REALM LEAGUE DIVISION 1

	P	W	D	L	F	A	P	H	A
KEYWORTH UNITED	24	18	2	4	112	34	38	3-5	2-5
FERRY RANGERS	24	16	3	5	82	38	35	4-1	0-5
NOTTS REGENT	24	15	3	6	94	54	33	1-1	2-4
NEWTHORPE UNITED	24	13	5	6	68	42	31	4-2	1-2
DALE VILLA	24	14	3	7	84	56	31	2-1	3-4
ARNOLD ROVERS	**24**	**12**	**5**	**7**	**59**	**53**	**29**		
WILFORD ROAD ATHLETIC	24	12	4	8	76	46	28	1-1	1-1
BULWELL FOREST VILLA	24	12	4	8	74	50	28	5-1	2-1
DAKEYNE STREET OLD BOYS	24	12	2	10	83	64	26	2-2	2-7
COTGRAVE	24	6	1	17	58	99	13	3-1	3-0
LONG EATON SPB	24	5	2	17	39	84	12	4-4	2-0
NOTTS CASUALS	24	2	0	22	39	135	4	3-2	1-0
HAZEL GROVE CELTIC	24	2	0	22	28	129	4	6-2	2-1
	312	139	34	139	896	884	312		

	P	W	D	L	F	A	P
ROVERS HOME	12	7	4	1	38	23	18
ROVERS AWAY	12	5	1	6	21	30	11

NOTTS REALM LEAGUE SENIOR CUP

R1 : KEYWORTH UNITED (A)	4-1
QF : NOTTS REGENT (H)	2-5

NOTTS INTERMEDIATE CUP

R1 : MAPPERLEY (H)	L

ARNOLD & DISTRICT BENEVOLENT CUP

R1 : MAPPERLEY VILLA (H)	W
QF : LAMBLEY VILLA (H)	4-0
SF : HENDON RISE (Church Lane)	W
F : BESTWOOD COLLIERY (Church Lane)	L

1949-50

NOTTM SPARTAN LEAGUE DIVISION 1

	P	W	D	L	F	A	P	H	A
ARNOLD ST MARYS	**27**	**25**	**2**	**0**	**138**	**36**	**52**		
SHERWOOD COLLIERY	28	19	4	5	105	39	42	2-1	4-2
ASPLEY OLD BOYS	28	20	0	8	86	49	40	7-3	5-0
STAPLEFORD VILLA	28	16	4	8	105	59	36	4-3	3-2
RUDDINGTON	28	12	10	6	95	59	34	3-3	3-0
ANNESLEY WELFARE	26	15	4	7	75	65	34	dnp	8-1
SUTTON COLLIERY	28	15	3	10	113	58	33	4-2	2-1
NETHERFIELD ROVERS	28	12	7	9	84	71	31	2-0	6-1
BALDERTON OLD BOYS	28	12	3	13	97	63	27	2-2	4-2
HUCKNALL COLLIERIES	28	10	4	14	66	72	24	4-1	3-1
BURTON JOYCE	28	7	3	18	72	108	17	3-1	7-1
WILFORD VILLAGE	28	6	4	18	64	104	16	6-0	8-2
COLWICK SUGAR FACTORY	28	6	4	18	64	115	16	6-2	5-1
SOUTHWELL ST MARYS	28	4	4	20	63	137	12	8-0	15-1
STAPLEFORD BROOKHILL	27	1	0	26	40	232	2	9-0	5-3
	416	180	56	180	1267	1267	416		
MARYS HOME	13	11	2	0	60	18	24		
MARYS AWAY	14	14	0	0	78	18	28		

NOTTM SPARTAN LEAGUE CUP

R1 : KIMBERLEY MINERS WELFARE (A) 6-0
R2 : STAPLEFORD VILLA (H) 5-1
QF : ASPLEY OLD BOYS (A) 4-5 (after extra time)

NOTTS INTERMEDIATE CUP

R1 : BRINSLEY (H) 3-1
R2 : BAGTHORPE ATHLETIC (H) W/O
R3 : BRAMCOTE & STAPLEFORD BRITISH LEGION (A) 4-4
R3R : BRAMCOTE & STAPLEFORD BRITISH LEGION (H) 5-0
QF : LENTON GREGORY (A) 3-2
SF : WILFORD (Formans Athletic Ground) 1-3

ARNOLD & DISTRICT BENEVOLENT CUP

R1 : MAPPERLEY (A) 2-4

1950-51

NOTTS REALM LEAGUE DIVISION 1

	P	W	D	L	F	A	P	H	A
BULWELL FOREST VILLA	20	17	0	3	76	21	34	3-2	0-2
WILFORD ROAD ATHLETIC	20	14	4	2	91	33	32	3-3	1-1
NOTTS REGENT	20	14	2	4	91	35	30	1-2	1-10
FERRY RANGERS	20	11	3	6	66	43	25	2-2	3-4
ARNOLD ROVERS	**20**	**8**	**6**	**6**	**47**	**48**	**22**		
DAKEYNE STREET OLD BOYS	20	9	2	9	59	55	20	1-3	4-3
BASFORD HALL OLD BOYS	20	8	4	8	49	47	18	4-2	1-1
AVRO	20	5	3	12	41	71	13	1-1	4-1
HENDON RISE	20	5	1	14	40	66	11	3-5	1-1
LODGE COLLIERY	20	3	1	16	24	90	7	2-1	3-2
NOTTS CASUALS	20	3	0	17	31	106	6	7-2	2-0
	220	97	26	97	615	615	218		
ROVERS HOME	10	4	3	3	27	23	11		
ROVERS AWAY	10	4	3	3	20	25	11		

BASFORD HALL OLD BOYS DEDUCTED TWO POINTS

NOTTS REALM LEAGUE SENIOR CUP

R1 : HENDON RISE (-)	2-1
QF : DALE VILLA (H)	W/O
SF : NEWTHORPE UNITED (Bulwell Forest Villa Ground)	2-1
F : NOTTS REGENT (Meadow Lane)	1-2

NOTTS INTERMEDIATE CUP

R1 : BOOTS ATHLETIC RESERVES (H)	L

ARNOLD & DISTRICT BENEVOLENT CUP

R1 : HOME BREWERY (H)	7-0
QF : tbc	L

1950-51

NOTTM SPARTAN LEAGUE DIVISION 1

	P	W	D	L	F	A	P	H	A
KEYWORTH UNITED	29	24	2	3	164	39	50	1-3	3-3
EAST KIRKBY WELFARE	30	23	2	5	109	44	48	2-4	4-1
ASPLEY OLD BOYS	30	21	4	5	114	43	46	0-3	2-5
ARNOLD ST MARYS	**30**	**20**	**4**	**6**	**120**	**54**	**44**		
STAPLEFORD VILLA	30	20	3	7	109	59	43	3-1	tbc
CHILWELL UNITED	30	18	2	10	107	62	38	4-1	tbc
SUTTON COLLIERY	30	13	5	12	102	79	31	4-3	2-2
RUDDINGTON	28	13	4	11	101	91	30	3-3	tbc
CITY TRANSPORT	29	13	3	13	85	101	29	tbc	2-3
BALDERTON OLD BOYS	30	11	6	13	90	88	28	7-1	7-1
NETHERFIELD ROVERS	30	10	1	19	78	105	21	7-3	5-1
SHERWOOD COLLIERY	28	7	2	19	56	88	16	2-1	2-1
RANGERS ATHLETIC	29	6	2	21	76	154	14	6-1	5-0
STAPLEFORD TOWN	30	6	1	23	53	163	13	6-2	6-0
BURTON JOYCE	29	5	2	22	43	117	12	7-0	7-2
WILFORD VILLAGE	30	3	3	24	52	170	9	5-0	6-3
	472	213	46	213	1459	1457	472		
MARYS HOME	15	10+	1+	3+	57+	26+	21+		
MARYS AWAY	15	8+	2+	2+	51+	22+	18+		

NOTTM SPARTAN LEAGUE CUP

R1 : RANGERS ATHLETIC (A) (Played at Church Lane)	9-1
R2 : SHERWOOD COLLIERY (H)	2-0
QF : BURTON JOYCE (A)	4-0
SF : RUDDINGTON (Formans Athletic Ground)	A *
SFR : RUDDINGTON (Formans Athletic Ground)	6-0
F : KEYWORTH UNITED (Meadow Lane)	2-4

* abandoned in extra time with Marys leading 3-2

NOTTS INTERMEDIATE CUP

R1 :	bye or W
R2 : BALDERTON OLD BOYS (-)	4-1
R3 : NEWSTEAD MINERS WELFARE (A)	5-2
QF : COSSALL COLLIERY (A)	2-4

ARNOLD & DISTRICT BENEVOLENT CUP

R1 :	bye or W
QF : tbc	W
SF : GEDLING COLLIERY (H)	L

1951-52

NOTTS REALM LEAGUE DIVISION 1

	P	W	D	L	F	A	P	H	A
ARNOLD ROVERS	**22**	**18**	**3**	**1**	**92**	**34**	**39**		
OAKDALE RANGERS	22	16	6	0	94	21	38	3-3	1-1
BULWELL FOREST VILLA	22	13	2	7	84	55	28	5-2	2-1
HENDON RISE	22	11	5	6	87	46	27	4-3	4-2
WILFORD ROAD ATHLETIC	22	12	2	8	70	45	26	1-2	4-2
FERRY RANGERS	22	11	2	9	103	59	24	3-1	6-2
EAST LEAKE	22	12	0	10	82	81	24	4-1	5-2
DAKEYNE STREET OLD BOYS	22	9	1	12	63	77	19	4-1	2-1
LODGE COLLIERY	22	6	3	13	54	105	15	3-1	7-1
RAF NEWTON	21	4	1	16	54	119	9	6-1	7-4
BASFORD HALL OLD BOYS	22	3	1	18	47	131	7	6-0	4-0
HOME BREWERY	21	2	2	17	35	104	6	9-1	2-2
	262	117	28	117	865	877	262		

	P	W	D	L	F	A	P
ROVERS HOMES	11	9	1	1	48	16	19
ROVERS AWAYS	11	9	2	0	44	18	20

NOTTS REALM LEAGUE SENIOR CUP

R1 : HENDON RISE (H)	6-3
QF : AVRO (H)	7-2
SF : WILFORD ROAD ATHLETIC (Mill Street, Basford)	4-1
F : FERRY RANGERS (Meadow Lane)	0-3

NOTTS INTERMEDIATE CUP

R1 : NUNCARGATE (A)	5-1
R2 : LENTON GREGORY (A)	L

ARNOLD & DISTRICT BENEVOLENT CUP

QF : SHERWOOD RANGERS (H)	W
SF : LAMBLEY VILLA (-)	W
F : GEDLING COLLIERY (Church Lane)	**2-1**

1951-52

NOTTM SPARTAN LEAGUE DIVISION 1

	P	W	D	L	F	A	P	H	A
RUDDINGTON	22	18	2	2	113	44	38	4-1	4-9
KEYWORTH UNITED	22	16	2	4	117	45	34	5-7	2-2
ASPLEY OLD BOYS	22	16	2	4	80	33	34	1-3	2-2
GROVE CELTIC	22	14	3	5	99	48	31	1-6	1-1
ARNOLD ST MARYS	**22**	**13**	**4**	**5**	**113**	**57**	**30**		
CHILWELL UNITED	22	10	2	10	64	63	22	6-1	4-5
EAST KIRKBY WELFARE	22	9	3	10	85	63	21	4-2	3-3
BURTON JOYCE	22	6	3	13	60	87	15	7-1	4-2
SUTTON COLLIERY	22	6	1	15	52	98	13	14-3	8-3
NETHERFIELD ROVERS	22	5	2	15	47	85	12	3-1	7-0
CASTLE BREWERY	22	5	2	15	42	120	12	8-2	5-0
WILFORD VILLAGE	22	1	0	21	31	159	2	8-1	12-2
	264	119	26	119	903	902	264		
MARYS HOME	11	8	0	3	61	28	16		
MARYS AWAY	11	5	4	2	52	29	14		

NOTTM SPARTAN LEAGUE CUP

R1 : CHILWELL UNITED (H)	12-5
R2 : EAST KIRKBY WELFARE (A)	3-4

NOTTS INTERMEDIATE CUP

R1 : EASTWOOD COLLIERIES (A)	2-1
R2 : BRIDGFORD ROVERS (H)	10-2 *
R2 : BRIDGFORD ROVERS (A)	0-7

* MATCH ORDERED TO BE REPLAYED FOR BREACH OF RULES

ARNOLD & DISTRICT BENEVOLENT CUP

QF : tbc	W
SF : GEDLING COLLIERY (A)	1-3

1952-53

NOTTS REALM LEAGUE DIVISION 1

	P	W	D	L	F	A	P	H	A
ARNOLD ROVERS	**18**	**17**	**0**	**1**	**88**	**17**	**34**		
OAKDALE RANGERS	18	12	4	2	56	23	28	6-1	4-0
BULWELL FOREST VILLA	18	12	2	4	65	29	26	4-0	4-1
DAKEYNE STREET OLD BOYS	18	10	5	3	45	31	25	4-2	2-4
FERRY RANGERS	18	8	1	9	50	46	17	3-0	6-3
TRENT RANGERS	18	5	2	11	34	52	12	7-0	2-0
BILBOROUGH UNITED	18	5	1	12	35	53	11	6-1	2-0
BESTWOOD	18	3	5	10	24	57	11	10-2	5-0
HENDON RISE	18	5	0	13	35	71	10	6-2	3-1
HOME BREWERY	18	1	4	13	18	69	6	6-0	8-0
	180	78	24	78	450	448	180		
ROVERS HOME	9	9	0	0	52	8	18		
ROVERS AWAY	9	8	0	1	36	9	16		

NOTTS REALM LEAGUE SENIOR CUP

R1 : bye	
QF : FERRY RANGERS (H)	5-0
SF : DAKEYNE STREET OLD BOYS (Bulwell Forest Villa Ground)	5-1
F : TRENT RANGERS (Meadow Lane)	**2-1**

NOTTS INTERMEDIATE CUP

R1 : OLD MUNDELLANS (A)	W
R2 : EVERLASTIC ATHLETIC (H)	W
R3 : AWSWORTH VILLA (A)	4-3
R4 : NETHERFIELD ROVERS (-)	3-0
QF : EASTWOOD COLLIERIES (H)	8-4
SF : RUDDINGTON (Meadow Lane)	3-1
F : SHEEPBRIDGE STEEL (City Ground)	**4-3**

ARNOLD & DISTRICT BENEVOLENT CUP

QF : tbc	W
SF : BESTWOOD COLLIERY (H)	2-1
F : ARNOLD ST MARYS (Church Lane)	**3-3 [TROPHY SHARED]**

1952-53

NOTTM SPARTAN LEAGUE DIVISION 1

	P	W	D	L	F	A	P	H	A
ASPLEY OLD BOYS	22	18	4	0	106	37	40	1-3	2-4
ARNOLD ST MARYS	**22**	**16**	**3**	**3**	**91**	**34**	**35**		
GROVE CELTIC	22	13	4	5	71	46	30	4-3	3-0
RUDDINGTON	22	13	3	6	83	44	29	3-1	2-2
KEYWORTH UNITED	22	8	7	7	66	55	23	6-3	0-0
BRINSLEY	22	9	5	8	55	47	23	5-2	2-2
NETHERFIELD ROVERS	22	8	3	11	57	71	19	6-1	3-1
HUCKNALL COLLIERIES	22	7	4	11	54	71	18	3-1	3-1
HUCKNALL BRITISH LEGION	22	8	1	13	43	84	17	5-0	0-2
MANOR FARM OLD BOYS	22	6	3	13	54	83	15	8-4	9-0
STAYTHORPE POWER STATION	22	3	3	16	51	96	9	4-3	6-1
BURTON JOYCE	22	4	0	18	36	94	8	8-0	8-0
	264	113	40	111	767	762	266		
MARYS HOME	11	10	0	1	53	21	20		
MARYS AWAY	11	6	3	2	38	13	15		

NOTTM SPARTAN LEAGUE CUP

R1 :	bye or W
R2 : HUCKNALL FOREST (H)	11-2
QF : HUCKNALL BRITISH LEGION (H)	3-2
SF : ERICSSON ATHLETIC (Gatehouse Ground, Linby)	0-2

NOTTS INTERMEDIATE CUP

R1 : MAPPERLEY (H)	7-2
R2 : GROVE CELTIC (A)	3-2
R3 : GAS SPORTS (A)	A *
R3R : GAS SPORTS (H)	5-1
R4 : EASTWOOD COLLIERIES (H)	L

* abandoned in extra time with Marys leading

ARNOLD & DISTRICT BENEVOLENT CUP

QF : tbc	W
SF : MAPPERLEY (H)	5-0
F : ARNOLD ROVERS (Church Lane)	**3-3 [TROPHY SHARED]**

1953-54

NOTTM SPARTAN LEAGUE DIVISION 1

	P	W	D	L	F	A	P	H	A
ARNOLD ROVERS	**22**	**19**	**2**	**1**	**111**	**28**	**40**		
ARNOLD ST MARYS	22	19	1	2	93	21	39	1-0	3-3
ASPLEY OLD BOYS	22	17	0	5	88	29	34	2-1	2-0
GROVE CELTIC	22	15	0	7	93	57	30	3-1	6-4
ERICSSON ATHLETIC	22	10	1	11	48	50	21	3-1	6-0
LINBY COLLIERY COLTS	22	10	1	11	45	60	21	8-2	2-5
RUDDINGTON	22	7	3	12	57	69	17	6-1	3-2
KEYWORTH UNITED	22	7	2	13	46	81	16	2-0	10-2
HUCKNALL COLLIERIES	22	6	3	13	51	64	15	1-1	5-2
NETHERFIELD ROVERS	22	6	2	14	43	88	14	9-0	12-0
BESTWOOD COLLIERY	22	4	4	14	30	86	12	7-3	5-0
BURTON JOYCE	22	2	1	19	26	100	5	9-0	6-0
	264	122	20	122	731	733	264		

	P	W	D	L	F	A	P
ROVERS HOME	11	10	1	0	51	10	21
ROVERS AWAY	11	9	1	1	60	18	19

NOTTM SPARTAN LEAGUE CUP

R1 : UNDERWOOD VILLA (H)	6-2
R2 : HUCKNALL COLLIERIES (H)	9-3
QF : LINBY COLLIERY COLTS (A)	4-1
SF : GROVE CELTIC (City Transport Ground, Aspley)	4-3 (after extra time)
F : ARNOLD ST MARYS (Plains Road)	**1-0**

NOTTS INTERMEDIATE CUP

R1 : ASPLEY OLD BOYS RESERVES (H)	9-3
R2 : LINBY COLLIERY COLTS (H)	5-4
R3 : BILBOROUGH (H)	6-0
R4 : MAPPERLEY VILLA (A)	4-1
QF : CHURCH WARSOP WELFARE (H)	3-1
SF : THORESBY COLLIERY (Gatehouse Ground, Linby)	5-0
F : ARNOLD ST MARYS (City Ground)	1-4

1953-54

NOTTM SPARTAN LEAGUE DIVISION 1

	P	W	D	L	F	A	P	H	A
ARNOLD ROVERS	22	19	2	1	111	28	40	3-3	0-1
ARNOLD ST MARYS	**22**	**19**	**1**	**2**	**93**	**21**	**39**		
ASPLEY OLD BOYS	22	17	0	5	88	29	34	4-1	1-2
GROVE CELTIC	22	15	0	7	93	57	30	3-0	3-0
ERICSSON ATHLETIC	22	10	1	11	48	50	21	3-1	4-1
LINBY COLLIERY COLTS	22	10	1	11	45	60	21	3-2	6-1
RUDDINGTON	22	7	3	12	57	69	17	6-1	6-0
KEYWORTH UNITED	22	7	2	13	46	81	16	3-1	6-0
HUCKNALL COLLIERIES	22	6	3	13	51	64	15	5-0	4-2
NETHERFIELD ROVERS	22	6	2	14	43	88	14	7-0	6-1
BESTWOOD COLLIERY	22	4	4	14	30	86	12	6-1	7-2
BURTON JOYCE	22	2	1	19	26	100	5	3-1	4-0
	264	122	20	122	731	733	264		
MARYS HOME	11	10	1	0	46	11	21		
MARYS AWAY	11	9	0	2	47	10	18		

NOTTM SPARTAN LEAGUE CUP

R1 : ERICSSON ATHLETIC (H)	7-4
R2 : NETHERFIELD ROVERS (A)	4-0
QF : DODGERS ATHLETIC (H)	3-1
SF : ASPLEY OLD BOYS (Formans Athletic Ground)	2-0
F : ARNOLD ROVERS (Plains Road)	0-1

NOTTS INTERMEDIATE CUP

R1 : BURTON JOYCE (H)	2-1
R2 : HUCKNALL BRITISH LEGION (H)	W
R3 : BESTWOOD OLD BOYS (A)	W
R4 : DAKEYNE STREET OLD BOYS (A)	4-2
QF : MANSFIELD ST AIDANS STAGS (-)	W
SF : LENTON GREGORY (Plains Road)	2-1
F : ARNOLD ROVERS (City Ground)	**4-1**

1954-55

NOTTM SPARTAN LEAGUE DIVISION 1

	P	W	D	L	F	A	P	H	A
ARNOLD ROVERS	**16**	**14**	**0**	**2**	**76**	**32**	**28**		
ARNOLD ST MARYS	16	13	0	3	67	29	26	4-1	2-6
ASPLEY OLD BOYS	16	12	0	4	57	32	24	4-2	2-4
SHEEPBRIDGE STEEL	16	9	1	6	65	43	19	8-4	4-2
NOTTINGHAM FOREST B	16	8	0	8	55	48	16	2-1	7-3
GROVE CELTIC	16	6	1	9	61	61	13	3-1	4-1
RUDDINGTON	16	5	0	11	42	72	10	4-2	4-1
KEYWORTH UNITED	16	2	0	14	32	77	4	8-2	5-0
HUCKNALL COLLIERIES	16	1	2	13	32	82	4	12-1	3-1
	144	70	4	70	487	476	144		
ROVERS HOME	8	8	0	0	45	14	16		
ROVERS AWAY	8	6	0	2	31	18	12		

NOTTM SPARTAN LEAGUE CUP

R1 : BURTON JOYCE (A)	5-2
R2 : NOTTINGHAM FOREST B (H)	3-8

NOTTS INTERMEDIATE CUP

R1 : BULWELL FOREST VILLA (A)	3-0
R2 : WORTHINGTON-SIMPSON RESERVES (H)	13-5
R3 : SHEEPBRIDGE STEEL (A)	3-1
R4 : OAKDALE RANGERS (H)	4-1
QF : OLLERTON COLLIERY (H)	3-0
SF : ARNOLD ST MARYS (Plains Road)	2-0
F : LENTON GREGORY (City Ground)	2-4

1954-55

NOTTM SPARTAN LEAGUE DIVISION 1

	P	W	D	L	F	A	P	H	A
ARNOLD ROVERS	16	14	0	2	76	32	28	6-2	1-4
ARNOLD ST MARYS	**16**	**13**	**0**	**3**	**67**	**29**	**26**		
ASPLEY OLD BOYS	16	12	0	4	57	32	24	4-3	3-1
SHEEPBRIDGE STEEL	16	9	1	6	65	43	19	3-1	4-2
NOTTINGHAM FOREST B	16	8	0	8	55	48	16	4-2	1-2
GROVE CELTIC	16	6	1	9	61	61	13	7-2	7-2
RUDDINGTON	16	5	0	11	42	72	10	5-2	5-0
KEYWORTH UNITED	16	2	0	14	32	77	4	2-0	9-2
HUCKNALL COLLIERIES	16	1	2	13	32	82	4	5-2	1-2
	144	70	4	70	487	476	144		
MARYS HOME	8	8	0	0	36	14	16		
MARYS AWAY	8	5	0	3	31	15	10		

NOTTM SPARTAN LEAGUE CUP

R1 : LENTON GREGORY RESERVES (H)	5-5 (after extra time)
R1R : LENTON GREGORY RESERVES (A)	4-1
R2 : MOORBRIDGE LANE (A) (Played at Church Lane)	12-0
QF : UNDERWOOD VILLA (H)	3-1
SF : SHEEPBRIDGE STEEL (Gatehouse Ground, Linby)	6-1
F : NOTTINGHAM FOREST B (City Ground)	**W**

NOTTS INTERMEDIATE CUP

R1 : NEWARK CENTRAL (H)	8-1
R2 : SHERWOOD AMATEURS B (H) (Played at Bestwood Colliery Ground)	4-1
R3 : KIMBERLEY YMCA (A)	1-0
R4 : WILFORD (H)	5-1
QF : CALVERTON COLLIERY (A)	3-2
SF : ARNOLD ROVERS (Plains Road)	0-2

1955-56

CENTRAL ALLIANCE DIVISION 2

	P	W	D	L	F	A	P	H	A
CRESWELL COLLIERY RESERVES	34	23	6	5	127	53	52	2-1	1-8
ILKESTON TOWN RESERVES	34	19	9	6	101	44	47	0-3	3-3
WILMORTON & ALVASTON	34	22	3	9	121	59	47	1-0	0-4
ARNOLD ST MARYS	34	21	4	9	102	74	46	3-3	8-0
OLLERTON COLLIERY	34	21	3	10	122	59	45	2-5	1-3
ARNOLD ROVERS	**34**	**20**	**4**	**10**	**109**	**83**	**44**		
KIMBERLEY YMCA	34	16	7	11	109	83	39	3-3	0-6
BELPER TOWN RESERVES	34	16	5	13	95	86	37	3-1	0-1
LONG EATON ZINGARI	34	15	5	14	83	85	35	1-3	1-2
STANTON IRONWORKS	34	12	6	16	76	85	30	4-2	3-5
IRONVILLE AMATEURS	34	13	4	17	103	127	30	5-3	7-4
HEANOR TOWN RESERVES	34	12	6	16	80	101	30	10-3	5-1
SHIREBROOK MINERS WELFARE RESERVES	34	12	5	17	90	104	29	1-2	5-2
SUTTON TOWN RESERVES	34	12	3	19	80	104	27	4-1	4-1
LINBY COLLIERY RESERVES	34	11	3	20	79	105	25	3-2	3-1
BRITISH ROPES RESERVES	33	7	4	22	75	158	18	4-3	2-2
LOSCOE MINERS WELFARE	34	7	3	24	52	121	17	7-1	2-1
AWSWORTH VILLA	33	5	2	26	50	123	12	5-2	3-1
	610	264	82	264	1654	1654	610		

	P	W	D	L	F	A	P
ROVERS HOME	17	12	2	3	61	38	26
ROVERS AWAY	17	8	2	7	48	45	18

NOTTS SENIOR CUP

1Q : bye	
2Q : ARNOLD ST MARYS (A)	3-1
3Q : RALEIGH ATHLETIC (H)	4-2
4Q : BRITISH ROPES (H)	2-1 (after extra time)
QF : ASPLEY OLD BOYS (H)	0-5

1955-56

CENTRAL ALLIANCE DIVISION 2

	P	W	D	L	F	A	P	H	A
CRESWELL COLLIERY RESERVES	34	23	6	5	127	53	52	4-6	0-4
ILKESTON TOWN RESERVES	34	19	9	6	101	44	47	1-1	1-7
WILMORTON & ALVASTON	34	22	3	9	121	59	47	0-1	6-1
ARNOLD ST MARYS	**34**	**21**	**4**	**9**	**102**	**74**	**46**		
OLLERTON COLLIERY	34	21	3	10	122	59	45	0-0	tbc
ARNOLD ROVERS	34	20	4	10	109	83	44	0-8	3-3
KIMBERLEY YMCA	34	16	7	11	109	83	39	4-3	5-2
BELPER TOWN RESERVES	34	16	5	13	95	86	37	5-1	2-4
LONG EATON ZINGARI	34	15	5	14	83	85	35	3-0	L
STANTON IRONWORKS	34	12	6	16	76	85	30	3-0	3-0
IRONVILLE AMATEURS	34	13	4	17	103	127	30	7-4	3-3
HEANOR TOWN RESERVES	34	12	6	16	80	101	30	6-1	4-0
SHIREBROOK MINERS WELFARE RESERVES	34	12	5	17	90	104	29	4-0	2-5
SUTTON TOWN RESERVES	34	12	3	19	80	104	27	tbc	2-1
LINBY COLLIERY RESERVES	34	11	3	20	79	105	25	3-0	4-3
BRITISH ROPES RESERVES	33	7	4	22	75	158	18	6-0	2-0
LOSCOE MINERS WELFARE	34	7	3	24	52	121	17	3-1	1-0
AWSWORTH VILLA	33	5	2	26	50	123	12	5-3	3-0
	610	264	82	264	1654	1654	610		

	P	W	D	L	F	A	P
MARYS HOME	17	11+	2	3+	54+	29+	24+
MARYS AWAY	17	9+	2	5+	40+	33+	20+

NOTTS SENIOR CUP

1Q : CINDERHILL COLLIERY (H)	10-1
2Q : ARNOLD ROVERS (H)	1-3

1956-57

CENTRAL ALLIANCE DIVISION 2

	P	W	D	L	F	A	P	H	A
HEANOR TOWN RESERVES	34	29	2	3	145	50	60	0-2	1-7
ILKESTON TOWN RESERVES	34	27	2	5	149	54	56	3-2	2-7
ARNOLD ST MARYS	34	22	6	6	160	72	50	4-2	4-4
ARNOLD ROVERS	**34**	**24**	**2**	**8**	**153**	**76**	**50**		
SUTTON TOWN RESERVES	34	23	4	7	118	74	50	2-3	5-2
RANSOME AND MARLES RESERVES	34	22	4	8	118	82	48	2-3	5-6
BELPER TOWN RESERVES	34	22	2	10	124	69	46	2-1	5-4
IRONVILLE AMATEURS	34	16	3	15	92	80	35	7-4	4-3
CRESWELL COLLIERY RESERVES	34	15	4	15	105	115	34	11-0	2-0
THORESBY MINERS WELFARE	34	14	5	15	87	98	33	6-2	1-2
KIMBERLEY TOWN	34	14	2	18	110	103	30	3-2	6-0
LONG EATON ZINGARI	34	11	3	20	107	121	25	6-4	6-2
SHIREBROOK MINERS WELFARE RESERVES	34	11	3	20	83	121	25	2-1	3-5
METAL BOX	34	7	5	22	68	134	19	1-1	8-0
STANTON IRONWORKS	34	5	6	23	55	125	16	3-2	7-2
LOSCOE MINERS WELFARE	34	6	4	24	66	150	16	6-0	9-1
BRITISH ROPES RESERVES	34	4	4	26	55	151	12	9-0	6-1
WILMORTON AND ALVASTON RESERVES	34	3	1	30	37	153	7	8-1	4-0
	612	275	62	275	1832	1828	612		

	P	W	D	L	F	A	P
ROVERS HOME	17	13	1	3	75	30	27
ROVERS AWAY	17	11	1	5	78	46	24

NOTTS SENIOR CUP

1Q : bye	
2Q : bye	
3Q : bye	
4Q : RETFORD TOWN (A)	1-4

1956-57

CENTRAL ALLIANCE DIVISION 2

	P	W	D	L	F	A	P	H	A
HEANOR TOWN RESERVES	34	29	2	3	145	50	60	3-3	3-5
ILKESTON TOWN RESERVES	34	27	2	5	149	54	56	5-2	2-6
ARNOLD ST MARYS	**34**	**22**	**6**	**6**	**160**	**72**	**50**		
ARNOLD ROVERS	34	24	2	8	153	76	50	4-4	2-4
SUTTON TOWN RESERVES	34	23	4	7	118	74	50	3-3	7-2
RANSOME AND MARLES RESERVES	34	22	4	8	118	82	48	5-3	3-6
BELPER TOWN RESERVES	34	22	2	10	124	69	46	2-3	2-2
IRONVILLE AMATEURS	34	16	3	15	92	80	35	3-0	2-0
CRESWELL COLLIERY RESERVES	34	15	4	15	105	115	34	4-2	1-2
THORESBY MINERS WELFARE	34	14	5	15	87	98	33	2-1	4-4
KIMBERLEY TOWN	34	14	2	18	110	103	30	5-3	4-2
LONG EATON ZINGARI	34	11	3	20	107	121	25	3-2	5-2
SHIREBROOK MINERS WELFARE RESERVES	34	11	3	20	83	121	25	9-1	7-0
METAL BOX	34	7	5	22	68	134	19	6-1	3-1
STANTON IRONWORKS	34	5	6	23	55	125	16	5-1	3-3
LOSCOE MINERS WELFARE	34	6	4	24	66	150	16	10-2	7-0
BRITISH ROPES RESERVES	34	4	4	26	55	151	12	11-0	3-1
WILMORTON AND ALVASTON RESERVES	34	3	1	30	37	153	7	14-0	8-1
	612	275	62	275	1832	1828	612		

	P	W	D	L	F	A	P
MARYS HOME	17	13	3	1	94	31	29
MARYS AWAY	17	9	3	5	66	41	21
	34	22	6	6	160	72	50

NOTTS SENIOR CUP

1Q : WARSOP MAIN (A)	5-4
2Q : BESTWOOD COLLIERY (A)	1-2

1957-58

CENTRAL ALLIANCE DIVISION 2

	P	W	D	L	F	A	P	H	A
SUTTON TOWN RESERVES	32	23	3	6	123	60	49	6-4	1-2
KIMBERLEY TOWN	32	23	3	6	122	60	49	3-0	2-1
ARNOLD ROVERS	**32**	**22**	**4**	**6**	**93**	**54**	**48**		
ILKESTON TOWN RESERVES	32	21	3	8	113	45	45	3-2	2-1
ARNOLD ST MARYS	32	20	4	8	121	64	44	1-1	1-3
ASPLEY OLD BOYS	32	20	4	8	94	68	44	4-1	0-2
HEANOR TOWN RESERVES	32	19	4	9	101	62	42	2-1	4-5
RANSOME AND MARLES RESERVES	32	16	4	12	94	92	36	3-0	3-1
NOTTINGHAM FOREST B	32	13	3	16	88	85	29	6-2	4-2
BELPER TOWN RESERVES	32	12	5	15	66	87	29	4-1	4-1
WILMORTON AND ALVASTON RESERVES	32	10	6	16	71	74	26	3-2	2-2
CRESWELL COLLIERY RESERVES	32	9	6	17	77	103	24	3-2	1-1
IRONVILLE AMATEURS	32	8	7	17	92	99	23	3-1	3-1
LONG EATON ZINGARI	32	11	1	20	82	110	23	5-2	2-5
SHIREBROOK MINERS WELFARE RESERVES	32	7	3	22	56	119	17	3-1	0-0
BRITISH ROPES RESERVES	32	6	2	24	47	123	14	2-1	1-2
STANTON IRONWORKS	32	0	2	30	39	174	2	4-2	8-2
	544	240	64	240	1479	1479	544		

	P	W	D	L	F	A	P
ROVERS HOME	16	15	1	0	55	23	31
ROVERS AWAY	16	7	3	6	38	31	17

CENTRAL ALLIANCE DIVISION 2 CUP

R1 : SUTTON TOWN RESERVES (A)	4-2
QF : BELPER TOWN RESERVES (A)	6-3
SF : ASPLEY OLD BOYS (H)	4-1
F : ARNOLD ST MARYS (Gedling Road)	0-2

NOTTS SENIOR CUP

1Q : LENTON GREGORY (A)	5-2
2Q : RUFFORD COLLIERY (A)	2-3

1957-58

CENTRAL ALLIANCE DIVISION 2

	P	W	D	L	F	A	P	H	A
SUTTON TOWN RESERVES	32	23	3	6	123	60	49	6-1	0-4
KIMBERLEY TOWN	32	23	3	6	122	60	49	2-1	1-2
ARNOLD ROVERS	32	22	4	6	93	54	48	3-1	1-1
ILKESTON TOWN RESERVES	32	21	3	8	113	45	45	4-6	2-0
ARNOLD ST MARYS	**32**	**20**	**4**	**8**	**121**	**64**	**44**		
ASPLEY OLD BOYS	32	20	4	8	94	68	44	2-3	1-2
HEANOR TOWN RESERVES	32	19	4	9	101	62	42	4-4	2-4
RANSOME AND MARLES RESERVES	32	16	4	12	94	92	36	4-4	7-2
NOTTINGHAM FOREST B	32	13	3	16	88	85	29	2-0	4-2
BELPER TOWN RESERVES	32	12	5	15	66	87	29	5-2	4-6
WILMORTON AND ALVASTON RESERVES	32	10	6	16	71	74	26	1-2	3-1
CRESWELL COLLIERY RESERVES	32	9	6	17	77	103	24	9-1	1-1
IRONVILLE AMATEURS	32	8	7	17	92	99	23	W	5-3
LONG EATON ZINGARI	32	11	1	20	82	110	23	4-3	4-2
SHIREBROOK MINERS WELFARE RESERVES	32	7	3	22	56	119	17	W	11-2
BRITISH ROPES RESERVES	32	6	2	24	47	123	12	W	5-1
STANTON IRONWORKS	32	0	2	30	39	174	2	6-0	7-0
	544	240	64	240	1479	1479	542		

	P	W	D	L	F	A	P
MARYS HOME	16	11	2	3	63	31	24
MARYS AWAY	16	9	2	5	58	33	20
	32	20	4	8	121	64	44

CENTRAL ALLIANCE DIVISION 2 CUP

R1 : THORESBY COLLIERY (H) W/O
QF : BRITISH ROPES RESERVES (H) 5-2
SF : HEANOR TOWN RESERVES (H) 6-2
F : ARNOLD ROVERS (Gedling Road) 2-0

FA AMATEUR CUP

EPR : LINBY COLLIERY (H) 3-1
PR : CLAY CROSS & DANESMOOR MINERS WELFARE (H) 2-3

NOTTS SENIOR CUP

1Q : NOTTINGHAMSHIRE (A) 5-1
2Q : BILSTHORPE COLLIERY (H) 6-0
3Q : KIMBERLEY TOWN (H) 7-1
4Q : BESTWOOD COLLIERY (H) 5-0
QF : EASTWOOD TOWN (A) 4-5 (after extra time)

ROVERS AND MARYS HEAD TO HEAD MEETINGS

SEASON	DATE	R-M	COMP	VENUE	ATT	P	R	D	M	R	M
1952-53	31-Aug-53	3-3	A&DBCF	CHURCH LANE		1	0	1	0	3	3
1953-54	26-Dec-53	3-3	NSL1	CHURCH LANE	3500	2	0	2	0	6	6
	28-Apr-54	1-0	NSL1	NOTTINGHAM ROAD		3	1	2	0	7	6
	1-May-54	1-0	NSLCF	PLAINS ROAD		4	2	2	0	8	6
	3-May-54	1-4	NICF	CITY GROUND		5	2	2	1	9	10
1954-55	16-Oct-54	2-6	NSL1	CHURCH LANE	2000	6	2	2	2	11	16
	9-Apr-55	4-1	NSL1	NOTTINGHAM ROAD		7	3	2	2	15	17
	11-Apr-55	2-0	NICSF	PLAINS ROAD	1356	8	4	2	2	17	17
1955-56	12-Nov-55	3-3	CA2	NOTTINGHAM ROAD		9	4	3	2	20	20
	3-Dec-55	3-1	NSC2Q	CHURCH LANE		10	5	3	2	23	21
	26-Dec-55	8-0	CA2	CHURCH LANE		11	6	3	2	31	21
1956-57	2-Feb-57	4-2	CA2	NOTTINGHAM ROAD*		12	7	3	2	35	23
	20-Apr-57	4-4	CA2	GEDLING ROAD		13	7	4	2	39	27
1957-58	22-Mar-58	1-3	CA2	GEDLING ROAD		14	7	4	3	40	30
	29-Mar-58	1-1	CA2	GEDLING ROAD		15	7	5	3	41	31
	3-May-58	0-2	CA2CF	GEDLING ROAD	2000+	16	7	5	4	41	33
* GEDLING ROAD UNFIT				LEAGUE		10	4	4	2	31	23
				CUP		6	3	1	2	10	10

MISCELLANEOUS RECORDS

MATCHES UNBEATEN FROM START OF SEASON

ROVERS	ALL GAMES	25	1953-54		
	LEAGUE	17	1946-47	&	1953-54
MARYS	ALL GAMES	24	1953-54		
	LEAGUE	27	1949-50 (unbeaten all season)		

CONSECUTIVE WINS

ROVERS	ALL GAMES	29	1952-53	to	1953-54
	LEAGUE	21	1952-53	to	1953-54
MARYS	ALL GAMES	16	1949-50		
	LEAGUE	15	1949-50		

CONSECUTIVE MATCHES UNDEFEATED

ROVERS	ALL GAMES	53	1952-53	to	1953-54
	LEAGUE	32	1952-53	to	1953-54
MARYS	ALL GAMES	28	1952-53	to	1953-54
	LEAGUE	35	1949-50	to	1950-51

BIGGEST MARGIN OF VICTORY

ROVERS	HOME	12-0	v	CARLTON STARS RESERVES	1946-47
	AWAY	13-0	v	ST SAVIOURS	1948-49
MARYS	HOME	14-0	v	WILMORTON & ALVASTON RESERVES	1956-57
	AWAY	15-1	v	SOUTHWELL ST MARYS	1949-50

(In 1953-54 Rovers and Marys beat Manor Farm Old Boys 17-1 and 16-1 respectively but the results were subsequently expunged from the official records)

BIGGEST MARGIN OF DEFEAT

ROVERS	HOME	3-8	v	NOTTINGHAM FOREST B	1954-55
	HOME	0-5	v	ASPLEY OLD BOYS	1955-56
	AWAY	1-10	v	NOTTS REGENT	1950-51
MARYS	HOME	0-8	v	ARNOLD ROVERS	1955-56
	AWAY	1-9	v	STAPLEFORD VILLA	1947-48

HIGHEST SCORING MATCH

ROVERS	18 GOALS	13-5	v	WORTHINGTON-SIMPSON RESERVES	1954-55
MARYS	17 GOALS	14-3	v	SUTTON COLLIERY	1951-52
	17 GOALS	12-5	v	CHILWELL UNITED	1951-52

(See note re: Manor Farm Old Boys games above)

MISCELLANEOUS RECORDS

INDIVIDUAL GOALS IN A GAME (WHERE PUBLISHED)

ROVERS	LES PEEL	6	v	WORTINGTON SIMPSON RESERVES	13-5	1954-55
	RON MADDOCKS	6	v	MANOR FARM OLD BOYS*	17-1	1953-54
MARYS	ALBERT ALLCOCK	7	v	BARLOCK TYPEWRITERS	8-4	1946-47
	RAY BENNETT	7	v	HUCKNALL BRITISH LEGION*	12-1	1953-54
	RAY BENNETT	7	v	MANOR FARM OLD BOYS*	16-1	1953-54

(* the results of these games were subsequently expunged from the official records)

PLAYERS APPEARING IN FIVE OR MORE SEASONS : 1946-47 to 1957-58

ROY 'FLY' CARTER	REGENT, ROVERS & MARYS	12 **
GEOFF PARR	REGENT & MARYS	12 **
BILL WHITT	REGENT, ROVERS & MARYS	12 **
RON HINSON	MARYS	10 **
DENNIS PARR	REGENT & MARYS	10 **
FRANCIS 'FRANNY' GREENSMITH	ROVERS	9 **
JACK BRACE	ROVERS & MARYS	9
JOHN CUNNINGHAM	REGENT, ROVERS & MARYS	9
JACK SURGEY	REGENT & ROVERS	9
SAM ARCHER	ROVERS & MARYS	7 **
ALEC CASTERTON	ROVERS	7 **
LES PEEL	ROVERS & MARYS	7 **
KEN ATHERLEY	ROVERS & MARYS	7
ERNIE BARBER	ROVERS & MARYS	7
CHARLIE MOORE	MARYS	7
HARRY 'JACK' WHARTON	MARYS	7
LEN ROCKLEY	MARYS	6 **
JIM ATKINSON	ROVERS & MARYS	6
KEN CUNNINGHAM	ROVERS & MARYS	6
RON MADDOCKS	ROVERS	5 **
KEITH MOORE	MARYS	5 **
RAY BENNETT	MARYS	5
TOMMY DICKINSON	MARYS	5
KEN DOVE	ROVERS	5
DON HAZLEDINE	REGENT & ROVERS	5
BILL HORTON	ROVERS & MARYS	5
CYRIL MIDDLETON	MARYS	5
REG ROCKLEY	MARYS	5
HERBERT 'DUKE' RYAN	REGENT, ROVERS & MARYS	5
JACK TULLEY	ROVERS	5

(** these players played for Rovers or Marys beyond 1957-58)

HIGHEST REPORTED ATTENDANCES

ATT	SEASON			COMPETITION	GROUND
4000	1946-47	MARYS	V 166 CAMP (WOLLATON PARK) POW XI	FRIENDLY	CHURCH LANE
3500	1953-54	MARYS	V ROVERS	NOTTM SPARTAN LEAGUE DIVISION 1	CHURCH LANE
3000	1952-53	ROVERS	V RUDDINGTON	NOTTS INTERMEDIATE CUP SEMI FINAL	MEADOW LANE
2000 +	1957-58	ROVERS	V MARYS	CENTRAL ALLIANCE DIVISION 2 CUP FINAL	GEDLING ROAD
2000	1948-49	REGENT	V KEYWORTH UNITED	NOTTS REALM LEAGUE SENIOR CUP FINAL	MEADOW LANE
2000	1954-55	MARYS	V ROVERS	NOTTM SPARTAN LEAGUE DIVISION 1	CHURCH LANE
2000	1955-56	ROVERS	V RALEIGH ATHLETIC	NOTTS SENIOR CUP 3RD QUALIFYING ROUND	NOTTINGHAM ROAD
1516	1953-54	MARYS	V LENTON GREGORY	NOTTS INTERMEDIATE CUP SEMI FINAL	PLAINS ROAD
1400	1950-51	ROVERS	V REGENT	NOTTS REALM LEAGUE SENIOR CUP FINAL	MEADOW LANE
1356	1954-55	ROVERS	V MARYS	NOTTS INTERMEDIATE CUP SEMI FINAL	PLAINS ROAD
1000	1949-50	MAPPERLEY	V MARYS	ARNOLD & DISTRICT BENEVOLENT CUP 1ST ROUND	
909	1953-54	ROVERS	V THORESBY COLLIERY	NOTTS INTERMEDIATE CUP SEMI FINAL	GATEHOUSE GROUND, LINBY

SOURCES

WEBSITES

WIKIPEDIA
MET OFFICE
BBC
GRANTHAM TODAY
NATIONAL PARKS
20TH CENTURY LONDON
UNIVERSITY OF NOTTINGHAM
BRITAIN EXPRESS
EDP24 (EASTERN DAILY PRESS)
NATIONAL PLAYING FIELDS ASSOCIATION
BODLEIAN MUSEUM
OUP (OXFORD UNIVERSITY PRESS)
MUNICH 58

BOOKS

FIFTIES BRITAIN POST-WAR LIFE by Nigel Perryman
PASSOVOTCHKA by David Downing
FOOTBALL AND ALL THAT by Norman Giller
THE LAWS OF ASSOCIATION FOOTBALL
THE YEARS WHEN BRITAIN SHIVERED by Ian McGaskill
NOTTINGHAM : LIFE IN THE POST WAR YEARS by Douglas Whitworth
NOTTINGHAM : A HISTORY by Chris Weir
TIN TACKS by Peter Turner

NEWSPAPERS

NOTTINGHAM GUARDIAN
NOTTINGHAM JOURNAL
NOTTINGHAM EVENING NEWS
NOTTINGHAM EVENING POST
FOOTBALL NEWS
FOOTBALL POST